Instructor's Manual with Test Bank

W9-CII-815

Introduction to Physical Anthropology

ELEVENTH EDITION

Robert Jurmain
Professor Emeritus, San Jose State University

Lynn Kilgore
University of Colorado, Boulder

Wenda Trevathan
New Mexico State University

Russell L. Ciochon
University of Iowa

Prepared by

Wesley A. Niewohner
California State University—San Bernadino
Instructor's Manual Portion

M. Leonor Monreal
Fullerton College
Test Bank Portion

THOMSON
WADSWORTH

Australia • Brazil • Canada • Mexico • Singapore • Spain • United Kingdom • United States

ISBN-13: 978-0-495-09990-1
ISBN-10: 0-495-09990-2

Thomson Higher Education
10 Davis Drive
Belmont, CA 94002-3098
USA

TABLE OF CONTENTS

PREFACE

This Instructor's Manual with Test Bank for *Introduction to Physical Anthropology*, 11th edition, by Jurmain, Kilgore, Trevathan, and Ciochon has been extensively revised. I hope that this manual will ease the burden of preparing lecture outlines and exam questions so that your teaching experience will be more enjoyable. Each chapter of the Instructor's Manual with Test Bank includes the following:

- *Chapter Outline*

- *Learning Objectives*

- *Key Terms and Concepts*

- *Lecture Suggestions and Enrichment Topics*

- *Student Media Exercises*

- *Multiple Choice Questions*

- *True/False Questions*

- *Short Answer Questions*

- *Essay Questions*

The test bank portion of this manual is available electronically in ExamView® Computerized Testing (Cross-platform ISBN# 0-495-09991-0), which allows you to create, deliver, and customize tests and study guides (both print and online) in minutes.

ExamView is a registered trademark of FSCreations, Inc. Used herein under license.

W. NIEWOEHNER

SAMPLE SYLLABUS
Integrating the Anthropology Resource Center

WEEK	READINGS	SUGGESTED EXERCISES
1	Chapter 1: Introduction to Physical Anthropology	Pick two sub-disciplines and click on the *Meet the Scientist* sub-section. Pick one scientist from each sub-discipline, read the interview, examine the photographs, and write a few paragraphs about your impressions of the research being done.
	Chapter 2: The Development of Evolutionary Theory	Go to the section *Researching Anthropology* found in each sub-discipline. Focus on the question *Is the Information on the Net Reliable?* and then write a paragraph discussing the key factors in assessing the reliability of websites.
2	Chapter 3: The Biological Basis of Life	
3	Chapter 4: Heredity and Evolution	
4	Chapter 5: Macroevolution: Processes of Vertebrate and Mammalian Evolution	Go to the *Physical Anthropology* section. Click on *Interactive Anthropology* and complete the exercises: *Label the Bones of Animals Who Share a Common Ancestor*
	Exam 1	
5	Chapter 6: Survey of the Living Primates	Go to the *Physical Anthropology* section. Click on *Interactive Anthropology* and complete the exercise: *Fill in the Taxonomy Categories*

	Chapter 7: Primate Behavior	Go to the *Physical Anthropology* section. Click on *Interactive Anthropology* and complete the exercise:
		
		    Identify the Primates' Skeletal Anatomy
		
		Go to the *Physical Anthropology* section. Click on *Map Exercises* and complete the following exercises:
		
		    Drag and Drop the Primate to its Geographic Region in Africa
		    Drag and Drop the Primate to its Geographic Region in Asia
		    Drag and Drop the Primate to its Geographic Region in Central and South America
		    Identify Where Modern African Apes Live

WEEK	READINGS	SUGGESTED EXERCISES
6	Chapter 8: Primate Models for Human Behavioral Evolution	Go to the *Physical Anthropology* section. Click on the *Meet the Scientist* sub-section, read about *Dr. Jonathan Marks* and complete the following: *Critical Thinking Questions*
7	Chapter 9: Overview of the Fossil Primates	Go to the *Physical Anthropology* section. Click on *Interactive Anthropology* and complete the following exercise: *Drag and Drop the Events in Early Primate Evolution to the Correct Place on the Timeline*
8	Chapter 10: Paleoanthropology: Reconstructing Early Hominid Behavior and Ecology	Go to the *Archaeology* section. Click on *Interactive Anthropology* and complete the following: *Learning Modules: Artifact Type Animations: Stratigraphy*
9	Chapter 11: Hominid Origins in Africa	Go to the *Archaeology* section. Click on the *Meet the Scientist* sub-section, read about *Dr. Fidelis T. Masao* and complete the following: *Critical Thinking Questions* Go to the *Physical Anthropology* section. Click on *Interactive Anthropology* and complete the following exercises: *Drag and Drop the Plio-Pleistocene Hominid Sites to the Correct Place on the Timeline* *Drag and Drop the Plio-Pleistocene Hominids to the Correct Place on the Timeline* Go to the *Archaeology* section. Click on *Map Exercises* and complete the following: *Drag and Drop the Hominid Sites to the Correct Place on the East African Rift Valley Map* *Drag and Drop the Early Homo Fossil Finds on the African Map* *Drag and Drop the Early Hominid Fossil Finds on the African Map*
10	Chapter 12: The Earliest Dispersal of the Genus *Homo*: *Homo erectus* and Contemporaries Exam 2	Go to the *Physical Anthropology* section. Click on the *Meet the Scientist* sub-section, read about *Dr. Josep Gibert Clols* and complete the following: *Critical Thinking Questions* Go to the *Archaeology* section. Click on *Map Exercises* and complete the following: *Drag and Drop the Homo Erectus Sites to the Correct Place on the Map of Europe and Africa* *Drag and Drop the Homo Erectus Sites to the Correct Place on the Map of Asia*
11	Chapter 13: Premodern Humans	
12	Chapter 14: The Origin and Dispersal of Modern Humans	

WEEK	READINGS	SUGGESTED EXERCISES
13	Chapter 15: Modern Human Biology: Patterns of Variation	

14	Chapter 16: Modern Human Biology: Patterns of Adaptation	Go to the *Cultural Anthropology* section. Click on *Map Exercises* and complete the following exercise:
		
		    The AIDS Epidemic
		
		Go to the *Cultural Anthropology* section. Click on *Video Exercises* and complete the following exercises:
		
		    AIDS in Africa: Overview
		    AIDS in Africa: Taking Action
		    AIDS in Africa: Marriage and Gender Issues
		
		Go to the *Cultural Anthropology* section. Click on the *Meet the Scientist* sub-section, read about ***Dr. Peter Biella*** and complete the following:
		
		    Critical Thinking Questions

15	Chapter 17 Legacies of Human Evolutionary History	Go to the *Cultural Anthropology* section. Click on *Map Exercises* and complete the following exercise:
		
		    Global Population and Life Expectancy
		    The Global Water Supply
		    The Global Environment

16	Final Exam	

CHAPTER 1: INTRODUCTION TO PHYSICAL ANTHROPOLOGY

Chapter Outline

I. Introduction
   a) Hominids are members of the family Hominidae.
      i) The Hominidae are distinguished by bipedal locomotion.
      ii) The 3.7 million year old footprints at the site of Laetoli are clear evidence for early hominids.
         (1) Other evidence for early hominids includes numerous fossil discoveries in Africa.
   b) *Homo sapiens* are the result of the same evolutionary forces that produced all other life forms on this planet.
      i) Evolution may be defined as a change in the genetic structure of a population.
         (1) Evolution can be studied at the microevolutionary or macroevolutionary level.
   c) Physical anthropologists do not limit their studies to biological systems only.
      i) The role of culture must also be considered.
         (1) In a broad sense, culture is the strategy by which humans adapt to the natural environment.
         (2) Culture has assumed an increasingly greater role throughout the course of human evolution and has interacted with biological evolution.
           (a) This is the concept of biocultural evolution.

II. What is Anthropology?
   a) Anthropology is the study of humankind.
      i) Anthropology has a broad focus and is divided into specialized subfields. In the United States these are:
         (1) Cultural (or social) anthropology.
         (2) Archaeology.
         (3) Physical (or biological) anthropology.
         (4) Some universities include linguistics.

III. Cultural Anthropology is the study of all aspects of human behavior.
   a) Early anthropologists concentrated on producing ethnographies.
      i) Later, cultural anthropologists broadened their scope to include cross-cultural studies.
   b) Ethnographic techniques are now used to study a variety of issues, including urban anthropology, medical anthropology, and economic anthropology.

IV. Archaeology is the study of earlier cultures and lifeways.
   a) The primary sources of information are artifacts and other material culture.
      i) Archaeologists ultimately strive to answer questions about human behavior, and these questions are answered by using precise excavation techniques.
         (1) Therefore, archaeology is not simply the digging up of valuable artifacts. It is a multidisciplinary approach to the study of human behavior.

V. Linguistic Anthropology is the study of human speech and language, including its origins.
   a) The spontaneous acquisition and use of language is a uniquely human characteristic.
      i) Linguistic anthropologists are interested in, among other things, the process of language acquisition and its implications for tracing the evolution of language.

VI. Physical Anthropology is the study human biology within an evolutionary framework.
   a) Physical anthropology and biological anthropology are synonymous.
      i) The use of the term biological anthropology reflects a shift away from the traditional emphasis on anthropometry towards other topics, including genetics, evolutionary biology, nutrition, adaptation, and growth and development.

b) Paleoanthropology is the study of human evolution as evidenced by the fossil record.
   i) Paleoanthropologists identify fossil hominid species and their evolutionary relationships and attempt to reconstruct their adaptations and behaviors.
   ii) Primate paleontology is the study of the primate fossil record.
c) Primatology is the study of nonhuman primate social behavior, ecology, and adaptations.
   i) Many of these insights help paleoanthropologists to model early hominid behavior.
      (1) Primate paleontology is the study of the nonhuman primate fossil record.
d) Osteology is the study of the skeleton.
   i) Knowledge of the structure and function of the skeletal system is key for understanding the fossil record, and it forms the foundation for the analysis of archaeologically derived human skeletal materials.
   ii) Paleopathology is a subfield of osteology.
      (1) Paleopathologists analyze skeletal samples, noting the incidence of trauma, diseases, nutritional deficiencies, and any other pathological conditions that leave traces on bones.
e) Forensic anthropology is the application of archaeological and osteological techniques to the law.
   i) Forensic anthropologists are often asked by law enforcement agencies to help identify and analyze skeletal remains that have legal significance.
   ii) They also aid in the identification of remains after mass disasters; the identification of the September 11 terrorist attack victims is a recent example.

VII. Physical Anthropology and the Scientific Method
   a) Biological anthologists follow the scientific method of hypothesis testing through data collection and analysis.
      i) A hypothesis is defined as a provisional statement of a phenomenon following initial data collection and careful observations.
      ii) The hypothesis must be tested through additional data collection and analysis. The goal is to reject the hypothesis through empirical research.
         (1) If the hypothesis cannot be falsified through rigorous testing, then it rises to the level of a theory.
            (a) A theory is a statement of scientific relationships that has been verified through hypothesis testing.
            (b) Theories are not absolute truths, since they may be disproved in light of new empirical evidence.

VIII. The Anthropological Perspective
   a) The anthropological perspective stresses that human beings can only be understood by broadening our perspectives over space and through time.
      i) Central to the anthropological perspective is relativistic view of cultural diversity.
   b) Anthropologists recognize that the evolution of human adaptive complexes encompasses hundreds of thousands to millions of years (broadening perspective through time). This evolutionary perspective is a core component of anthropology and a major theme throughout the text.

Learning Objectives

After reading Chapter 1, the student should be able to:
1. Define anthropology and list its major subfields.
2. Identify the major research areas within physical/biological anthropology.
3. Demonstrate an understanding of the scientific method and its application to physical anthropology.
4. Discuss the anthropological perspective.

Key Terms and Concepts

Lecture Suggestions and Enrichment Topics

1. Describe your own research interests in order to demonstrate that anthropology has many specialized sub-fields.
2. Compare and contrast the adaptive nature of biological change with that of cultural change. Emphasize that culture is learned, and therefore can change rapidly, whereas biological adaptation requires genetic change and cannot occur as rapidly.
3. Elaborate on the changing emphasis in physical anthropology away from anthropometry towards an emphasis on human biology and adaptation.
4. Expand the discussion of the scientific method. Explore how most people tend to generalize from isolated events and anecdotal information, and point out that this approach differs significantly from that of data collection and hypothesis testing.
5. Emphasize that there are many sources of so-called facts, including those found on the Internet. Point out that people who do not have adequate scientific backgrounds author some human evolution websites.

Student Media Exercises

1. Have students go to the Wadsworth Anthropology Resource Center, look through the sub-disciplines and then click on *Meet the Scientist*. Students should choose two scientists from different sub-disciplines and answer the critical thinking questions.
2. Guide students to the Wadsworth Anthropology Resource Center's *Researching Anthropology* section, found in each sub-discipline. Have them read through it and focus on the question *Is the Information on the Net Reliable* and then discuss the key factors in assessing the reliability of websites.
3. Visit the American Anthropological Association's web site, http://www.aaanet.org/, to learn more about the discipline of anthropology. What non-academic careers are available for anthropologists? (Use the link http://www.aaanet.org/careers.htm).

4. The official web site for the American Association of Physical Anthropology is http://www.physanth.org. What careers are available to physical anthropologists? (Use the link http://www.physanth.org/careers/).

5. Log on to Wadsworth's *Forensic Anthropology Module* (http://www.wadsworth.com/ anthropology_d/special_features/forensics/) and click on Careers in Forensic Anthropology. Write a paragraph describing the career opportunities in this field.

Multiple Choice Questions

1. At present, the members of the family Hominidae includes
   A. apes.
   B. monkeys.
   C. all primates.
   D. humans.
   E. none of these

   ANS: D
   PG: 2

2. A group of organisms that can interbreed and produce fertile offspring is called
   A. the Hominidae.
   B. a species.
   C. a family.
   D. a hominid.
   E. B and C only

   ANS: B
   PG: 3

3. Human evolution
   A. is NOT subject to the same factors that have produced other species.
   B. has been the result of cultural factors alone.
   C. is subject to the same forces that have acted upon other organisms.
   D. has NOT been influenced by cultural factors.
   E. none of these .

   ANS: C
   PG: 3

4. The term *evolution* refers to
   A. changes in the genetic make-up of a population from one generation to the next.
   B. the process of speciation.
   C. ongoing biological processes, including genetic changes within populations and the appearance of new species.
   D. all of these
   E. B and C only

   ANS: D
   PG: 3

5. The strategy humans developed that helped them to adapt to the natural environment is
   A. evolution.
   B. culture.
   C. biological adaptation.
   D. walking on two legs.
   E. genetic change.

   ANS: B
   PG: 4

6. Cultural behaviors
   A. have become less important throughout human evolution.
   B. are genetically determined.
   C. includes only those aspects of human lifestyle that relate to the arts.
   D. are NOT genetically determined.
   E. A and B only

   ANS: D
   PG: 4

7. The term *biocultural evolution* refers to
   A. biological changes in a species over time.
   B. changes in human culture from generation to generation.
   C. the interaction between biology and culture in human evolution.
   D. biological evolution in all species except humans.
   E. none of these

   ANS: C
   PG: 5

8. In the United States, anthropology is comprised of _____ major subfields.
   A. 2
   B. 5
   C. 6
   D. 3
   E. 1

   ANS: D
   PG: 5

9. The Greek word *anthropos* means
   A. primate.
   B. ape.
   C. human.
   D. life.
   E. behavior.

   ANS: C
   PG: 5

10. Cultural anthropology
    A. was first developed in the 17th century.
    B. includes the recovery and analysis of material culture from earlier civilizations.
    C. focuses solely upon the study of traditional societies.
    D. has no practical application in modern society.
    E. is the study of all aspects of human behavior.

    ANS: E
    PG: 5

11. Ethnographies
    A. focus only on Western European societies.
    B. are studies of nonhuman primates.
    C. emphasize, among other topics, subsistence strategies, religion, and ritual.
    D. are studies done by archaeologists.
    E. involve the study of the human skeleton.

    ANS: C
    PG: 5

12. Medical anthropologists
    A. often receive most of their training in physical anthropology.
    B. examine the relationship between culture and health and disease.
    C. never collaborate with medical doctors.
    D. all of these
    E. A and B only

    ANS: E
    PG: 5

13. Archaeology
    A. primarily involves the recovery of valuable artifacts.
    B. does NOT examine issues relating to human culture.
    C. is the study of earlier human groups as evidenced by cultural remains.
    D. has no relationship to physical anthropology.
    E. generally does NOT require collaboration with experts from other disciplines.

    ANS: C
    PG: 6

14. The most important source of data for archaeologists are
    A. material culture left by earlier societies.
    B. interviews with living people.
    C. DNA preserved in fossils.
    D. early hominid fossils.
    E. human skeletal remains.

    ANS: A
    PG: 6

15. In the United States, the greatest expansion in archaeology in recent years has been in the area of
    A. paleoanthropology.
    B. ethnographies.
    C. medical anthropology.
    D. cultural resource management.
    E. none of these

    ANS: D
    PG: 6

16. The applied branch of archaeology that evaluates sites threatened with destruction is
    A. ethnology.
    B. classical archaeology.
    C. ethnography.
    D. paleontology.
    E. cultural resource management.

    ANS: E
    PG: 6

17. The subdiscipline of anthropology concerned with various aspects of human language is called
    A. primatology.
    B. linguistic anthropology.
    C. ethnology.
    D. paleoanthropology.
    E. anthropometry.

    ANS: B
    PG: 6

18. The study of human biology within the framework of human evolution is the domain of
    A. cultural anthropology.
    B. physical/biological anthropology.
    C. primatology.
    D. osteology.
    E. archaeology.

    ANS: B
    PG: 6

19. The origins of physical anthropology arose from which two areas of interest among 19th century scientists?
    A. the origins of species and human variation.
    B. the genetic determinants of behavior and osteology.
    C. nonhuman primates and origins of modern species.
    D. human variation and osteology.
    E. human evolution and nonhuman primates.

    ANS: A
    PG: 6-8

20. Most people, including scientists, until the 19th century, did NOT consider the possibility that humans had evolved from earlier forms. Which of the following stimulated interest in this concept?
    A. The discovery of Neandertal fossils in the 1800s.
    B. The publication of Charles Darwin's *Origin of Species*.
    C. The discovery of *Australopithecus afarensis* in the late 1800s.
    D. all of these
    E. A and B only

    ANS: E
    PG: 6-8

21. The subfield of physical anthropology that is concerned with the study of human evolution as evidenced in the fossil record is
    A. osteology.
    B. paleoanthropology.
    C. anthropometry.
    D. ethnography.
    E. paleopathology.

    ANS: B
    PG: 7

22. _____ anthropologists help us to understand relationships between extinct and living species by comparing DNA sequences.
    A. DNA
    B. Osteological
    C. Molecular
    D. Cultural
    E. none of these

    ANS: C
    PG: 6-8

23. Primatology is the study of
    A. human evolution.
    B. human skeletal material.
    C. skeletal remains at crime scenes.
    D. disease in earlier human groups.
    E. nonhuman primates.

    ANS: E
    PG: 9

24. The study of the primate fossil record is known as
    A. osteology.
    B. primate anthropology.
    C. paleopathology.
    D. forensic anthropology.
    E. primate paleontology.

    ANS: E
    PG: 9

25. _____ is the subdiscipline of osteology that is concerned with disease and trauma in earlier
    populations.
    A. Forensic anthropology
    B. Primatology
    C. Anthropometry
    D. Paleoanthropology
    E. Paleopathology

    ANS: E
    PG: 9

26. Forensic anthropologists
    A. study disease and trauma in ancient populations.
    B. apply anthropological techniques to the law.
    C. are primarily concerned with the recovery of material culture remains.
    D. examine the relationships between medical treatment and culturally determined views of
       disease.
    E. study nonhuman primates.

    ANS: B
    PG: 10

27. Who uses anthropological techniques to assist in crime investigations and to identify skeletal remains
    in cases of disaster?
    A. paleoanthropologists
    B. primatologists
    C. archeologists
    D. cultural anthropologists
    E. forensic anthropologists

    ANS: E
    PG: 10

28. The probably the majority of applied anthropologists are trained as
    A. cultural anthropologists.
    B. forensic anthropologists.
    C. biological anthropologists.
    D. archaeologists.
    E. primatologists.

    ANS: A
    PG: 5

29. Within biological anthropology, the best example of applied anthropology is
    A. cultural anthropology.
    B. forensic anthropology.
    C. paleoanthropology.
    D. archaeology.
    E. primatology.

    ANS: B
    PG: 10

30. A hypothesis
    A. is a statement that has been proven to be true.
    B. is equivalent to a theory.
    C. is a provisional statement regarding certain scientific facts or observations.
    D. A and B only
    E. none of these

    ANS: C
    PG: 12

31. A provisional explanation for a phenomenon is called
    A. a theory.
    B. a datum.
    C. empirical.
    D. scientific testing.
    E. a hypothesis.

    ANS: E
    PG: 12

32. The initial step in the scientific method is
    A. the formation of a theory.
    B. the formation of a hypothesis.
    C. to perform an experiment.
    D. to publish a scientific article.
    E. to collect data and establish facts.

    ANS: E
    PG: 12

33. A scientific theory is
    A. an untested hypothesis.
    B. a hypothesis that has yet to be falsified.
    C. a provisional explanation for a phenomenon.
    D. none of these
    E. A and C only

    ANS: B
    PG: 12

34. The goal of the scientific method is to
    A. establish the absolute truth.
    B. support preconceived notions.
    C. generate the most accurate explanations possible.
    D. A and B only
    E. none of these

    ANS: C
    PG: 12

35. Which branch/branches of anthropology uses/use the anthropological perspective?
    A. archaeology
    B. cultural anthropology
    C. paleoanthropology
    D. A and B only
    E. all of these

    ANS: E
    PG: 13-14

True/False Questions

1. The 3.7 million year old footprints of two hominids were discovered in a riverbed in Texas.

   ANS: False
   PG: 2

2. The earliest hominids, such as *Australopithecus afarensis* manufactured stone tools.

   ANS: False
   PG: 2

3. The "culture gene" transmits culture from generation to generation.

   ANS: False
   PG: 4

4. The focus of anthropology is very narrow, and has only two subfields.

   ANS: False
   PG: 5

5. In the United States, the greatest expansion in archaeology has been in historic archaeology.

   ANS: False
   PG: 6

6. Physical anthropologists are interested only in the study of biological phenomena and are not interested in the study of culture.

    ANS: False
    PG: 6

7. Linguistic anthropologists have failed to identify past relationships between human populations based on the study of languages.

    ANS: False
    PG: 6

8. Some physical anthropologists focus on the relationships between cultural practices and health and disease.

    ANS: True
    PG: 6-7

9. Anthropology CANNOT be applied to practical issues outside the university setting.

    ANS: False
    PG: 5-8

10. Physical anthropologists must understand anatomy in order to assess the structure and function of fossil remains.

    ANS: True
    PG: 5-8

11. Anthropologists strive to be as ethnocentric as possible.

    ANS: False
    PG: 5

12. Ethnocentrism often results in cultures being seen as inferior to one's own.

    ANS: True
    PG: 14

Short Answer Questions

1. Define biocultural evolution.
   (p. 4)

2. What are three major subfields of anthropology? Describe each in terms of their subject matter.
   (pp. 5-11)

3. In a biological sense, what is adaptation?
   (Key Term p. 3)

4. Briefly describe the major goals of archaeology.
   (p. 6)

5. Why are physical/biological anthropologists interested in human biological variation?
   (p. 6-11)

6. What can molecular anthropologists tell us about human evolution?
   (p. 8)

Essay Questions

1. Define osteology and then discuss which subfields of physical anthropology require knowledge of osteology.

2. Discuss the role of the scientific method in physical anthropology.

3. Explain what "the anthropological perspective" means.

CHAPTER 2: THE DEVELOPMENT OF EVOLUTIONARY THEORY

Chapter Outline

I. **Introduction**
   a) Evolution is often denigrated as being "only" a theory.
      i) Evolution is, in fact, a scientific theory that has a wealth of support, and is <u>the</u> unifying theory of the biological sciences.
   b) Evolution is of central importance to physical anthropology, and evolutionary thought has had a long history of development.

II. **A Brief History of Evolutionary Thought**
   a) Charles Darwin is credited with formulating the theory of natural selection, although Alfred Russel Wallace independently duplicated Darwin's ideas.
   b) The predominant European worldview throughout the Middle Ages was one of stasis and the fixity of the species.
      i) Christian teachings that God created all life were taken literally.
      ii) The universe was perceived as being part of the Grand Design.
         (1) Additionally, most believed that life could be ranked in a hierarchy called the Great Chain of Being, an idea that was first proposed by Aristotle in the 4th century B.C.
         (2) Archbishop James Ussher calculated that the world had been created in 4004 B.C.
      iii) The belief that the earth was very young, coupled with the notion of fixity of the species was a significant obstacle to the development of evolutionary thought.
   c) **The Scientific Revolution**
      i) The scientific revolution developed as fundamental ideas of the earth and the biological world were overturned.
         (1) In 1514, Copernicus challenged Aristotle's idea that the earth was the center of the universe by arguing that the solar system was heliocentric.
         (2) The laws of physics, motion and gravity were developed in the 17th century.
         (3) Europeans began to investigate nature as though it was mechanistic, and sought to discover its fundamental laws without reference to supernatural intervention.
   d) **Precursors to the Theory of Evolution**
      i) John Ray (1627-1705), an ordained minister at Cambridge University, was first to recognize that groups of plants and animals could be distinguished from other groups by their ability and produce offspring.
         (1) These groups were termed species.
         (2) Ray also coined the term genus, recognizing that similar species could be grouped together.
      ii) Carolus Linnaeus (1707-1778), a Swedish naturalist and believer in the fixity of species, developed the binomial system of classification plants in his publication, *Systema Naturae* (1735).
         (1) He added the taxonomic levels class and order and classified humans as *Homo sapiens*.
      iii) Comte de Buffon (1707-1788) stressed the importance of change in the universe and the dynamics between nature and living forms in *Natural History* (1749).
      iv) Erasmus Darwin (1731-1802), Charles Darwin's grandfather, was a freethinking physician who wrote about evolutionary ideas composed in verse but the degree to which he influenced his grandson's ideas is unclear.

v) Jean-Baptiste Lamarck (1744-1829) was the first to propose an explanation of the evolutionary process.
    (1) He proposed a theory of the inheritance of acquired characteristics in which an animal's body parts are altered through use or disuse and these altered characteristics are transmitted to their offspring.
        (a) Although this is biologically impossible, he nevertheless is credited with being the first to recognize the importance of the interaction between organisms and their environment in the evolutionary process.

vi) Georges Cuvier (1769-1832), a French vertebrate paleontologist, was an opponent of Lamarck's evolutionary ideas.
    (1) Cuvier introduced the concept of extinction to explain the existence of hitherto unknown fossil forms.
    (2) Cuvier was a proponent of catastrophism, the idea that the earth's geological features are a result of catastrophic events, the most recent being the biblical flood.
        (a) These events destroyed old life forms, and the newer forms were the result of creation events.

vii) Charles Lyell (1797-1875), author of *Principles of Geology* (1830-1833), is considered the founder of modern geology.
    (1) He demonstrated that uniform processes (uniformitarianism) could account for present geological features.
        (a) His ideas provided the time depth necessary for biological evolution to have occurred.

viii) Thomas Malthus (1766-1834), an English clergyman and economist wrote *An Essay on the Principles of Population* (1798).
    (1) He noted that population sizes increase exponentially but food supplies remain stable.
        (a) This concept inspired both Charles Darwin and Alfred Wallace.

ix) Alfred Russel Wallace (1823-1913) developed his own theory of natural selection after collecting bird and insect specimens in Southeast Asia.
    (1) He first published some of his ideas in 1855, and then in 1858 Wallace wrote "On the Tendency of Varieties to Depart Indefinitely from the Original Type".

x) Mary Anning (1799-1847), an amateur geologist and famous "fossilist", unknowingly contributed significantly to the field of paleontology by discovering hundreds of fossils including the first complete fossil of an *Ichthyosaurus*.

III. The Discovery of Natural Selection

a) Charles Darwin (1809-1882) proposed the first credible mechanism for evolutionary change, natural selection, in *On the Origin of the Species* (1859).
    i) After graduating from Christ's College, where he studied theology, but also cultivated his interests in natural science and geology, he was recommended to join the five-year expedition of the HMS *Beagle*.
        (1) Darwin began the voyage as a believer in the fixity of species, but his observations of, among other things, fossils of giant ancient versions of living animals and varieties of Galápagos finches eventually convinced him to the contrary.
        (2) After his return to England in October 1836, he began to formulate his theory of natural selection.
            (a) He wrote summaries of his ideas in 1842 and 1844, but felt he needed more evidence before he published.
            (b) He was sent both of Wallace's papers, and Darwin was spurred to put all of his ideas in writing.
            (c) Initial reaction to *On the Origin of Species* was mostly negative, but scientific opinion gradually shifted to Darwin's favor.

IV. Natural Selection

a) Darwin envisioned it as a process in which individuals with favorable variations survive and reproduce at a higher rate than those with unfavorable variations. The key elements in Darwin's formulation include:

  i) The potential for reproductive rates that outpace the rate of increase of food supplies.

  ii) The presence of biological variation within all species.

  iii) Constant competition among individuals for survival.

  iv) Individuals with favorable traits are more likely to survive and reproduce.

  v) The environment "determines" which traits are favorable.

  vi) Favorable traits are passed on to offspring at a higher rate than non-favorable traits, thus increasing in frequency through time and eventually producing new species.

  vii) Geographical isolation may lead to the formation of new species.

V. Natural Selection in Action

a) Natural selection is an empirically studied phenomenon.

  i) Industrial melanism is a documented case of evolutionary shifts in frequencies of pigmentation patterns in peppered moth populations near Manchester, England.
    (1) Evolutionary shifts in response to the environment are called adaptations.

  ii) Natural selection has been demonstrated on the (Galápagos) island of Daphne Major.
    (1) Measurements of beak thickness changes through time among the medium ground finch indicate that thicker-beaked individuals had greater reproductive success during droughts.

  iii) Natural selection, through the use of antibiotics, is responsible for the increased number of antibiotic-resistant strains of microorganisms.

b) These examples of natural selection in action indicate that certain common principles apply:

  i) A trait must be inherited to have importance in natural selection.

  ii) Natural selection cannot occur without variation in inherited characteristics.

  iii) Fitness is a relative measure that will change as the environment changes

c) Natural selection can act through not only differential death rates, but also through differential fertility rates.

VI. Constraints on Nineteenth Century Evolutionary Theory

a) Darwin argued that natural selection acts on variation within species, yet no one could explain the source of this variation.

b) Darwin also didn't know how favorable traits were passed from generation to generation.

  i) The laws of heredity were unknown, and most believed that parental traits were blended in the offspring.

  ii) Gregor Mendel had worked out the modern principles of heredity, but his work was not recognized until the beginning of the 20th century.

VII. Opposition to Evolution Today

a) Darwin's formulation of evolution was offensive to Christians because it was in conflict with biblical versions of the creation.

b) The mechanisms of evolution are complex, and many people do not understand them.

  i) Many are not comfortable with the principles of biology and genetics and have little scientific background.

  ii) Most Americans are raised in belief systems that do not emphasize the biological continuity between life forms.

c) Yet, evolutionary theories are accepted, in part, by the Catholic Church and most mainstream Protestants.

d) **A Brief History of Religious-Based Opposition to Evolution in the United States** reveals why most fundamentalists reject all scientific explanations of evolution.
    (1) Historically, religious fundamentalists opposed the teaching of evolution in public schools at the pre-baccalaureate level, and some states prohibited any mention of evolution until 1968.
        (a) Proponents of *creation science* now prefer to use the term *intelligent design*.
        (b) Many attempts to legislate the teaching of evolution have been overturned, such as the attempted takeover of the Dover Area School Board that was thwarted when none of the eight members of the School Board were reelected in 2004.
    (2) The state and federal courts have consistently ruled that laws that require the teaching of ID violate the First Amendment of the Constitution.

Learning Objectives

After reading Chapter 2, the student should be able to:
1. Trace the development of theories of biological evolution in light of advances in the natural sciences, resulting in part from the age of discovery and exploration.
2. Understand Western European world views, particularly the notions of fixity of species and a general sense of stasis, and how these concepts inhibited the development of theories of biological evolution.
3. Discuss the contributions of 18th and 19th century scientists to evolutionary theory.
4. Discuss the contributions of Charles Darwin and Alfred Russel Wallace to the theory of evolution by means of natural selection.
5. Give examples of natural selection.
6. Trace the history of the opposition to evolution in the United States starting in the 1920s through to the present.

Key Terms and Concepts

Binomial nomenclature	p. 22	Natural selection	p. 20
Biological continuity	p. 32	Reproductive success	p. 28
Catastrophism	p. 24	Reproductively isolated	p. 22
Christian fundamentalists	p. 33	Selective pressures	p. 29
Fertility	p. 31	Taxonomy	p. 22
Fitness	p. 28	Transmutation	p. 26
Fixity of species	p. 20	Uniformitarianism	p. 24
Genome	p. 32		

Lecture Suggestions and Enrichment Topics

1. From Jurmain *et al. Basic Genetics for Anthropology* CD: Use the animations of evolution and natural selection to introduce these concepts for your lecture.
2. Often, beginning students have little knowledge of the history of science, and are therefore unaware that creationist/evolutionist debates have been ongoing for over 150 years. It is enlightening to demonstrate that many current "creationist" arguments are merely recycled, previously rejected old ideas.
3. Most students have heard of Darwin, but few really understand the full impact of his ideas not only on scientific thought, but also on his personal life. This author has found that, rather than lecturing, showing a video on Darwin's life brings home these points. The video *Charles Darwin: Evolution's Voice* from A & E's *Biography* series is particularly relevant. Be sure to point out that Darwin waited over 20 years to publish his ideas after returning from the voyage of the HMS *Beagle*, mostly because he was aware that his theories ran contrary to widely accepted biblical doctrines.

Student Media Exercises

1. From Jurmain *et al. Basic Genetics for Anthropology* CD: Have students go through section I, *Evolution and Natural Selection*, and complete the quiz.
2. From J. Kappelman's *Virtual Laboratories for Physical Anthropology* CD: Students should complete Section I of Lab 2: *Evolution and Natural Selection* to reinforce their conceptual understanding of natural selection.
3. Visit the National Center for Science Education's website, http://www.ncseweb.org/, and read about creationist attempts to teach "creation science" in public schools. First click on "Links" and then the "Critiques of Creationism" link and write a paragraph summarizing one of the critiques.
4. One historical figure that vehemently opposed Darwin's ideas was Louis Agassiz (1807-1873). Go to the University of California - Berkeley's Museum of Paleontology website for information on Agassiz (http://www.ucmp.berkeley.edu/history/agassiz.html) and write a brief paragraph on his life and ideas.

Multiple Choice Questions

1. In Europe during the Middle Ages, it was believed that
   A. all species had evolved from a common ancestor.
   B. evolution was the result of natural selection acting upon genetic variation.
   C. all forms were created by God and did not change over time.
   D. most species had become extinct over time.
   E. life was created slowly, over millions of years.

   ANS: C
   PG: 20

2. Among the widely held beliefs in 19th century Europe that prevented the acceptance of biological evolution were the
   A. notion that species did not change.
   B. belief in the recent origin of life on earth.
   C. concept that species were continuously changing.
   D. all of these
   E. A and B only

   ANS: E
   PG: 20-21

3. The belief that species do not change but are the same as when first created is known as
   A. fixity of species.
   B. the Great Chain of Being.
   C. heliocentrism.
   D. uniformitarianism.
   E. natural selection.

   ANS: A
   PG: 20

4. The concept that life was organized into a fixed hierarchy from simple to complex was prevalent well into the 19th century in Europe and the United States. This is referred to as
   A. the binomial system.
   B. natural selection.
   C. uniformitarianism.
   D. the Great Chain of Being.
   E. Lamarckism.

   ANS: D
   PG: 20-21

5. Several events had combined to alter Western Europeans' ideas about the earth by the 18th century. These included
   A. the circumnavigation of the globe.
   B. the discovery of the New World.
   C. the discovery of the heliocentric universe.
   D. all of these
   E. A and B only

   ANS: D
   PG: 20

6. The fact that anatomical structures appear to be uniquely fitted to the functions they serve was the basis for the
   A. theory of uniformitarianism.
   B. theory of natural selection.
   C. theory of the inheritance of acquired characteristics.
   D. theory of catastrophism.
   E. argument from design.

   ANS: E
   PG: 20-21

7. By the 17th century, some scientists were beginning to break with long-held traditions and sought to discover
   A. the physical laws of physics, motion, and gravity.
   B. the supernatural forces that created life.
   C. the structure of the DNA molecule.
   D. how genetic mutations occurred.
   E. none of these

   ANS: A
   PG: 20-21

8. Who first recognized that species were groups of organisms that were distinguished from other such groups by their ability to reproduce?
   A. John Ray
   B. Charles Darwin
   C. Carolus Linnaeus
   D. Alfred Russel Wallace
   E. Jean-Baptiste Lamarck

   ANS: A
   PG: 22

9. Who developed the binomial system of classifying biological organisms?
   A. Jean-Baptiste Lamarck
   B. Georges Cuvier
   C. Carolus Linnaeus
   D. Comte de Buffon
   E. Erasmus Darwin

   ANS: C
   PG: 23

10. Carolus Linnaeus
    A. developed a binomial system of classification for plants and animals.
    B. was a proponent of evolutionary change.
    C. opposed all notions of fixity of species.
    D. was a supporter of Charles Darwin.
    E. developed theories of natural selection.

    ANS: A
    PG: 22

11. _____ was an 18th century thinker who believed that living forms changed in response to the environment. Although he did not think nature was perfect or had a grand purpose, he still rejected the idea that one species could give rise to another.
    A. Alfred Russel Wallace
    B. Comte de Buffon
    C. Erasmus Darwin
    D. John Ray
    E. Georges Cuvier

    ANS: B
    PG: 22

12. Charles Darwin was not the first to conceive of evolutionary change. Those who preceded him included
    A. Jean Baptiste Lamarck.
    B. Erasmus Darwin.
    C. Comte de Buffon.
    D. all of these
    E. none of these

    ANS: D
    PG: 22-24

13. Who was the first to offer a scientific explanation for how species changed?
    A. Carolus Linnaeus
    B. Jean-Baptiste Lamarck
    C. Charles Lyell
    D. Charles Darwin
    E. Erasmus Darwin

    ANS: B
    PG: 23

14. The theory that the frequent use of an organ caused it to be enhanced was developed by
    A. Charles Darwin.
    B. Carolus Linnaeus.
    C. Georges Cuvier.
    D. Charles Lyell.
    E. Jean-Baptiste Lamarck.

    ANS: B
    PG: 22

15. The role of the environment as a significant factor in evolutionary change was first recognized and stated by
    A. Jean-Baptiste Lamarck.
    B. Georges Cuvier.
    C. Thomas Malthus.
    D. Charles Darwin.
    E. Charles Lyell.

    ANS: A
    PG: 23

16. The term "biology" was coined by
    A. Jean-Baptiste Lamarck.
    B. Georges Cuvier.
    C. Thomas Malthus.
    D. Charles Darwin.
    E. Charles Lyell.

    ANS: A
    PG: 23

17. The theory that characteristics acquired during the lifetime of an individual could be passed on to that individual's offspring is termed
    A. natural selection.
    B. catastrophism.
    C. the inheritance of acquired characteristics.
    D. uniformitarianism.
    E. fixity of species.

    ANS: C
    PG: 23

18. The view that the extinction and the subsequent appearance of more modern forms could be explained by a series of disasters and creations is known as
    A. natural selection
    B. catastrophism.
    C. use-disuse theory.
    D. uniformitarianism.
    E. descent with modification

    ANS: B
    PG: 24

19. The opponent of Jean-Baptiste Lamarck who proposed the theory of catastrophism was
    A. Charles Lyell.
    B. Alfred Russel Wallace.
    C. Thomas Malthus.
    D. Erasmus Darwin.
    E. Georges Cuvier.

    ANS: E
    PG: 24

20. Thomas Malthus
    A. proposed that population size is kept in check by the limited availability of resources.
    B. wrote *An Essay on the Principle of Population*.
    C. influenced the development of Charles Darwin's and Alfred Russel Wallace's theories of natural selection.
    D. all of these
    E. A and B only

    ANS: D
    PG: 24

21. Who proposed that population size increases at a faster rate than food supplies?
    A. Erasmus Darwin
    B. Alfred Russel Wallace
    C. Thomas Malthus
    D. Charles Lyell
    E. Jean-Baptiste Lamarck

    ANS: C
    PG: 24

22. Who wrote *Principles of Geology* and emphasized the principle of uniformitarianism?
    A. Charles Darwin
    B. Charles Lyell
    C. Alfred Russel Wallace
    D. Jean-Baptiste Lamarck
    E. Thomas Malthus

    ANS: B
    PG: 24

23. The principle of uniformitarianism
    A. stated that the geological processes that operated in the past are still occurring in the present.
    B. was a problem for the development of evolutionary theories.
    C. proposed that the earth was only a few thousand years old.
    D. was the same as the theory of catastrophism.
    E. was first proposed by Georges Cuvier.

    ANS: A
    PG: 24

24. Which concept, proposed by Charles Lyell, was to have a profound effect on 19th century scientific thought?
    A. Recent origins for earth.
    B. The role of catastrophic events in producing geological phenomena.
    C. Natural selection.
    D. The immense age of the earth and uniform processes.
    E. The inheritance of acquired characteristics.

    ANS: D
    PG: 24

25. Mary Anning is credited with
    A. the principle of uniformitarianism.
    B. being the co discoverer of natural selection.
    C. finding numerous important fossils during the **19th century**.
    D. being married to Charles Darwin.
    E. none of these

    ANS: C
    PG: 25

26. Charles Darwin
    A. grew up in modest circumstances.
    B. began to doubt the fixity of species during a voyage around the world in the 1830s.
    C. received no formal education.
    D. spent two years in Africa where he developed the theory of natural selection.
    E. was a physician who studied natural history as a hobby.

    ANS: B
    PG: 25-26

27. In formulating his theory of natural selection, Charles Darwin
    A. recognized the importance of biological variation within a population.
    B. applied his knowledge of domesticated species to undomesticated ones.
    C. appreciated the fact that population size is limited by availability of food.
    D. all of these
    E. none of these

    ANS: D
    PG: 25-26

28. Charles Darwin
    A. was reluctant to publish his theories.
    B. wrote his theory of natural selection while still on board the *Beagle*.
    C. published his theories as soon as he returned from his voyage on the *Beagle*.
    D. was not concerned with public opinion and did not mind if his theories were criticized.
    E. knew his friends and colleagues would not be affected by the publication of his theory.

    ANS: A
    PG: 25-28

29. Which contemporary of Charles Darwin also developed a theory of evolution by means of natural selection?
    A. Charles Lyell
    B. Jean-Baptiste Lamarck
    C. Erasmus Darwin
    D. Alfred Russel Wallace
    E. Georges Cuvier

    ANS: D
    PG: 28

30. The fact that individuals who possess favorable traits are more likely to survive and reproduce than those who possess less favorable traits is the basis for the theory of
    A. uniformitarianism.
    B. natural selection.
    C. the inheritance of acquired characteristics.
    D. catastrophism.
    E. the fixity of species.

    ANS: B
    PG: 28-29

31. Which of the following concepts DID NOT influence Darwin in developing his theory of evolution?
    A. Population size increases more rapidly than food supplies.
    B. There is competition among individuals for resources.
    C. Species are unchanging types, and individual variation within a species is not important.
    D. There is biological variation in all members of a species.
    E. Favorable variations are passed on and accumulate in populations over time.

    ANS: C
    PG: 25-28

32. Darwin based his evolutionary ideas on
    A. the religious views of the time of a very young earth.
    B. the reality of the concept of fixity of species.
    C. an understanding of modern genetic principles.
    D. all of these
    E. none of these

    ANS: E
    PG: 25-28

33. Selective pressures
    A. remain constant, regardless of the environment.
    B. are unimportant in the evolutionary process.
    C. can change if environmental conditions change.
    D. are directionless and random.
    E. are not related to adaptation.

    ANS: C
    PG: 28-29

34. "Fitness" in an evolutionary sense, refers to an individual's
    A. strength.
    B. reproductive success.
    C. aggressiveness.
    D. size.
    E. age at death.

    ANS: B
    PG: 28

35. According to natural selection theory
    A. traits that confer a reproductive advantage will be selected for.
    B. mutations in somatic cells can be passed on to offspring.
    C. natural selection only acts on hereditary traits.
    D. all of these
    E. A and C only

    ANS: E
    PG: 28-29

36. When it came to explaining the origins of variation within species, Darwin
    A. used Mendel's theory of heredity.
    B. agreed with Lamarck that it was caused by an animal's inner needs.
    C. argued it was caused by differential use of an animals body parts.
    D. had no idea of the true causes.
    E. none of these

    ANS: D
    PG: 31

True/False Questions

1. Evolution is a theory that has little scientific support.

    ANS: False
    PG: 19

2. The Great Chain of Being was first proposed by Charles Darwin..

    ANS: False
    PG: 20

3. Erasmus Darwin is credited with heavily influencing Charles Darwin's evolutionary thinking.

    ANS: False
    PG: 25

4. Use-disuse theory has recently displaced natural selection as mainstream science's most accepted theory of evolutionary change.

    ANS: False
    PG: 24

5. Georges Cuvier, author of *Principles of Geology*, is considered the founder of modern geology.

    ANS: False
    PG: 24

6. Charles Darwin formulated his theory of natural selection while visiting the Galápagos Islands and observing its finches.

    ANS: False
    PG: 24-25

7. Charles Darwin acknowledged the importance of sexual reproduction when formulating his theory of natural selection.

    ANS: True
    PG: 24-25

8. Charles Darwin refrained from immediately publishing his theory of natural selection because he was aware of its controversial nature.

    ANS: True
    PG: 24-28

9. There are no well-documented examples of natural selection operating in natural populations.

    ANS: False
    PG: 24-28

10. Proponents of "creation science" hold that their ideas are absolute and infallible.

    ANS: True
    PG: 32

Short Answer Questions

1. Explain how traditionally held views prevented wide acceptance of evolutionary theories in 19th century Europe and America. Give a specific example.
(pp. 20-21)

2. Outline Lamarck's theory of inheritance of acquired characteristics. According to this theory, what was the environment's role in biological change?
(pp. 20-25)

3. Discuss the ideas of two individuals who significantly affected Darwin's formulation of the theory of natural selection.
(pp. 25-26)

4. How is natural selection related to environmental factors? How can selective pressures change? Give an example.
(pp. 28-31)

5. Discuss the definition of fitness as it pertains to natural selection.
(p. 28)

Essay Questions

1. Many people argue that evolution is "only a theory". Define *theory* and then describe how evolution does or does not fit the definition.

2. Discuss the role of differential fertility in natural selection.

3. Many people in the United States believe in the biblical creation. What factors may account for the fact that many people do not accept evolution as an explanation for the origins and diversity of life?

4. Explain why Charles Lyell's principle of uniformitarianism was important to Charles Darwin and Alfred Russel Wallace as they developed their theories of biological evolution.

CHAPTER 3: THE BIOLOGICAL BASIS OF LIFE

Chapter Outline

I. Introduction
    a) Genetics is the study of how traits are transmitted from generation to generation.
        i) Understanding genetics is crucial to understanding the process of evolution and is a crucial link to the sub disciplines of biological anthropology.

II. The Cell
    a) Cells are the basic units of life for all organisms.
        i) Some organisms are single-celled, others, called multicellular organisms, are composed of up to 1 billion cells.
        ii) Prokaryotic cells appeared about 3.7 billion years ago.
            (1) These are single-celled organisms such as bacteria and blue-green algae.
        iii) Eukaryotic cells appeared about 1.2 billion years ago.
            (1) These cells have a membrane-bound nucleus and distinct organelles.
                (a) The nucleus contains genetic information in the form of DNA and RNA.
                (b) The cytoplasm surrounds the nucleus and contains various organelles that have metabolic functions. Among these organelles are the mitochondria and the ribosomes.
                    (i) The mitochondria function in energy production and have their own DNA (mtDNA).
                    (ii) The ribosomes function in protein synthesis.
        iv) There are two cell types.
            (1) Somatic cells are the cellular components of body tissues.
            (2) Gametes are sex cells, either sperm or ova, and two gametes fuse to form a zygote.

III. DNA Structure
    a) The chemical and physical properties of DNA were discovered in 1953.
    b) The DNA molecule is composed of two complementary chains of nucleotides.
        i) A single nucleotide is composed of a deoxyribose sugar, a phosphate group, and one of four nitrogenous bases.
            (1) The bases are adenine, guanine, thymine, and cytosine.
            (2) The double helix forms because adenine bonds to thymine, and guanine bonds to cytosine.
            (3) This complementary base bonding is the key to DNA's ability to replicate itself.

IV. DNA Replication
    a) DNA replication occurs before the cell divides.
        i) Initially, enzymes break the bonds between the two DNA strands.
        ii) The exposed bases attract unattached complementary DNA nucleotides.
        iii) The two parental nucleotide chains serve as models for the growing replicated strands.
            (1) Thus, each new DNA molecule consists of one original nucleotide chain joined to one new nucleotide chain.

V. Protein Synthesis
    a) Proteins are complex, three-dimensional molecules composed of amino acids with the ability to bind to other molecules.
        i) The protein hemoglobin, found in red blood cells, is able to transport oxygen through the body because of its ability to bind to oxygen.
    b) Some proteins are structural while others (such as enzymes and hormones) are functional.
        i) Enzymes initiate and enhance chemical reactions.

ii) Specialized cells produce hormones, which target tissues and have specific effects.
    (1) Physiological development and metabolic activities can be altered or prevented from occurring if protein synthesis does not occur accurately.
iii) Regulatory proteins can enter a cell's nucleus, bind to the DNA and regulate its activity.
c) Proteins are composed of amino acids.
    i) There are 20 amino acids; 8 of these must be obtained through the diet.
    ii) A protein's function is determined by its sequence of amino acids.
        (1) The sequence of DNA bases taken three at a time (a triplet) ultimately specifies which amino acids are to be used to synthesize a protein.
d) Protein synthesis occurs at the ribosomes.
    i) The first step is called transcription. This occurs in the nucleus as a complementary strand of mRNA is produced from the DNA strand.
        (1) The mRNA triplets are referred to as codons.
        (2) mRNA differs from DNA in that it is single-stranded, it contains a different type of sugar, and it contains uracil instead of thymine.
    ii) The second step, translation, occurs at the ribosomes.
        (1) Here, the mRNA strand is "read" by the ribosomes three bases (one codon) at a time.
        (2) This step requires the carrier molecule, transfer RNA (tRNA).
            (a) Each tRNA has the ability to bind to one amino acid.
            (b) Particular tRNA molecules (matching the mRNA codon) carry the appropriate amino acid to the ribosomes to be incorporated into the growing polypeptide chain.

VI. What Is a Gene?

a) A gene is the sequence of DNA bases responsible for the synthesis of a protein or a portion of a protein.
    i) New genetic research indicates that we must modify the above definition, since DNA is known to also code for RNA and DNA nucleotides.
        (1) Some proteins are composed of more than one polypeptide chain, each of which results from the action of a single gene.
        (2) A change in the DNA sequence is a mutation.
b) Gene action is complex, since not all segments of DNA are expressed during protein synthesis.
    i) Exons are DNA segments that are transcribed into mRNA and are expressed in protein synthesis.
    ii) Introns are DNA segments that are transcribed into mRNA but eliminated before transcription.
c) **Regulatory genes** produce regulatory proteins that can switch on or turn off other segments of DNA.
    i) Alterations in regulatory genes may be responsible for the physical differences between closely related species.
        (1) Changes in the regulatory genes of chimpanzees and/or humans may be responsible for our comparatively large physical differences, despite the fact that humans and chimpanzees share about 98% of their DNA.
        (2) The most important regulatory genes are the *Hox* genes.
            (a) These highly conserved genes direct the development of the body plan and the segmentation of the embryonic tissues.

VII. Mutation: When a Gene Changes

a) Sickle-cell anemia is a well-known disorder that is the result of a point mutation.
    i) Normal adult hemoglobin A is composed of 2 alpha and 2 beta chains of amino acids.
    ii) Abnormal hemoglobin S results when valine is substituted for glutamic acid at the sixth position of the beta chain.

(1) If a person has two copies of the Hb^S gene, they will have sickle-cell anemia.

    (a) This occurs because hemoglobin S causes red blood cells to collapse and form a sickle-shape under oxygen stress.

(2) If a person has one Hb^A gene and one Hb^S gene, they have the sickle-cell trait and only about 40% of their hemoglobin is abnormal. They are less severely affected during times of oxygen stress and have normal life spans.

  b) Mutations have evolutionary consequences only if they are passed on to the offspring in the gametes.

VIII. Chromosomes

  a) DNA exists during much of the cell cycle as chromatin, the uncoiled form of DNA.

  b) Chromosomes become visible during cell division as the DNA forms complex coils.

    i) They appear as two strands joined at the centromere because the DNA has replicated during interphase.

    ii) Humans have 46 chromosomes, whereas gorillas and chimpanzees have 48.

  c) Chromosomes generally occur in pairs in eukaryotes.

    i) Homologous chromosomes are pairs that carry genes influencing the same traits, although their alleles may differ.

      (1) The locus is the location of a gene on a chromosome. For example, the ABO locus is on chromosome 9.

    ii) The two basic types of chromosomes are autosomes and sex chromosomes.

      (1) The sex chromosomes are designated X and Y; whereas the X functions more like an autosome, the Y chromosome primarily functions in sex determination in mammals.

    iii) All autosomes occur in pairs, and abnormal numbers often result in death soon after conception.

      (1) Abnormal numbers of sex chromosomes may result in sterility or other non-fatal consequences.

IX. Karyotyping Chromosomes

  a) Photomicrographs of dividing cells are used to produce a karyotype.

    i) Individual chromosomes are identified by the characteristic position of the centromere and banding patterns produced by colored stains.

X. Cell Division

  a) **Mitosis** occurs in somatic cells.

    i) Human somatic cells contain 46 double-stranded chromosomes in the early stages of mitosis.

    ii) Chromosomes line up along the center of the cell and the chromosomes are pulled apart at the centromere.

      (1) The result is a genetically identical daughter cell with the diploid number of chromosomes.

  b) **Meiosis** occurs in gametes.

    i) Meiosis has two divisions: a reduction division and a second cell division.

      (1) In the first division, pairs of homologous chromosomes line up at the center of the cell. As division proceeds, the double-stranded chromosomes are not pulled apart; rather, the members of pairs migrate to opposite sides of the cell.

        (a) The result is two cells, each of which contains 23 double-stranded chromosomes.

        (b) Crossing-over also occurs during the reduction division.

      (2) In the second division, the 23 double-stranded chromosomes align at the center of the cell and then are pulled apart at the centromere.

        (a) This reduction is similar to mitosis.

        (b) The result is four daughter cells, each with the haploid number of chromosomes.

XI. The Evolutionary Significance of Meiosis

a) Meiosis (and sexual reproduction) increases genetic variation in populations very quickly.

    i) The random assortment of chromosomes at the center of the cell during the first meiotic division can result in 8 million genetically different gametes.

        (1) The number rises to 70 trillion when the mating of two individuals is considered.

        (2) This, in part, provides the genetic diversity for natural selection to act on.

b) Genetic variation is essential for the process of adaptation.

    i) If all individuals were genetically identical, evolution could not proceed.

c) **Problems with meiosis** can have significant consequences.

    i) About 98% of newborns have the correct number of chromosomes.

        (1) Yet, about 50% of pregnancies terminate in miscarriages.

        (2) Of these miscarriages, about 70% are the result of abnormal chromosome number.

    ii) Failure of homologous chromosomes or chromosome strands to separate during meiosis is termed nondisjunction.

        (1) Nondisjunction leads to a monosomy or trisomy.

        (2) Down syndrome (trisomy 21) occurs when there are three copies of chromosome 21 present in the individual.

           (a) This occurs in about 1/1,000 live births and the incidence of trisomy 21 increases with increased maternal age.

        (3) Nondisjunction may also occur in sex chromosomes.

           (a) Observed karyotypes are XXY, XO, XXX, and XYY, some of which are associated with impaired mental function and/or sterility.

           (b) It is not possible to survive without an X chromosome.

XII. New Frontiers

a) The discovery of DNA's structure and function has revolutionized biology.

    i) The PCR technique was developed in 1986 and is used to analyze nucleotide sequences from very small segments of DNA.

        (1) With PCR very small samples of DNA can be examined for the patterns of repeated DNA sequences unique to each individual. This process is called DNA fingerprinting and is used by forensic scientists.

    ii) Recombinant DNA technology is used to insert genes from one species into another to produce large quantities of gene products.

    iii) Genetic manipulation has become increasingly controversial.

        (1) There are concerns over long-term exposure to genetically altered products.

        (2) The first successful clone of an animal (an African toad) was accomplished in the 1960s.

           (a) Dolly, the sheep, was cloned in 1997. She became ill with arthritis and a virus-caused lung tumor and was euthanized in 2003.

           (b) A more recently cloned species is the horse; a foal named Prometea was born in May 2003.

    iv) The Human Genome Project, begun in 1990, attempts to sequence all 30,000 of our genes.

        (1) About 87% of the genome had been sequenced (in rough form) by 2000 and the project was completed in 2003

           (a) A rough draft of the chimpanzee genome was announced in 2003.

        (2) Work will continue for years to discover the identity and functions of the proteins produced by the identified genes.

        (3) The genomes of over 600 species (mostly viruses) have already been sequenced.

    v) Ultimately, we will begin comparative analyses of human and nonhuman primate genomes to further assess their evolutionary relationships.

Learning Objectives

After reading Chapter 3, the student should be able to:

1. Identify the basic cell types and discuss the function of the mitochondria and ribosomes.
2. Discuss the structure and function of DNA and RNA.
3. Outline the steps of protein synthesis.
4. Discuss the nature of chromosomes, karyotyping, and the concept of a gene.
5. Compare and contrast mitosis with meiosis.
6. Discuss the importance of meiosis to the evolutionary process.
7. Identify the cause of nondisjunction during meiosis and discuss the resultant problems.
8. Discuss the "new frontiers" of genetic research, including the significance of recombinant DNA technology and the Human Genome Project.

Key Terms and Concepts

Alleles	p. 52	Mitochondrial DNA (mtDNA)	p. 38
Amino acids	p. 42	Mitosis	p. 53
Autosomes	p. 50	Molecules	p. 38
Centromere	p. 50	Mutation	p. 44
Chromatin	p. 49	Nondisjunction	p. 56
Chromosomes	p. 49	Nucleotides	p. 38
Clones	p. 54	Nucleus	p. 37
Complementary	p. 40	Organelles	p 37
Cytoplasm	p. 38	Point mutation	p. 49
Deoxyribonucleic acid (DNA)	p. 38	Polymerase chain reaction (PCR)	p. 58
Enzymes	p. 40	Polypeptide chain	p. 44
Exons	p. 46	Protein synthesis	p. 38
Gametes	p. 38	Proteins	p. 38
Gene	p. 44	Random assortment	p. 54
Genome	p. 59	Recombinant DNA technology	p. 58
Hemoglobin	p. 40	Recombination (crossing over)	p. 54
Homeobox genes	p. 46	Regulatory proteins	p. 41
Hormones	p. 41	Replicate	p. 40
Human Genome Project	p. 59	Ribonucleic acid (RNA)	p. 38
Introns	p. 46	Ribosomes	p. 38
Karyotype	p. 52	Sex chromosomes	p. 50
Locus (*pl.*, loci)	p. 50	Sickle-cell anemia	p. 49
Meiosis	p. 53	Somatic cells	p. 38
Messenger RNA (mRNA)	p. 42	Transfer RNA (tRNA)	p. 43
Mitochondria (mitochondrion)	p. 38	Zygote	p. 38

Lecture Suggestions and Enrichment Topics

1. From Jurmain *et al. Basic Genetics for Anthropology* CD: Use the animations of DNA and cell divisions to introduce these concepts for your lecture.
2. Elaborate on cell function and the specialization of cells. Point out that although all cells carry the same DNA, much of the DNA is "switched off" during fetal development.
3. Elaborate on the universal nature of the genetic code to emphasize the concept of biological continuity. Reinforce the fact that chimpanzees and humans share about 98% of their DNA.
4. Provide examples of other autosomal trisomies, such as trisomy 13 (Patau syndrome), and trisomy 18 (Edwards syndrome). Contrast the severity of autosomal trisomies with trisomies or monosomies of the sex chromosomes.
5. Elaborate on the process of DNA fingerprinting; most students are mystified by the subject.

Student Media Exercises

1. Log on to Wadsworth's *Molecular Methods in Anthropology Module* (http://www.wadsworth.com/ anthropology_d/special_features/ext/molecular_methods/), read the section *Molecular Anthropology and the Human Genome* and then answer *Discussion Question 1.*
2. Log on to Wadsworth's *Molecular Methods in Anthropology Module* (http://www.wadsworth.com/ anthropology_d/special_features/ext/molecular_methods/), read the section *DNA Extraction*, and then write a short summary explaining the method.
3. From J. Kappelman's *Virtual Laboratories for Physical Anthropology* CD: Students should complete Section II of Lab 2: *Genetic Basis of Inheritance* to reinforce their conceptual understanding of DNA structure and function.
4. From Jurmain *et al. Basic Genetics for Anthropology* CD: Have students go through section II, *DNA*, and complete the quiz.
5. From Jurmain *et al. Basic Genetics for Anthropology* CD: Have students go through section III, *Cell Division*, and complete the quiz.
6. Watson and Crick's original 1953 article, *A Structure for Deoxyribose Nucleic Acid*, can be found at http://www.watsoncrombie.com/watson_crick_nature.html. Read the article and list the most important points that are made by the authors.

Multiple Choice Questions

1. Cells
   A. are the basic units of life.
   B. usually do not have DNA.
   C. only have a nucleus and no cytoplasm.
   D. are only inherited from one parent.
   E. originated on earth approximately 5 million years ago.

   ANS: A
   PG: 37

2. The cell nucleus
   A. is the same thing as the cytoplasm.
   B. is not distinct from the cytoplasm.
   C. contains only X and Y chromosomes.
   D. is made up of ribosomes.
   E. contains genetic information.

   ANS: E
   PG: 37

3. Which of the following is NOT a function of cells?
   A. protein synthesis
   B. storing DNA
   C. breaking down nutrients
   D. storing PCR
   E. storing energy

   ANS: D
   PG: 37,38

4. Ribosomes are
   A. the sex chromosomes.
   B. gametes.
   C. found only in prokaryotes.
   D. only present when the cell divides.
   E. important to protein synthesis.

   ANS: E
   PG: 38

5. Somatic cells are
   A. one type of eukaryotic cell.
   B. not gametes.
   C. the cellular components of tissue.
   D. all of these
   E. A and B only

   ANS: D
   PG: 38

6. The two basic types of eukaryotic cells are somatic cells and
   A. zygotes.
   B. gametes.
   C. autosomes.
   D. polar bodies.
   E. organelles.

   ANS: B
   PG: 38

7. Gametes
   A. are egg and sperm cells.
   B. are also called zygotes.
   C. transmit genetic information from parent to offspring.
   D. all of these
   E. A and C only

   ANS: E
   PG: 38

8. A zygote
   A. is formed by the union of two somatic cells.
   B. has only half the full complement of genetic material.
   C. is part of a nucleotide.
   D. undergoes meiosis.
   E. is a fertilized egg.

   ANS: E
   PG: 38

9. DNA
   A. is single-stranded.
   B. is composed of nitrogenous bases, sugars and gametes.
   C. directs cellular functions.
   D. contains the base uracil.
   E. contains six different nitrogenous bases.

   ANS: C
   PG: 38

10. A DNA nucleotide
    A. is composed of a nitrogenous base, a sugar, and a phosphorous unit.
    B. is the same thing as an RNA molecule.
    C. codes for the production of an amino acid.
    D. can include the nitrogenous base uracil.
    E. A and B only

    ANS: A
    PG: 38

11. Which of the following is not a nitrogenous base found in DNA?
    A. Uracil
    B. Guanine
    C. Thymine
    D. Adenine
    E. Cytosine

    ANS: A
    PG: 38

12. The DNA base adenine always pairs with which other DNA base(s)?
    A. Guanine
    B. Thymine
    C. Cytosine
    D. Uracil
    E. B and D only

    ANS: B
    PG: 40

13. Enzymes
    A. are proteins.
    B. are major constituents of body tissues.
    C. initiate and enhance chemical reactions.
    D. A and C only
    E. none of these

    ANS: D
    PG: 40

14. Which of the following is FALSE?
    A. Proteins are composed of amino acids.
    B. The first step in protein synthesis is translation.
    C. The number and sequence of amino acids determines protein function.
    D. Proteins are manufactured by the ribosomes.
    E. The sequence of amino acids in a protein is ultimately determined by the sequence of DNA bases.

    ANS: B
    PG: 40-41

15. Which of the following statements concerning RNA is FALSE?
    A. It contains the base uracil instead of thymine.
    B. It is single-stranded.
    C. It contains the same sugar that is found in DNA.
    D. It is able to pass through the nuclear membrane.
    E. It is involved in the synthesis of proteins.

    ANS: C
    PG: 42-43

16. In protein synthesis, the process called transcription is the
    A. manufacture of tRNA.
    B. assembly of polypeptide chains.
    C. assembly of a mRNA molecule.
    D. production of amino acids.
    E. manufacture of ribosomal RNA.

    ANS: C
    PG: 43

17. The entire sequence of DNA bases responsible for the manufacture of a protein or part of a protein is called a (an)
    A. helix.
    B. codon.
    C. polypeptide
    D. amino acid.
    E. gene.

    ANS: E
    PG: 44

18. The component of red blood cells responsible for oxygen transport is
    A. valine.
    B. hemoglobin.
    C. proline.
    D. the cell membrane.
    E. the ribosomes.

    ANS: B
    PG: 48

19. The substitution of one DNA base for another is a (an)
    A. point mutation.
    B. genome.
    C. trisomy.
    D. allele.
    E. locus.

    ANS: A
    PG: 49

20. Sickle-cell anemia results from
    A. a single amino acid substitution in the hemoglobin molecule.
    B. a defect in the normal hemoglobin molecule.
    C. a point mutation.
    D. all of these
    E. none of these

    ANS: D
    PG: 48-49

21. Which of the following statements is FALSE?
    A. Sickle-cell anemia can result in impaired blood circulation.
    B. Individuals with sickle-cell anemia inherited an abnormal allele from each parent that causes
       the production of an altered form of hemoglobin.
    C. People with sickle-cell trait are as severely affected as those with sickle-cell anemia.
    D. The abnormal form of hemoglobin in people with sickle-cell anemia is called hemoglobin S.
    E. The mutation that results in sickle-cell anemia affects the hemoglobin beta chain.

    ANS: C
    PG: 48

22. That portion of a cell's existence during which metabolic processes occur is called
    A. interphase.
    B. metaphase.
    C. anaphase.
    D. telophase.
    E. prophase.

    ANS: A
    PG: 53-54

23. When DNA occurs as an uncoiled, uncondensed filamentous substance, it is called
    A. a chromosome.
    B. mitochondrial DNA.
    C. a ribosome.
    D. chromatin.
    E. an autosome.

    ANS: D
    PG: 49

24. Chromosomes are
    A. made up of DNA and protein.
    B. visible only during certain stages of cell division.
    C. composed of two strands during certain stages of cell division.
    D. all of these
    E. B and C only

    ANS: D
    PG: 49-50

25. The two strands of a chromosome are joined at a constricted region called the
    A. autosome.
    B. ribosome.
    C. centromere.
    D. nucleotide.
    E. cytoplasm.

    ANS: C
    PG: 51-53

26. Homologous chromosomes
    A. are member of different pairs.
    B. are genetically identical.
    C. carry genetic information that influences the same traits.
    D. are only inherited from the mother.
    E. are only inherited from the father.

    ANS: C
    PG: 51-53

27. How many chromosomes occur in a normal human somatic cell?
    A. 23
    B. 48
    C. 46
    D. 53
    E. 50

    ANS: C
    PG: 49-50

28. How many chromosome **pairs** occur in a normal human somatic cell?
    A. 24
    B. 23
    C. 26
    D. 25
    E. 22

    ANS: B
    PG: 49-50

29. Alleles are
    A. segments of tRNA that code for polypeptide chains.
    B. only present on X and Y chromosomes.
    C. the entire genetic make-up of an individual.
    D. alternative forms of a gene.
    E. proteins.

    ANS: D
    PG: 52

30. The X and Y chromosomes are called
    A. autosomes.
    B. gametes.
    C. centromeres.
    D. sex chromosomes.
    E. karyotypes.

    ANS: D
    PG: 50

31. The Y chromosome
    A. is found in both sexes, males have two, females have one.
    B. influences numerous characteristics in addition to sex determination.
    C. can be inherited form either parent.
    D. carries genes that cause the fetus to develop as a male.
    E. causes a fetus to develop as female if there are two present.

    ANS: D
    PG: 50

32. Which statement is TRUE of autosomes?
    A. It is not necessary for them to occur in pairs for normal physiological functions to occur.
    B. A person can be missing an autosome and not exhibit any abnormalities.
    C. Having extra autosomes is not a problem for most people.
    D. Over half the autosomes an individual possesses are inherited from the mother.
    E. Abnormal numbers of autosomes always result in serious problems, and most result in death.

    ANS: E
    PG: 50

33. An arrangement of chromosomes in terms of size, position of the centromere, and similarity of banding patterns is called a (an)
    A. homology.
    B. random assortment.
    C. karyotype.
    D. gamete.
    E. genome.

    ANS: C
    PG: 52

34. Meiosis
    A. is the cell division process in somatic cells.
    B. replaces cells during growth and development.
    C. permits healing of injured tissue.
    D. all of these
    E. none of these

    ANS: E
    PG: 54

35. Which of the following is true of mitosis?
    A. The process requires only one cell division to be complete.
    B. There are two cell divisions before the process is complete.
    C. The result is gamete formation.
    D. Crossing-over occurs between homologous chromosomes.
    E. Homologous chromosomes come together as pairs.

    ANS: A
    PG: 53

36. After mitosis, daughter cells contain the same amount of DNA as in the original cell. This is due to
    A. protein synthesis.
    B. recombination.
    C. pairing of homologous chromosomes.
    D. meiosis
    E. DNA replication.

    ANS: E
    PG: 53-54

37. Which of the following is FALSE regarding the process of meiosis?
    A. Meiosis produces gametes.
    B. Meiosis produces daughter cells with half the original amount of DNA found in the original cell.
    C. There are two cell divisions.
    D. Meiosis produces daughter cells with the same amount of DNA found in the original cell.
    E. Homologous chromosomes exchange genetic information.

    ANS: D
    PG: 54-55

38. The number of chromosomes found in a somatic cell is called the _____ number.
    A. diploid
    B. somatic
    C. gametic
    D. haploid
    E. trisomic

    ANS: A
    PG: 49-50

39. Reduction division occurs during
    A. crossing over.
    B. mitosis.
    C. meiosis.
    D. protein synthesis.
    E. none of these.

    ANS: C
    PG: 54

40. Which of the following produces varying combinations of genes in populations?
    A. recombination
    B. meiosis
    C. nondisjunction
    D. all of these
    E. A and B only

    ANS: E
    PG: 54-55

41. Which of the following is FALSE?
    A. Nondisjunction occurs when homologous chromosomes fail to separate.
    B. Nondisjunction occurs when strands of the same chromosome fail to separate.
    C. Nondisjunction can result in a daughter cell with an extra chromosome.
    D. Nondisjunction can result in a daughter cell completely lacking a chromosome.
    E. Nondisjunction occurs only in mitosis.

    ANS: E
    PG: 53-54

42. Trisomy 21
    A. occurs more frequently with advancing age of the mother.
    B. is caused by nondisjunction.
    C. is caused by having three X chromosomes.
    D. all of these
    E. A and B only

    ANS: E
    PG: 57

43. Scientists use _____ to produce many copies of small DNA fragments, such as those obtained at crime scenes or from fossils.
    A. transcription
    B. polymerase chain reactions
    C. nondisjunction
    D. trisomies
    E. random assortment of alleles

    ANS: B
    PG: 58

44. A major goal of the Human Genome Project is to
    A. facilitate human cloning.
    B. map the chromosomes of every human on the planet.
    C. sequence the entire human genome.
    D. trace evolutionary relationships among primates.
    E. prevent overpopulation.

    ANS: C
    PG: 59

True/False Questions

1. A eukaryotic cell is composed of carbohydrates, lipids, and proteins, but lacks nucleic acids.

    ANS: False
    PG: 38

2. Mitochondrial DNA has the same molecular structure and function as nuclear DNA.

    ANS: True
    PG: 38

3. A triplet is a series of three DNA bases.

    ANS: True
    PG: 38-40

4. The process of transcription during protein synthesis occurs at the ribosomes.

    ANS: False
    PG: 43

5. Regulatory genes produce enzymes and other proteins that either switch on or turn off other segments of DNA.

    ANS: True
    PG: 40

6. Homeotic genes are expressed only during adulthood.

    ANS: False
    PG: 44-47

7. Individuals who inherit only one of the hemoglobin S alleles have sickle-cell anemia.

    ANS: False
    PG: 48

8. Karyotype analysis is often used in the prenatal diagnosis of chromosomal abnormalities.

    ANS: True
    PG: 52

9. Nondisjunction can occur in the autosomes but never occurs in the sex chromosomes.

    ANS: False
    PG: 56-57

10. Turner syndrome females have three X chromosomes.

    ANS: False
    PG: 57

Short Answer Questions

1. Describe the structure of the DNA molecule; include as much detail as you can.
   (pp. 40-41)

2. How do DNA and RNA differ in structure and function?
   (pp. 41-43)

3. What are the two steps in protein synthesis? Where does each occur?
   (pp. 40-43)

4. Compare and contrast the processes and end products of mitosis and meiosis.
   (pp. 53-56)

5. Describe reduction division and explain why it is necessary to meiosis.
   (pp. 54-55)

6. Discuss the evolutionary significance of meiosis.
   (p. 54-55)

7. Explain how nondisjunction can occur. Give one example of nondisjunction of the autosomes.
   (pp. 56-57)

8. Give two examples of how the field of genetics has revolutionized biological science.
   (pp. 58-59)

Essay Questions

1. Humans and chimpanzees share about 98% of their DNA. What might be the role of regulatory genes in producing the anatomical differences between these two lineages?

2. Discuss whether it is possible for a human to have the following combinations of sex chromosomes: XYY; XO (only one X and no Y); XXX.

3. Using your knowledge of the principles of natural selection, explain why genetic variation is central to the evolutionary process.

CHAPTER 4: HEREDITY AND EVOLUTION

Chapter Outline

I. **Introduction**
   a) The genetic principles described by Mendel form the basis of modern genetics.
      i) Although farmers and herders realized they could manipulate the frequency and expression of desired traits in plants and animals, no one previous to Mendel could explain how these traits were affected through selective breeding.
      ii) The predominant belief centered on the blending of parental traits in the offspring.
      iii) Even Darwin believed in some aspects of blending inheritance, since he was unaware of Mendel's work.

II. **The Genetic Principles Discovered by Mendel**
   a) Gregor Mendel (1822-1884) developed his theory of heredity while working with garden pea hybrids.
      i) Purebred strains were crossed to produce hybrids, and Mendel calculated the frequencies of traits in each generation.
      ii) These results were the empirical basis for his theory.
   b) **Segregation**
      i) The parental (P) generation was crossed to produce the first filial (F_1) generation.
         (1) The F_1 generation did not have intermediate traits.
         (2) The F_1 generation was then crossed to produce the F_2 generation.
            (a) One expression of the trait, shortness of the stem or wrinkling of the seeds, for example, disappeared in the F_1 generation, but reappeared in the F_2 generation.
            (b) The expression that was present in the F_1 generation occurred more often in the F_2 generation (in a 3:1 ratio).
         (3) Mendel concluded that discrete units, occurring in pairs and separating into different sex cells, must control the traits.
            (a) This is Mendel's **principle of segregation**.
   c) **Dominance and Recessiveness**
      i) Mendel used these terms to account for the fact that the expression of one (recessive) trait in the F_1 generation was masked by the expression of the other (dominant) trait.
         (1) Variations of genes at a locus are termed alleles.
         (2) Plant height, stem length, and other traits in Figure 4-2 are controlled by two alleles at one locus.
            (a) When two copies of the same allele occur at one locus, the individual is homozygous.
            (b) When two different alleles are paired at the same locus, the individual is heterozygous.
         (3) The actual genetic makeup is called the genotype and the observed manifestation of the genotype is the phenotype.
      ii) A Punnett square can be used to predict the proportions of F_2 phenotypes and genotypes.
         (1) When two individuals are crossed, both heterozygous at a given locus, typical Mendelian ratios are produced in the next generation.
            (a) The phenotypic ratio is 3:1 and the genotypic ratio is 1:2:1.
   d) **Independent Assortment**
      i) Mendel made crosses with two traits simultaneously, such as plant height and seed color.
      ii) The results indicated that the proportion of F_2 traits did not affect each other.
         (1) Mendel stated this relationship as the **principle of independent assortment**.
            (a) The loci coding for height and seed color happened to be on different chromosomes that assort independently of each other during meiosis and were therefore not linked.

III. Mendelian Inheritance in Humans

a) Mendelian traits are also called discrete traits or traits of simple inheritance.

b) There are over 17,000 Mendelian traits in humans.

    i) Most are biochemical in nature and the result of harmful alleles.

    ii) Traits may be inherited either as dominant or recessive alleles.

    iii) Recessive conditions are typically associated with the lack of a substance.

        (1) Individuals who are heterozygous are termed carriers.

        (2) The probability of having an affected child when both parents are carriers is 25%.

c) The ABO blood groups are inherited in a Mendelian fashion.

    i) Dominance, recessiveness, as well as codominance are illustrated in this system.

d) **Misconceptions Regarding Dominance and Recessiveness**

    i) Some traits, such as eye color, are mistakenly described as having Mendelian inheritance.

        (1) Eye color is in fact determined by alleles occurring at two or three loci.

    ii) Dominance and recessiveness are not all-or-nothing situations.

        (1) Recessive alleles may have an effect on the phenotype in the heterozygous condition.

        (2) Several alleles are known to have effects on the phenotype at the biochemical level.

    iii) Dominant alleles are not "stronger", "better", or more common than recessive alleles.

e) **Patterns of Inheritance**

    i) Six different modes of Mendelian inheritance have been identified in humans through the use of pedigree analysis: autosomal dominant, autosomal recessive, X-linked recessive, X-linked dominant, Y-linked, and mitochondrial.

        (1) **Autosomal dominant traits** are governed by loci on the autosomes.

            (a) All affected family members have at least one affected parent.

            (b) Males and females are equally affected.

        (2) **Autosomal recessive traits** are also influenced by loci on autosomes.

            (a) Pedigrees for autosomal recessive traits differ from those for autosomal dominant traits.

                (i) Recessive traits may appear to skip generations if both parents are carriers.

                (ii) Most affected individuals have unaffected parents.

                (iii) The frequency of affected offspring from most matings is less than 50%.

                (iv) As in autosomal dominant traits, males and females are equally affected.

        (3) **Sex-linked traits** are affected by loci on either the X or Y chromosome.

            (a) Most of the approximately 450 known sex-linked traits have loci on the X chromosome.

                (i) Because females have two X chromosomes, they have an autosomal-like pattern of expression.

                (ii) Males, having only one X chromosome, are hemizygous, and cannot express dominance or recessiveness for X-linked traits.

IV. Non-Mendelian Patterns of Inheritance

a) **Polygenic inheritance** refers to traits that are influenced by alleles at two or more loci.

    i) For example, melanin production is influenced by between 3 and 6 genetic loci.

        (1) The alleles coding for melanin production have additive effects.

        (2) The effect of multiple alleles at several loci produces continuous variation in skin tone.

    ii) Much of the variation in human phenotypes used in traditional racial classifications is produced by polygenic, not Mendelian, traits.

    iii) Polygenic traits are continuous in nature. They can be measured and then analyzed with traditional statistical methods using means and standard deviations.

        (1) Many Mendelian traits have known loci. However, polygenic traits cannot be traced to specific loci.

b) **Pleiotropy**
   i) Pleiotropic effects, where one gene influences more than one phenotypic expression, are probably very common.
   ii) There are many examples of pleiotropic genes, such as the sickle-cell allele and the autosomal recessive disorder phenylketonuria (PKU).
      (1) Individuals who are homozygous for PKU do not produce the enzyme phenylketonurase, which converts phenylalanine into tyrosine.
         (a) Without phenylketonurase, phenylalanine breaks down into other substances that accumulate in the central nervous system, potentially resulting in mental retardation.

c) **Mitochondrial Inheritance**
   i) mtDNA is transmitted to the offspring only from the mother because sperm cells lose their mitochondria prior to fertilization of the egg.
   ii) mtDNA mutation rates have been used to construct evolutionary relationships between primate species and between living human populations.

V. **Genetic and Environmental Factors**
   a) For polygenic traits, many aspects of the phenotype are influenced by genetic-environmental interactions.
   b) Mendelian traits are less likely to be influenced by the environment.

VI. **Modern Evolutionary Theory**
   a) Modern evolutionary theory has its roots in the principles of natural selection formulated by Darwin and Wallace, plus the rediscovery of Mendelian principles of inheritance. The competing explanations of evolution offered by mutationists and selectionists were synthesized into a single theory in mid-1930.
      i) **The Modern Synthesis**
         (1) Julian Huxley coined the term "Modern Synthesis" – the comprehensive theory of evolution that incorporates two processes: natural selection and mutation.
         (2) Evolution is defined as a two stage process consisting of:
            (a) The production and redistribution of variation.
            (b) The process of natural selection.

VII. **A Current Definition of Evolution**
   a) Evolution can be defined as a change in allele frequency from one generation to the next.
      i) Allele frequencies only refer to populations, since individuals cannot change alleles.
   b) Short-term evolutionary changes, such as allele frequency changes from one generation to the next, are termed microevolution.
   c) Long-term evolutionary effects evident in the fossil record are termed macroevolution.

VIII. **Factors That Produce and Redistribute Variation**
   a) **Mutations** are alterations in the genetic material.
      i) Mutations must occur in the gametes (sperm or egg) in order to have evolutionary consequences.
      ii) Mutation rates tend to be low, and mutations alone tend to have little impact on changes in allele frequencies.
         (1) Evolutionary changes can occur rapidly when mutations are coupled with natural selection.
         (2) Mutations produce new genetic variation, so they have a key role in evolutionary change.
   b) **Gene Flow** is the exchange of genes between populations.
      i) Population movements (and the resulting exchange of genes) have been very high during the past 500 years, but this does not mean that gene flow was reduced in ancient hunting and gathering populations.
         (1) Gene flow between human populations during the past 1 million years helps to explain why human speciation has been rare.

c) **Genetic Drift** is caused by random alterations of allele frequencies in populations, and is tied to population size.
   i) Founder effect is a particular kind of drift that may occur when a small founding population colonizes a new area or when a large population is reduced to a much smaller size through war, famine, disease, or other factors.
   ii) Genetic drift has played an important role in human evolution since ancient hunter-gatherer groups were probably small in size.
      (1) Small population sizes may produce sudden fluctuations in allele frequencies.
      (2) If many small populations experience genetic drift, the pace of evolution can increase significantly.
   iii) Genetic evidence suggests that *Homo sapiens* experienced a bottleneck in the last 100,000 to 200,000 years, indicating modern humans may be a product of founder effect.
d) **Recombination** is the reshuffling of genes in the offspring every generation as a result of sexual reproduction.
   i) This does not cause evolution, but it provides genetic combinations upon which natural selection can act.

IX. **Natural Selection Acts on Variation**
   a) Natural selection acts on variation produced by mutation, gene flow, genetic drift and recombination.
      i) Directional changes in allele frequencies are a function of the environmental context.
   b) The best example of natural selection in human populations involves the allele for hemoglobin S.
      i) The Hb^S mutation occurs at a low frequency in all human populations.
      ii) In some populations, especially in western and central Africa, the Hb^S allele occurs in frequencies approaching 20%.
         (1) The geographical correlation between the distribution of malaria and high frequencies of the Hb^S allele indicates a biological relationship between the two.
         (2) Heterozygotes for the Hb^S allele have a greater resistance to malaria and higher reproductive success in malarial environments than do non-heterozygotes.

X. **Review of Genetics and Evolutionary Factors**
   a) The evolutionary process occurs at five different levels:
      i) Mutations of the DNA in the gametes (the molecular level).
      ii) These molecular mutations are carried on the chromosomes (the chromosomal level).
      iii) The chromosomes assort during meiosis and are passed on to the offspring (the cellular level).
      iv) The individual is subject to natural selection (the level of the organism).
      v) Populations are composed of individuals, and evolution is said to occur when allele frequencies change (the level of the population).
         (1) Genetic drift and gene flow may act to change allele frequencies in populations.

Learning Objectives
After reading Chapter 4, the student should be able to:
1. Discuss the basic principles of Mendelian inheritance; including the concepts of dominant, recessive, and codominant alleles, and the principles of segregation and independent assortment.
2. List some of the common Mendelian characteristics known in humans and indicate their mode of inheritance (i.e. autosomal dominant, autosomal recessive, x-linked).
3. Contrast the patterns of inheritance for autosomal dominant and recessive traits, and sex-linked traits.
4. Describe the differences between Mendelian and non-Mendelian modes of inheritance (polygenic, pleitropy, and mitochondrial) and list some polygenic traits.

5. Understand the mechanisms that produce genetic variation in populations and explain the processes by which selection and other evolutionary forces (mutation, genetic drift, gene flow, and recombination) produce and redistribute variation.
6. Describe how altered forms of hemoglobin are maintained in some human populations by natural selection acting on mutations that increase the reproductive success of certain genotypes.

Key Terms and Concepts

Allele frequency	p. 80	Mendelian traits	p. 68
Antigens	p. 71	Microevolution	p. 81
Assort	p. 68	Pedigree chart	p. 72
Codominance	p. 71	Phenotype	p. 68
Dominant	p. 67	Phenotypic ratio	p. 68
Evolution	p. 80	Pleiotropy	p. 77
Founder effect	p. 82	Point mutation	p. 81
Gene flow	p. 81	Polygenic	p. 76
Gene pool	p. 80	Population	p. 80
Genetic drift	p. 82	Principle of independent assortment	p. 68
Genotype	p. 67	Principle of segregation	p. 66
Heterozygous	p. 67	Recessive	p. 66
Homozygous	p. 67	Selective breeding	p. 65
Hybrids	p. 65	Variation (genetic)	p. 79
Macroevolution	p. 81		

Lecture Suggestions and Enrichment Topics

1. You can illustrate Mendelian principles in your class by calculating the frequencies for various Mendelian traits, such as hitchhiker's thumb or earlobe form. Then, demonstrate the nature of continuous traits by calculating stature or forearm length. The data can then be used to illustrate the different statistical approaches to Mendelian versus polygenic traits.
2. Collecting information from students regarding ABO and Rh blood groups is another useful approach to illustrating Mendelian principles. Often, biology departments have blood typing supplies, usually with "fake blood" to demonstrate blood typing to students. You may be able to borrow some for a demonstration. Most schools have strict policies regarding the use of biological materials, and they rarely allow the use of real blood for class demonstrations.
3. Explore the advances in the field of genetics and genetic testing which permit more accurate diagnosis of individual carrier status. Point out that these advances will eventually eliminate the need for pedigree analysis as more accurate methods of diagnosis become available.
4. Discuss the genealogy of the blue Fugates of Kentucky (search for "blue Fugates" on the Internet). They carry a recessive allele causing an enzyme deficiency that results in blue skin tones. This case illustrates Mendelian principles of inheritance as well as a phenotypic effect of an enzyme deficiency.

Student Media Exercises

1. From J. Kappelman's *Virtual Laboratories for Physical Anthropology* CD: Students should complete the lab exercise *Virtual Experiment: Sickle-Cell Allele Frequency* in Lab 2: *Genetics and Evolution of Human Populations* to reinforce their conceptual understanding of natural selection in action.
2. From Jurmain *et al. Basic Genetics for Anthropology* CD: Have students go through section IV, *Basic Concepts in Heredity*, and complete the quiz.

3. Log on to Online Mendelian Inheritance in Man (http://www.ncbi.nlm.nih.gov/entrez/query.fcgi?db=OMIM) and click on the link "Genes and Disease." Pick one genetic disease and write a short paragraph describing its clinical expression and mode of inheritance.
4. In *InfoTrac* access the article *Gene mutation for color blindness found* (*Science News*, July 22, 2000 v158 i4 p63). Answer this question: What evolutionary force is responsible for the high frequency of this genetic disorder in this particular population?
5. Have students construct their own family pedigree for a particular Mendelian trait. Again, the ABO blood group is simple to explore. Even if they do not know their own blood type, they may be able to determine their parents' and siblings' types and calculate their own possibilities and/or probabilities using Punnett squares.

Multiple Choice Questions

1. Gregor Mendel
   A. developed theories of evolutionary change.
   B. discovered the structure of the DNA molecule.
   C. studied characteristics that are influenced by several genetic loci.
   D. discovered the fundamental principles of how traits are inherited.
   E. developed the theory of inheritance of acquired characteristics.

   ANS: D
   PG: 65

2. How do the basic principles of inheritance, identified by Mendel in plants, differ from those in humans?
   A. They are simpler.
   B. Plants don't have alleles.
   C. There are no differences since the basic principles are the same.
   D. There are no Mendelian traits in humans.
   E. The number of chromosomes is different; therefore the genetic principles are different.

   ANS: C
   PG: 65

3. When Mendel crossed true breeding tall and short parental plants
   A. all the offspring were tall.
   B. half the offspring were tall, the other half were short.
   C. all the offspring were short.
   D. the offspring were intermediate in height relative to the two parent plants.
   E. about 90 percent were tall, but the rest were short.

   ANS: A
   PG: 66

4. In Mendel's experiments, the ratio of tall to short plants in the F_2 generation was
   A. 15 to 1
   B. 3 to 1.
   C. ½ tall, ½ short.
   D. 4 to 1.
   E. 5 to 1.

   ANS: B
   PG: 67

5. Which is FALSE regarding the F_1 plants in Mendel's experiments?
    A. They were hybrids.
    B. They were heterozygous for the traits in question.
    C. Their parents were homozygous for the traits in question.
    D. All F_1s displayed the dominant trait in their phenotype.
    E. All F_1s displayed the recessive trait in their phenotype.

    ANS: E
    PG: 69

6. A person who is homozygous recessive at a locus has
    A. two copies of the recessive allele.
    B. two copies of the dominant allele.
    C. an autosomal trisomy.
    D. a recessive allele on the X chromosome only.
    E. a recessive allele on the Y chromosome only.

    ANS: A
    PG: 69

7. When an allele is NOT expressed in heterozygotes, but is only expressed in homozygotes, it is said
    to be
    A. dominant.
    B. codominant.
    C. recessive.
    D. homozygous dominant.
    E. segregated.

    ANS: C
    PG: 68-69

8. In Mendel's experiments, the tall parental (P) plants
    A. were homozygous for the allele for tallness.
    B. were heterozygous at the locus controlling height.
    C. could NOT be crossed with short plants.
    D. were homozygous for the allele for shortness.
    E. none of these

    ANS: A
    PG: 69

9. An individual's actual genetic make-up is called the
    A. phenotype.
    B. homozygosity.
    C. recessiveness.
    D. phenotypic ratio.
    E. genotype.

    ANS: E
    PG: 67

10. The detectable manifestation of gene action is the
    A. genotype.
    B. phenotype.
    C. phenotypic ratio.
    D. genotypic ratio.
    E. independent assortment.

    ANS: B
    PG: 68

11. Gregor Mendel
    A. published his results and won the Nobel Prize for his discoveries.
    B. was trained as a geneticist.
    C. died before the importance of his research was recognized.
    D. was a professor at the University of Vienna.
    E. never published his work.

    ANS: C
    PG: 65

12. The fact that both green and yellow peas were produced by both tall and short pea plants in predictable frequencies led Mendel to propose the
    A. principle of segregation.
    B. principle of independent assortment.
    C. concept of dominance.
    D. concept of codominance.
    E. blending theory of inheritance.

    ANS: B
    PG: 66

13. When Mendel crossed plants and considered two traits simultaneously (e.g. height and seed color in peas), what proportion of the F_2 generation offspring expressed both recessive phenotypes?
    A. 9/16
    B. 8/16
    C. 12/16
    D. 3/16
    E. 1/16

      ANS: E
      PG: 67

14. Two people (BOTH heterozygotes) are able to taste a chemical substance called PTC. The ability to taste PTC is caused by a dominant allele (T). The inability to taste PTC is caused by a recessive allele (t). What proportion of their children would be expected to have the ability to taste PTC?
    A. 3/4
    B. 1/2
    C. All
    D. 1/4
    E. 2/3

    ANS: A
    PG: 68

15. Two people (BOTH heterozygotes) are able to taste a chemical substance called PTC. The ability to taste PTC is caused by a dominant allele (T). The inability to taste PTC is caused by a recessive allele (t). What proportion of their children would be expected NOT to be able to taste PTC?
    A. 3/4
    B. All
    C. 1/4
    D. 2/3

    ANS: D
    PG: 68 (use a Punnett Square)

16. Two people (BOTH heterozygotes) are able to taste a chemical substance called PTC. The ability to taste PTC is caused by a dominant allele (T). The inability to taste PTC is caused by a recessive allele (t). What proportion of their offspring would be expected to be heterozygous?
    A. 3/4
    B. 1/2
    C. All
    D. 1/4
    E. 2/3

    ANS: B
    PG: 68(Use a Punnett square)

17. Two people (BOTH heterozygotes) are able to taste a chemical substance called PTC. The ability to taste PTC is caused by a dominant allele (T). The inability to taste PTC is caused by a recessive allele (t). What proportion of their children would be expected to have the tt genotype?
    A. 3/4
    B. 1/2
    C. All
    D. 1/4
    E. 2/3

    ANS: D
    PG: 68 (Use a Punnett square)

18. Dominant alleles
    A. usually cause the underproduction of an enzyme.
    B. always produce the most desirable phenotype.
    C. can mask the expression of other alleles at the same locus.
    D. are always the most common allele in a population.
    E. were discovered by Charles Darwin.

    ANS: C
    PG: 68

19. Which of the following is NOT inherited in a Mendelian fashion?
    A. ABO blood type
    B. Marfan syndrome
    C. achondroplasia
    D. phenylketonuria
    E. skin color

    ANS: E
    PG: 71-72

20. The ABO blood type system consists of _____ alleles.
    A. 6
    B. 4
    C. 3
    D. 2
    E. 5

    ANS: C
    PG: 71

21. Which of the following is NOT a polygenic trait?
    A. stature
    B. skin color
    C. eye color
    D. ABO blood type
    E. hair color

    ANS: D
    PG: 76

22. When a person possesses two different alleles at the same locus, and both alleles are expressed in the phenotype, this is called
    A. recessiveness.
    B. codominance.
    C. dominance.
    D. homozygosity.
    E. X-linkage.

    ANS: B
    PG: 71

23. Type AB blood is an example of
    A. codominance.
    B. blending.
    C. recessiveness.
    D. dominance.
    E. polygenic inheritance.

    ANS: A
    PG: 71

24. How many ABO phenotypes are there?
    A. 4
    B. 2
    C. 3
    D. 6
    E. 1

    ANS: A
    PG: 71

25. A person with blood type B is heterozygous. What is that person's genotype?
   A. BB
   B. OO
   C. BO
   D. AB
   E. none of these

   ANS: C
   PG: 71

26. A man who has type A blood has the AO genotype. His wife, with type B blood, has the BO genotype. Which of the following blood types is/are possible for their children?
   A. type O
   B. type AB
   C. type B
   D. all of these
   E. A and C only

   ANS: D
   PG: 71 (use a Punnett square)

27. All individuals who express a dominant trait
   A. could be heterozygous.
   B. must have at least one parent who expressed the trait.
   C. have no parents who expressed the trait (assuming no mutations).
   D. All of these are possible.
   E. A and B only

   ANS: E
   PG: 72-73

28. In a hypothetical situation, B is the allele that causes brachydactyly. If a man who has normal fingers (bb) and a woman with brachydactyly (Bb) have children, what proportion of these children would you expect to have normal fingers? (Hint: Use a Punnett square).
   A. None
   B. All
   C. 1/4
   D. 3/4
   E. 1/2

   ANS: E
   PG: 73

29. At a hypothetical locus, a man's genotype is Aa. What proportion of his gametes would be expected to receive the A allele?
    A. All
    B. 1/2
    C. 3/4
    D. 1/4
    E. None

    ANS: B
    PG: 73 (use a Punnett square)

30. Sex-linked traits
    A. have their loci on the sex chromosomes.
    B. are expressed more often in males than in females.
    C. are expressed in females in the same fashion as autosomal traits.
    D. all of these
    E. none of these

    ANS: D
    PG: 74

31. Which statement(s) concerning polygenic traits is/are TRUE?
    A. They are governed by more than one genetic locus.
    B. Their expression is often influenced by genetic/environmental interactions.
    C. The alleles have an additive effect on the phenotype.
    D. all of these
    E. A and B only

    ANS: D
    PG: 76-77

32. Mendelian traits
    A. are governed by more than one genetic locus.
    B. occur only in some people.
    C. are always dominant.
    D. are governed by one genetic locus.
    E. are always recessive.

    ANS: D
    PG: 68,76

33. Polygenic traits
    A. are discrete.
    B. have a continuous range of expression.
    C. are controlled by only one genetic locus.
    D. include the ABO blood type system and cystic fibrosis.
    E. are also called Mendelian traits.

    ANS: B
    PG: 76

34. Which of the following types of traits are governed by more than one genetic locus?
    A. polygenic
    B. dominant
    C. Mendelian
    D. recessive
    E. pleiotropic

    ANS: A
    PG: 76

35. Mendelian traits
    A. are governed by several genetic loci.
    B. are more likely to have identifiable loci than polygenic traits.
    C. have continuous distributions.
    D. can be described by statistics such as the average and standard deviation.
    E. have phenotypic expressions that are often the result of genetic and environmental interactions.

    ANS: B
    PG: 78

36. Evolution can be described as a two-stage process that includes
    A. genetic drift followed by migration.
    B. natural selection followed by migration.
    C. recombination followed by mutation.
    D. production of variation followed by natural selection.
    E. none of these

    ANS: D
    PG: 79

37. Evolution can be most succinctly defined as
    A. the appearance of new species.
    B. the change from one species to another in one generation.
    C. a change in allele frequencies from one generation to the next.
    D. any type of genetic mutation.
    E. genetic drift.

    ANS: C
    PG: 80

38. What produces new alleles at a locus?
    A. natural selection
    B. recombination
    C. mutation
    D. migration
    E. genetic drift

    ANS: C
    PG: 80

39. In order for a mutation to be passed on to an offspring, the mutation must
    A. occur in a gamete.
    B. be beneficial.
    C. occur in a somatic cell.
    D. result in additional chromosomes.
    E. A and B only

    ANS: A
    PG: 81

40. The only source(s) of new genetic material in any population is/are
    A. mutations.
    B. genetic drift.
    C. founder effect.
    D. migration.
    E. natural selection.

    ANS: A
    PG: 81

41. Gene flow is defined as the
    A. production of new alleles.
    B. production of new genetic material.
    C. chance loss of alleles in a population.
    D. exchange of genes between populations.
    E. differential reproductive success of individuals.

    ANS: D
    PG: 81-82

42. Genetic drift
    A. is a random change in allele frequencies.
    B. has its greatest effect in small populations.
    C. includes the phenomenon of founder effect.
    D. all of these
    E. A and B only

    ANS: D
    PG: 82-83

43. If two people with the sickle-cell trait have children, some of their offspring would be expected to have
    A. sickle-cell anemia.
    B. the sickle-cell trait.
    C. normal hemoglobin.
    D. some hemoglobin S in their red blood cells.
    E. all of these

    ANS: E
    PG: 85 (Use a Punnett square)

44. Which of the below is FALSE regarding the relationship between malaria and the Hb^S allele?
    A. There is no geographic correlation between the distribution of the Hb^S allele and malaria.
    B. Heterozygotes have greater resistance to malaria than homozygous individuals.
    C. The malarial parasite does not reproduce very well in the red blood cells of heterozygotes.
    D. Malaria is caused by the *Plasmodium* parasite.
    E. The Hb^S mutation probably occurs occasionally in all human populations.

    ANS: A
    PG: 85-86

45. The Hb^S allele increased in frequency in West African populations due to
    A. sickle-cell anemia.
    B. genetic drift.
    C. migration.
    D. increased mutation rates.
    E. natural selection.

    ANS: E
    PG:85-86

True/False Questions
1. Recessive conditions are usually associated with the lack of production of an enzyme.

    ANS: True
    PG: 66

2. All human genetic disorders are inherited as recessive traits.

    ANS: False
    PG: 70-71

3. Dominance and recessiveness are all-or-nothing situations because the recessive allele has NO phenotypic effects in heterozygotes.

    ANS: False
    PG: 71

4. The majority of sex-linked traits have loci on the X chromosome.

    ANS: True
    PG: 74

5. X-linked traits affect males and females in equal frequencies.

    ANS: False
    PG: 74

6. Melanin production is a polygenic trait that is influenced by between three and six genetic loci.

   ANS: True
   PG: 76

7. Polygenic traits account for few, if any, of the readily ob servable phenotypic variation seen in humans.

   ANS: False
   PG: 76

8. The genotype sets limits and potentials for development and interacts with the environment to produce the phenotype.

   ANS: True
   PG: 77

9. Genetic pleiotropy refers to the fact that multiple genes influence a single phenotypic expression.

   ANS: False
   PG: 77

10. The most important aspect of mtDNA is the fact that it is not subject to mutation.

    ANS: False
    PG: 78

Short Answer Questions

1. Explain Mendel's principle of segregation.
   (p. 66)

2. Explain Mendel's principle of independent assortment.
   (p. 68)

3. What are the typical Mendelian phenotypic and genotypic ratios in the F_2 generation for a cross of purebred tall and short plants? Why are these ratios typical?
   (p. 67-69)

4. Explain the concepts of dominance, codominance, and recessiveness as used in modern genetics.
   (pp. 67, 71-72)

5. Explain why a woman with type O blood and a man with type A blood could potentially have children with either type A or O blood.
   (p. 71)

6. Explain how two parents who do NOT express a particular trait in their phenotype can nevertheless produce children who express the trait. Give an example of a specific trait or disease where this could occur.
   (pp. 71-73)

7. Define genetic drift. How are founder effect and genetic drift related?
    (p. 82)

8. What is the effect of genetic bottlenecks on human and nonhuman species?
    (pp. 82-85)

9. List two evolutionary factors and their level of organization in the evolutionary process.
    (p.88, Table 4.4)

Essay Questions
1. Why is genetic variation necessary for the process of natural selection to operate? What are the
    sources of genetic variation?

2. Using the Hb^S allele to illustrate, describe why fitness levels are a function of the environment.

3. Discuss the differences between Mendelian and polygenic modes of inheritance. Provide an
    example of a Mendelian and a polygenic trait.

4. How have new molecular techniques been applied to forensic anthropology?

CHAPTER 5: MACROEVOLUTION: PROCESSES OF VERTEBRATE AND MAMMALIAN EVOLUTION

Chapter Outline

I. **Introduction**
   a) Macroevolution refers to large-scale evolutionary processes.
      i) These processes can be understood in light of geological history, the principles of classification, and hypotheses concerning modes of evolutionary change.

II. **The Human Place in the Organic World**
   a) Biologists deal with the complexity of the living world by grouping, or classifying organisms.
      i) Classification reduces the apparent complexity and is meant to indicate evolutionary relationships.
   b) Multicelled animals are grouped into the Metazoa.
      i) The Metazoa are further divided into more than 20 major *phyla*.
         (1) The phylum Chordata includes animals with a nerve chord, gill slits (present during development), and a notochord.
            (a) Most chordates are vertebrates.
            (b) The vertebrates are composed of six classes, one of which is the mammals.

III. **Principles of Classification**
   a) Taxonomy is the science of classification.
      i) The only useful traits in taxonomy are those that are indicative of evolutionary descent.
         (1) Homologies are structures shared by species because of common descent.
         (2) Similar structures (analogies) may arise in different lineages not because of common descent, but because they are the product of similar functional demands.
         (3) The process that produces analogies is called homoplasy.
   b) **Constructing classifications and interpreting evolutionary relationships**
      i) The two major schools of classification are evolutionary systematics and cladistics.
         (1) Evolutionary systematics and cladistics have some features in common.
            (a) Both schools trace evolutionary relationships and construct classifications.
            (b) Both schools recognize that some features (characters) are more informative of evolutionary relationships than others.
            (c) Both schools focus exclusively on homologies.
         (2) These two schools differ in how characters are chosen, which groups are compared, and how the results are ultimately interpreted.
            (a) Cladistics is concerned with ancestral and derived characters.
               (i) Ancestral traits (those traits shared through common distant ancestry) do not provide useful information in a cladistic analysis.
               (ii) Derived, or modified, traits are more informative when distinguishing evolutionary lineages because they are modified from the ancestral condition; cladistics concentrates on these traits.
               (iii) Cladistics has been used to clarify the evolutionary relationship between modern birds and theropod dinosaurs.
                  1. For example, some theropods share feathers (a derived trait) with modern birds.

(b) Phylogenetic systematics uses a phylogenetic tree to illustrate evolutionary relationships, whereas cladistics uses a cladogram.
  (i) A phylogenetic tree incorporates the dimension of time, but a cladogram does not.
  (ii) Phylogenetic trees use hypothesized ancestor-descendant relationships, but cladograms do not.
  (iii) Ultimately, most physical anthropologists use the information from cladistic analyses to produce phylogenetic trees.

IV. Definition of Species
a) The biological species concept is the definition accepted by most zoologists.
b) Speciation is the macroevolutionary process that produces new species.
  i) The **biological species concept** emphasizes geographic isolation during speciation.
    (1) The combined effects of genetic drift and natural selection followed by behavioral isolation are central to the speciation process.
  ii) The **recognition species concept** emphasizes the role of mate recognition in the speciation process.
    (1) Potential mates from different populations may not recognize each other due to differing patterns of body coloration, or different patterns of estrus swellings.
    (2) This concept also emphasizes the role of less fit hybrids in reinforcing species boundaries.
  iii) The **ecological species concept** emphasizes the role of ecological niche exploitation and natural selection in reinforcing species boundaries.
    (1) This concept assumes there is an "adaptive gap" separating ecological zones, preventing intermediate types from being successful in between ecological zones.
c) **Process of speciation**: There are four different hypothesized modes of speciation: allopatric, parapatric, sympatric, and instantaneous speciation.
  i) Allopatric speciation requires the complete geographic isolation of insipient species.
  ii) Parapatric speciation requires partial reproductive isolation.
    (1) Hybrid zones form between adjacent populations.
    (2) Mate recognition and selective breeding serve to help complete the speciation process.
  iii) Sympatric speciation has been suggested as a theoretical model, but has yet to be supported by observations of populations.
    (1) This model requires no reproductive isolation.
  iv) Instantaneous speciation is thought to occur by chromosomal mutation.
    (1) In plants, this mode has been observed to occur when problems in meiosis results in varieties with different chromosomal numbers.
    (2) Large-scale chromosomal alterations leading to speciation have been difficult to demonstrate in mammals.
d) **Interpreting species and other groups in the fossil record** is difficult.
  i) The goal is to make meaningful biological statements about the amount of variation present.
    (1) In addition to individual variation, we also have to assess other sources of variation such as age changes and differences between individuals due to sexual dimorphism.
  ii) The smallest taxonomic unit is the species.
    (1) Since the biological species concept cannot be tested in fossil species, we have to refer to the levels of variation present in living animals.
      (a) Intraspecific variation is caused by individual, age, and/or sex differences within the species.
      (b) Interspecific variation is between-species variation.
      (c) Fossil species are constructed in such a way as to approximate the levels of intraspecific and interspecific morphological variation observed in extant species.

iii) The paleospecies concept is used for fossil species in order to account for variation both through time and over space.

    (1) Constructing paleospecies is a subjective process.

iv) The next larger taxonomic unit is the genus.

    (1) The genus is defined as a group of species composed of members more closely related to each other than they are to species from any other genus.

    (2) Grouping species into genera is also a subjective process, especially when fossils are considered.

        (a) Members of the same genus share the same broad adaptive zone.

        (b) Members of the same genus also share derived characters not seen in members of other genera.

V. Vertebrate Evolutionary History: A Brief Summary

a) The geological time scale divides the earth's history into eras, periods, and epochs.

    i) The first vertebrates appear in the fossil record in the early Paleozoic (500 mya).

    ii) Mammal-like reptiles diversified at the close of the Paleozoic (250 mya).

        (1) These forms are probably ancestors of modern mammals.

b) Continental drift had profound evolutionary effects during the Paleozoic and the Mesozoic; groups of animals were separated from each other and mammals and reptiles were redistributed around the globe.

    i) During the late Paleozoic, the continents came together to form Pangaea.

    ii) Gondwanaland, consisting of South America, Africa, Antarctica, Australia, and India, began to split off from Pangaea during the early Mesozoic.

        (1) The other continents (North America, Greenland, Europe, and Asia) formed Laurasia.

    iii) The continents continued to move and began to assume their present positions by the end of the Mesozoic (c. 65 mya).

c) The dominant form of land vertebrates during the Mesozoic was the dinosaur.

    i) Most went extinct at the end of the Mesozoic due to collisions of asteroids or comets with the earth.

    ii) The earliest mammals also existed during the early Mesozoic.

        (1) The first placental mammals appeared about 70 mya and were extremely successful during the Cenozoic.

d) The Cenozoic is divided into seven epochs: the Paleocene, Eocene, Oligocene, Miocene, Pliocene, Pleistocene, and Holocene.

VI. Mammalian Evolution

a) The Cenozoic is known as the Age of Mammals.

    i) The diversification of the mammals followed the extinction of the dinosaurs, since new ecological niches became available.

    ii) Mammals were successful because they evolved a complex brain and had flexible behaviors.

        (1) Mammals are viviparous.

        (2) Reptiles have homodont dentition, whereas mammals have heterodont dentition that allows them to process a wide variety of foods.

            (a) The primitive mammalian dental formula is 3.1.4.3.

        (3) Mammals (and birds) maintain a constant internal body temperature (they are endothermic).

VII. The Emergence of Major Mammalian Groups
a) The three major subgroups of mammals are monotremes, marsupials, and placental mammals.
  i) The monotremes are the most primitive mammals because they lay eggs.
  ii) In marsupials, the young are born extremely immature and complete their development in the mother's pouch.
  iii) Placental mammals nourish the fetus with a specialized tissue, the placenta.
    (1) The placenta permits a longer gestation period resulting in a more completely developed central nervous system in the fetus.

VIII. Processes of Macroevolution
a) An **adaptive radiation** is the rapid expansion and diversification of new life forms into new ecological niches.
  i) A species will diverge into as many variations as allowed by its adaptive potential and the adaptive opportunities of the ecosystem.
    (1) For example, the evolution of the reptilian egg caused the adaptive radiation of the reptiles by opening new adaptive niches on land.
b) **Generalized and specialized characteristics**
  i) An adaptive radiation involves the transformation of generalized characteristics into specialized characteristics.
    (1) Traits that are adapted for many functions are generalized.
    (2) Generalized and specialized can also refer to the entire organism.
      (a) Species that are generalized have the greatest adaptive potential.
c) **Modes of evolutionary change**
  i) The recent consensus has been that accumulated microevolutionary changes can produce large-scale macroevolutionary changes, including speciation. This view is called gradualism.
  ii) Others argue that species exist unchanged for thousands of years, and then undergo rapid bursts of evolutionary change. This is called punctuated equilibrium.
    (1) This school of thought posits that speciation is the major agent of evolutionary change.
  iii) The best support for punctuated evolutionary change comes from the fossilized remains of marine invertebrates, which generally lack transitional forms.
  iv) The primate fossil record is consistent with gradualism, although the pace of evolution within lineages is not constant.

Learning Objectives

After reading Chapter 5, the student should be able to:
1. Understand the concepts of taxonomy and distinguish between cladistics and evolutionary systematics.
2. Understand the use of generalized, specialized, derived (modified), and ancestral (primitive) traits in cladistics and evolutionary systematics.
3. Define the concepts of genus and species and discuss the criteria for making taxonomic designations for fossil material.
4. Discuss the models for macroevolution. Include the roles of geographic isolation and natural selection.
5. Discuss the geologic time scale and place the major events of vertebrate evolution within that time scale.
6. List and define the major living mammalian groups.
7. Contrast gradualism with punctuated equilibrium.

Key Terms and Concepts

Adaptive radiation	p. 114	Geological time scale	p. 108
Allopatric	p. 105	Heterodont	p. 113
Analogies	p. 98	Homologies	p. 98
Ancestral (primitive)	p. 99	Homoplasy	p. 98
Biological species concept	p. 102	Interspecific	p. 107
Chordata	p. 95	Intraspecific	p. 107
Clade	p. 98	Paleospecies	p. 107
Cladistics	p. 98	Phylogenetic species concept	p. 105
Cladogram	p. 101	Phylogenetic tree	p. 101
Classification	p. 95	Placental	p. 110
Continental drift	p. 108	Punctuated equilibrium	p. 115
Derived (modified)	p. 98	Recognition species concept	p. 103
Ecological niches	p. 110	Sexual dimorphism	p. 107
Ecological species concept	p. 103	Shared derived	p. 101
Endothermic	p. 113	Speciation	p. 103
Epochs	p. 110	Therapods	p. 101
Evolutionary systematics	p. 98	Vertebrates	p. 95
Genus (pl., genera)	p. 107		

Lecture Suggestions and Enrichment Topics

1. Most students are interested in dinosaurs. You can draw them into a discussion of the adaptive radiation of the mammals (including the primates) by presenting the current hypotheses concerning the extinction of the dinosaurs at the end of the Cretaceous. One place to find current information is on the University of California Museum of Paleontology website http://www.ucmp.berkeley.edu/diapsids/extinction.html.

2. Students often think that the fossil record generally lacks transitional forms. For a discussion of transitional forms in the fossil record see http://www.talkorigins.org/faqs/comdesc/.

3. The tabloid press often presents fantastic stories about primate and human evolution such as "bat boy", the famous half-bat half-boy, or the "discovery" of Adam and Eve's skeletons. These stories can provide the basis for serious and meaningful class discussion, not only the biological fallacies presented, but the distortion of evolutionary principles that routinely find their way to supermarket check-out stands. Also, always keep your eyes open for these stories and begin building your own collection!

Student Media Exercises

1. From J. Kappelman's *Virtual Laboratories for Physical Anthropology* CD: Students should complete Section III of Lab 7: *Primate Phylogeny* to reinforce their conceptual understanding of phylogenetic and cladistic analysis.

2. Go online to the University of California – Berkeley's Museum of Paleontology Hall of Mammals (http://www.ucmp.berkeley.edu/mammal/mammal.html) to better understand the evolution and classification of mammals.

3. In *InfoTrac* find the article Did Darwin get it all right? (Richard A. Kerr. *Science*, March 10, 1995 v267 n5203 p1421). Read the article and answer this question: What is the nature of the evidence supporting punctuated equilibrium?

4. In *InfoTrac* do a keyword search on "dinosaur extinction" and read some of the articles. Do any of them challenge the theory that an asteroid collision caused the extinction of the dinosaurs?

Multiple Choice Questions

1. The ordering of organisms into categories, such as orders or families is termed
   - A. evolution.
   - B. classification.
   - C. parallelism.
   - D. analogy.
   - E. generalization.

   ANS: B
   PG: 95

2. Ideally, taxonomic classification
   - A. reflects evolutionary relationships.
   - B. is based on the presence of acquired characteristics.
   - C. is always based solely on between-species behavioral similarities.
   - D. reflects the current geographic distribution of species.
   - E. is only applicable to nonhuman species.

   ANS: A
   PG: 95

2. Animals with a nerve cord along the back and gill slits during some developmental stage are called
   - A. insects.
   - B. invertebrates.
   - C. chordates.
   - D. metazoans.
   - E. all of these

   ANS: C
   PG: 95

3. Which of the following are vertebrates?
   - A. birds
   - B. reptiles
   - C. amphibians
   - D. all of these
   - E. A and B only

   ANS: D
   PG: 95

4. Structural similarities shared by species that are acquired by descent from a common ancestor are
   - A. analogies.
   - B. homologies.
   - C. acquired.
   - D. uncommon.
   - E. uninformative of evolutionary relationships.

   ANS: B
   PG: 95

5. Structural similarities between species that are based on common function and not on common evolutionary descent are called
   A. acquired.
   B. generalized.
   C. non-adaptive.
   D. analogies.
   E. homologies.

   ANS: D
   PG: 98

6. The evolutionary process that produced analogous structures in New and Old World monkeys is called
   A. speciation.
   B. homology.
   C. homoplasy.
   D. founder effect.
   E. none of these

   ANS: C
   PG: 98

7. The two primary schools of classification discussed in the text are
   A. generalized and specialized.
   B. organic and inorganic.
   C. evolutionary systematics and cladistics.
   D. cladistics and non-cladistics.
   E. ancestral and derived (modified).

   ANS: C
   PG: 98

8. Structural similarities shared by a wide array of distantly related species that are inherited from a common ancestor, such as the number of bones in the forelimb, are termed
   A. specialized.
   B. ancestral (primitive).
   C. adaptive radiations.
   D. analogies.
   E. derived (modified).

   ANS: B
   PG: 99

9. Traits that reflect specific evolutionary lineages and can be informative of evolutionary relationships are called
   A. ancestral (primitive).
   B. acquired.
   C. derived (modified).
   D. convergent characters.
   E. analogies.

   ANS: C
   PG: 99

10. When assessing evolutionary relationships, one approach is to interpret patterns of ancestral (primitive) and derived (modified) characteristics. This approach is called
    A. taxonomy.
    B. phylogeny.
    C. classification.
    D. cladistics.
    E. none of these

    ANS: D
    PG: 99

11. In grouping organisms together in a cladistic classification, the most important characteristics are those that are
    A. ancestral.
    B. derived (modified).
    C. primitive.
    D. analogous.
    E. homologous.

    ANS: B
    PG: 99

12. The presumed evolutionary link between theropod dinosaurs and birds is based on
    A. homoplasies only.
    B. general analogous characteristics.
    C. a few shared ancestral characteristics.
    D. derived (modified) characteristics such as the presence of feathers in both lineages.
    E. all of these

    ANS: D
    PG: 99-100

13. A hypothesis regarding ancestor-descendant relationships that includes a time-scale is called a
    A. cladogram.
    B. phylogenetic tree.
    C. phylogram tree.
    D. hypogram tree.
    E. none of these

    ANS: B
    PG: 101

14. A phylogenetic tree _____ whereas a cladogram does not.
    A. includes the dimension of time
    B. indicates ancestral-descendant relationships
    C. uses only analogous character traits
    D. all of these
    E. A and B only

    ANS: E
    PG: 101

15. Speciation can occur as a result of
    A. geographic isolation.
    B. natural selection acting on populations.
    C. behavioral isolation.
    D. all of these
    E. A and B only

    ANS: D
    PG: 103-105

16. Assigning fossil remains to a particular primate species
    A. is an uncomplicated process.
    B. requires splitting samples into as many species as possible.
    C. requires making comparisons to well-known living species of primates.
    D. can be accomplished only if the species is sexually dimorphic.
    E. none of these

    ANS: C
    PG: 106-108

17. Morphological variation between individuals WITHIN a species
    A. may be the product of male/female morphological differences.
    B. is called interspecific variation.
    C. is of no concern to anthropologists.
    D. is unimportant when interpreting the fossil record.
    E. produces large numbers of identical individuals.

    ANS: A
    PG: 106-108

18. A genus may be defined as a group of
    A. individuals who interbreed but are reproductively isolated from other such groups.
    B. closely related species.
    C. species that share the same broad adaptive zone.
    D. all of these
    E. B and C only

    ANS: E
    PG: 107

19. Grouping contemporaneous species into genera
    A. is to some extent a subjective process.
    B. can be facilitated by identifying which species can interbreed and produce live but perhaps non-fertile hybrid offspring.
    C. is not always easy and may not be accurate.
    D. B and C only
    E. all of these

    ANS: E
    PG: 106-108

20. The first vertebrates appear in the fossil record during the
   A. Pleistocene.
   B. Paleozoic.
   C. Paleocene.
   D. Mesozoic.
   E. none of these

   ANS: B
   PG: 111

21. Continental drift
   A. had no real impact on the evolutionary history of vertebrates.
   B. never occurred.
   C. is the movement of the continents on the Earth's surface.
   D. ceased to occur several million years ago.
   E. occurs only in the Old World.

   ANS: C
   PG: 108

22. The evolutionary consequences of long-term continental drift include:
   A. the isolation of populations of organisms.
   B. the altered geographic distribution of life forms.
   C. lowered mutation rates.
   D. all of these
   E. A and B only

   ANS: E
   PG: 108-109

23. Reptiles were the dominant form of land vertebrate during the
   A. Cenozoic.
   B. Paleozoic.
   C. Mesozoic.
   D. Precambrian.
   E. Permian.

   ANS: C
   PG: 111

24. The environmental setting to which a species is adapted is its
   A. adaptive radiation.
   B. geographic isolation.
   C. geographic barrier.
   D. geological time.
   E. ecological niche.

   ANS: E
   PG: 110

25. Which of the following is/are epochs of the Cenozoic?
    A. Paleocene
    B. Oligocene
    C. Eocene
    D. all of these
    E. A and C only

    ANS: D
    PG: 109

26. The adaptive radiation of the mammals occurred mostly during the
    A. Pleistocene.
    B. Mesozoic.
    C. Quaternary.
    D. Cenozoic.
    E. Paleozoic.

    ANS: D
    PG: 114

27. Giving birth to live young is termed
    A. viviparous.
    B. oviparous.
    C. homeothermy.
    D. nulliparous.
    E. heterodont.

    ANS: A
    PG: 114

28. Mammals, in contrast to reptiles,
    A. have larger brains.
    B. are homodont.
    C. are oviparous.
    D. lack fur.
    E. are ectothermic.

    ANS: A
    PG: 113

29. Endothermy refers to
    A. mammalian tooth shapes.
    B. the loss of heat in animals without fur.
    C. using physiology to maintain a constant internal body temperature.
    D. staying warm by lying in the sun.
    E. all of these

    ANS: C
    PG: 113

30. Modern endothermic animals include
    A. fish.
    B. amphibians.
    C. birds.
    D. mammals.
    E. C and D only

    ANS: E
    PG: 113

31. Monotremes are
    A. marsupials.
    B. viviparous reptiles.
    C. egg-laying fish.
    D. placental mammals.
    E. egg-laying mammals.

    ANS: E
    PG: 114

32. In _____ the young are born in an extremely immature state and complete development in their mother's external pouch.
    A. placental mammals
    B. monotremes
    C. marsupials
    D. reptiles
    E. none of these

    ANS: C
    PG: 114

33. The rapid expansion and diversification of groups of organisms into newly available ecological niches is termed
    A. generalization.
    B. homology.
    C. parallel evolution.
    D. an adaptive radiation.
    E. specialization.

    ANS: D
    PG: 114

34. The diversification of reptiles facilitated by the evolution of the reptilian egg is a good example of
    A. parallel evolution.
    B. specialization.
    C. homology.
    D. adaptive radiation.
    E. devolution.

    ANS: D
    PG: 114

35. The theory that macroevolution proceeds as the result of gradual microevolutionary change
    A. is the only explanation of speciation accepted by biologists today.
    B. is called the theory of punctuated equilibrium.
    C. has been refuted.
    D. has been questioned as the exclusive mode of speciation.
    E. postulates rapid evolutionary change followed by long periods of stasis.

    ANS: D
    PG: 115

36. The theory that species persist unchanged for long periods and then undergo rapid evolutionary change is known as
    A. gradualism.
    B. punctuated equilibrium.
    C. parallel evolution.
    D. homology.
    E. microevolution.

    ANS: B
    PG: 115

True/False Questions
1. Cladistics is an approach to classification that makes evolutionary interpretations based solely on shared ancestral characters.

    ANS: False
    PG: 101

2. The evolutionary modifications possible in any species are NOT limited to that species' evolutionary legacy. In other words, all things are made possible by evolution.

    ANS: False
    PG: 102

3. Therapods were a group of small- to medium-sized ground-living carnivorous dinosaurs.

    ANS: True
    PG: 99-101

4. If dinosaurs and birds both evolved feathers independent of one other, then the presence of feathers would be considered a homoplasy in both lineages.

    ANS: True
    PG: 101

5. Both the recognition species concept and the ecological species concept include natural selection as a factor in separating species from one another.

    ANS: True
    PG: 102-103

6. Savannah baboons and hamadryas baboons living in east Africa have NEVER been observed to produce viable, fertile hybrid offspring.

    ANS: False
    PG: 102-106

7. The minimum biological category defined in fossil primates is the genus.

    ANS: False
    PG: 102-103

8. Reptiles were the dominant land vertebrates during the Paleozoic.

    ANS: False
    PG: 111

9. The Paleocene, Eocene, and Oligocene are all epochs of the Mesozoic.

    ANS: False
    PG: 109

10. The mammals achieved rapid evolutionary success because they possessed several characteristics related to learning and general behavioral flexibility.

    ANS: True
    PG: 113-114

Short Answer Questions

1. Define analogous and homologous traits and provide an example of each.
    (pp. 97-98)

2. Contrast ancestral traits with derived traits.
    (p. 99)

3. Why is geographic isolation important to the process of speciation?
    (pp. 105-106)

4. What are the influences of long-term continental drift on the evolution of terrestrial life forms?
    (pp. 108-109)

5. Define the term "adaptive radiation".
    (p. 114)

6. How does the punctuated equilibrium view of speciation differ from the gradualist view?
    (p. 115)

Essay Questions

1. Contrast the two schools of taxonomy: evolutionary systematics and cladistics.

2. What are the features of the major models of speciation discussed in the text?

3. Discuss the problems faced by scientists when attempting to assign species and genus names to fossils.

CHAPTER 6: SURVEY OF THE LIVING PRIMATES

Chapter Outline

I. Introduction

a) This chapter is an overview of the living primates: prosimians, monkeys, and apes.

   i) The fact that prosimians evolved before the anthropoids does not mean that evolution is a goal directed process, or that anthropoids are more advanced than prosimians.

   ii) Each primate group evolved unique morphologies as they adapted to their environments, so no one group should be thought of as the final stage or apex of evolution.

II. Primate Characteristics

a) Primates share traits with other mammals such as: body hair, a long gestation period and live births, mammary glands, different types of teeth, homeothermy, increased brain size, and the capacity for learning and behavioral flexibility.

   i) Primates are generalized, having retained many primitive (or ancestral) mammalian traits.

b) A few traits that set primates apart from other mammals are:

   i) A tendency toward erect posture.

   ii) A flexible, generalized limb structure.

   iii) Lack of dietary specialization and generalized dentition.

   iv) Color vision (in diurnal species).

   v) Decreased reliance on the sense of smell.

   vi) Expansion and increased complexity of the brain.

   vii) Delayed maturation and extension of the lifespan.

   viii) Greater dependence on learned behaviors.

   ix) The tendency to live in social groups and the permanent association of adult males with the group.

III. Primate Adaptations

a) **Evolutionary Factors**

   i) The primate adaptive niche is in the trees, so, traditionally, primate characteristics have been explained as the result of adaptation to arboreality (the arboreal hypothesis).

   ii) An alternative is the visual predation hypothesis that argues that primates first adapted to the lowest tiers of the forest canopy and captured prey items through stealth.

   iii) Another scenario proposes that primates developed in conjunction with the rise of the angiosperms (flowering plants).

b) **Geographic Distribution and Habitats**

   i) Primates are found primarily in tropical or semitropical habitats of the New and Old Worlds.

     (1) Most primates are arboreal, although a few (such as some Old World monkeys, chimpanzees, and gorillas) are semi-terrestrial.

c) **Diet and Teeth**

   i) Primates are generally omnivorous.

   ii) Most primates have four kinds of teeth: incisors, canines, premolars, and molars.

     (1) The dental formula describes the number of each tooth type in each quadrant of the mouth.

       (a) The generalized placental mammal dental formula is 3.1.4.3.

       (b) In primates and other mammal groups, there has been a general trend towards the reduction in the number of teeth.

       (c) Most New World monkeys have a dental formula of 2.1.3.3.

       (d) Humans, apes, and all Old World monkeys have a dental formula of 2.1.2.3.

     (2) Most primate molars and premolars have low, rounded cusps for processing a wide variety of foods.

d) **Locomotion**
   i) Even though most primates are quadrupedal to some degree, many primates employ more than one form of locomotion.
      (1) Terrestrial quadrupeds possess forelimbs and hind limbs that are approximately equal in length.
         (a) Arboreal quadrupeds possess forelimbs that are shorter than their hind limbs.
         (b) Quadrupeds also have long, flexible lumbar spines.
      (2) Vertical clinging and leaping is a form of locomotion seen in many prosimians.
      (3) Brachiation is a form of suspensory locomotion in which the body is alternately supported under either forelimb.
         (a) Some monkeys are termed semibrachiators, since they use a combination of leaping along with arm swinging.
         (b) Apes and humans are capable of true brachiation.
         (c) Habitual brachiators have arms that are longer than their legs, a short lumbar spine, long curved fingers, and reduced thumbs.
         (d) In some New World monkeys, suspensory behaviors are enhanced by the use of their prehensile tail.

IV. **Primate Classification**
   a) Primate classification is changing due to information from comparative studies of protein structure, DNA sequences, and karyotypes.
   b) It is clear now that chimpanzees and humans are more similar to each other genetically than either is to the gorilla.
      i) Comparisons of the banding patterns of chimpanzee and human chromosomes indicate the possibility that the chimpanzee chromosomes 12 and 13 fused to produce the human chromosome 2.
      ii) Some anthropologists now support placing all great apes in the family Hominidae.
   c) Tarsiers are difficult to classify because they possess a number of prosimian and anthropoid features and biochemically, tarsiers are more closely related to anthropoids.
      i) Some support the creation of two new suborders: Haplorhini (tarsiers plus all anthropoids) and Strepsirhini (lemurs and lorises only).

V. **A Survey of the Living primates**
   a) **Prosimians (Lemurs, Lorises, and Tarsiers)** exhibit more ancestral mammalian characteristics than any other primate group.
      i) Prosimians are distinguished from the anthropoids by a number of features: more laterally placed eyes, differences in reproductive physiology, shorter gestation and maturation periods, a "dental comb", and the retention of a "grooming claw".
         (1) **Lemurs** are found only on the island of Madagascar.
            (a) Larger lemurs are diurnal and eat a variety of foods (leaves, fruit, bark, and shoots), while smaller lemurs are nocturnal and insectivorous.
            (b) Several species live in large social units, while others live in monogamous family units or are solitary.
         (2) **Lorises** are found in the tropical forests and woodlands of India, Sri Lanka, Southeast Asia, and Africa.
            (a) Some are almost entirely insectivorous, while others eat fruit, leaves, gums, and slugs.
         (3) **Tarsiers** are only found on the islands of Southeast Asia.
            (a) They are nocturnal and insectivorous and the social unit consists of a mated pair and their offspring.

b) **Anthropoids (Monkeys, Apes, and Humans)**
   i) Anthropoids differ from prosimians in a number of features including: larger body sizes, larger brains, reduced reliance on olfaction, increased reliance on vision, fully enclosed eye orbits, fusion of the mandible, longer gestation and maturation periods, and increased parental care.
      (1) **New World Monkeys** (the platyrrhines) exhibit a wide range of size, diet, and ecological adaptations.
         (a) They are traditionally divided into two families: Callitrichidae (marmosets and tamarins) and Cebidae (all others).
         (b) The callitrichids retain claws and usually give birth to twins.
         (c) The cebids vary in body size and diet and some possess a prehensile tail.
      (2) **Old World Monkeys** are the most widely distributed of the living non-human primates and are generally less arboreal than New World monkeys.
         (a) The single family of Cercopithecoidea is divided into the cercopithecines (omnivorous cheek-pouched monkeys), and colobines (the leaf-eating monkeys).
         (b) Depending on the species, locomotor behaviors include terrestrial quadrupedalism, arboreal quadrupedalism, leaping and jumping, and semibrachiation.
         (c) Some terrestrial species are sexually dimorphic in body size.
         (d) Monogamous pairs are uncommon among Old World monkeys; colobines live in small groups and baboons and most macaques live in large social groups.
   ii) **Old and New World Monkeys: A Case of Homoplasy**
      (1) Old and New World monkeys are the product of lineages that split some 30 mya.
         (a) Currently, most researchers believe that both lineages arose in Africa from a common monkey ancestor.
         (b) Conditions existed 50-30 mya that would have facilitated an over-water dispersal of monkeys from Africa to South America.
c) **Hominoids (Apes and Humans)**, relative to monkeys, have larger body sizes (except gibbons and siamangs), lack a tail, have a shorter trunk and shoulders adapted for suspensory behaviors, have more complex behaviors and brains, and an increased period of infant dependency.
   i) The superfamily Hominoidea includes the family Hylobatidae (gibbons and siamangs), the family Pongidae (orangutans, gorillas, bonobos, and chimpanzees), and the family Hominidae (humans).
      (1) **Gibbons and Siamangs** are the smallest of the apes.
         (a) Many of their body features are adaptations to brachiation.
         (b) Their basic social unit is an adult male and female, plus their offspring.
         (c) They are highly territorial.
      (2) **Orangutans** are found only on the Indonesian islands of Borneo and Sumatra.
         (a) They have pronounced sexual dimorphism in body size.
         (b) They are primarily frugivorous and lead solitary lives.
      (3) **Gorillas** are the largest of all the living primates.
         (a) They live in western and eastern equatorial Africa.
         (b) Gorillas, like orangutans, have marked sexual dimorphism in body size. Adult males are primarily terrestrial because of their great weight (up to 400 pounds).
         (c) Mountain gorillas live in groups with one to two adult silverback males, plus several females and their subadult offspring.
         (d) Gorillas are almost exclusively vegetarian.

(4) **Chimpanzees** are the best known of the nonhuman primates.
   (a) Chimpanzees live in equatorial Africa, but their present distribution is patchy.
   (b) They have less pronounced sexual dimorphism and smaller body sizes.
   (c) They are morphologically similar to gorillas, and both gorillas and chimpanzees are knuckle walkers, although chimpanzees can walk bipedally for short distances.
   (d) They have a more varied diet than gorillas, including fruit, leaves, insects, and small mammals (which they hunt).
   (e) Chimpanzees live in large communities and have complex social interactions.
(5) **Bonobos** are found only in an area south of the Zaire River.
   (a) Bonobos and chimpanzees are morphologically similar but bonobos have a more linear body build.
   (b) Bonobos live in fluid communities, but bonobo society is centered on male-female bonds (rather than the close male-male bonds observed in chimpanzees).
   (c) Unlike all other nonhuman primates, bonobos copulate throughout the female's estrous cycle.
(6) **Humans** are the only living member of the habitually bipedal hominids.
   (a) Humans retain generalized primate dentition, but with reduced canines, and they also retain mobile shoulder joints that enable them to brachiate.
   (b) Humans are omnivorous and have generalized digestive systems
   (c) Humans are unique among primates in that they possess a very large, neuronally complex brain that (along with specialized anatomical structures) predisposes them to use spoken language.
   (d) Humans possess many adaptations of the pelvis, leg, and foot that enable habitual bipedalism.

VI.   Endangered Primates

   a) The Miss Waldron's red colobus monkey is the first nonhuman primate to be officially declared extinct.
   b) Many primate species now number only in the hundreds to the thousands of individuals due to habitat loss, being hunted as food, and/or being captured for export.
      i) Habitat loss is one of the most pressing problems, but hunting pressures in both Africa and South America are a significant threat.
      ii) Many countries are attempting to ensure the survival of a few species.
      iii) In addition, there is international pressure to curb the bush meat trade.
   c) Unfortunately, many primate species will continue to go extinct despite our best efforts.

Learning Objectives

After reading Chapter 6, the student should be able to:
1. Discuss the primates both in terms of their ancestral mammalian traits as well as the evolutionary trends that define the order *Primates*.
2. Discuss the geographical distribution and habitat preferences of the primates.
3. Discuss primate diet, teeth, and locomotor patterns and their morphological correlates.
4. Understand the basics of primate taxonomic classification, emphasizing the major taxa: suborder, superfamily, family, genus and species.
5. List the distinguishing features of prosimians, anthropoids, and hominoids.
6. List the members of the superfamily *Hominoidea* and describe their morphological traits and social structures.
7. Discuss the endangered status of the nonhuman primate species mentioned in the text.

Key Terms and Concepts

Adaptive niche	p. 127	Lumbar	p. 132
Anthropoids	p. 122	Morphology	p. 124
Arboreal	p. 127	Natal group	p. 145
Binocular vision	p. 124	Neocortex	p. 125
Brachiation	p. 132	Nocturnal	p. 124
Callitricidae	p. 138	Olfaction	p. 124
Cebidae	p. 138	Omnivorous	p. 124
Cercopithecidae	p. 140	Polyandry	p. 138
Cercopithecines	p. 140	Prehensility	p. 124
Colobines	p. 140	Primates	p. 122
Dental formula	p. 131	Primatologists	p. 124
Diurnal	p. 124	Prosimians	p. 122
Frugivorous	p. 144	Quadrupedal	p. 131
Hemispheres	p. 125	Rhinarium	p. 136
Hominoidea	p. 143	Sensory modalities	p. 125
Hylobatidae	p. 143	Sexual dimorphism	p. 142
Intelligence	p. 148	Stereoscopic vision	p. 124
Ischial callosities	p. 140	Territorial	p. 143

Lecture Suggestions and Enrichment Topics

1. If your college or university is near a zoo with a good primate collection, you should arrange a class trip. Be sure they can distinguish a monkey from an ape. Have them pay particular attention to locomotor patterns, noting their anatomical correlates. If there is an infant in any of the exhibits, have them observe the mother/infant interactions and have them note the similarities between these interactions and those of human mothers and infants.
2. Since this course will probably be the student's only exposure to nonhuman primates, it is important to point out the serious threats to the survival of most free-ranging nonhuman primate populations. Certainly, within the lifetime of many students, several primate species will become extinct in the wild.
3. Discuss the hypothesis that HIV was transmitted to humans through the eating of bonobo bush meat. Bonobos carry the SIV virus, but do not become ill, therefore they could be useful in solving the AIDS crisis.

Student Media Exercises

1. From J. Kappelman's *Virtual Laboratories for Physical Anthropology* CD: Students should complete Lab 3: *Primate Functional Morphology* to help them understand the fundamentals of primate functional morphology.
2. From J. Kappelman's *Virtual Laboratories for Physical Anthropology* CD: Students should complete Lab 4: *Primates in Motion* to help them understand the fundamentals of primate locomotion.
3. From J. Kappelman's *Virtual Laboratories for Physical Anthropology* CD: Students should complete Lab 5: *Primate Diets and Feeding Behavior* to help them understand the fundamentals of the relationships between primate diets and their masticatory morphology.
4. In *InfoTrac* search for the article Seduced by Sifakas (*National Wildlife*, **June-July 2002 pNA**). Answer the following question: The Madagascar natives do not kill Sifakas for meat, yet Sifakas are an endangered species; why then, are they endangered?

5. In *InfoTrac* search for the article <u>The global decline of primates</u> (John Tuxill. *World Watch*, Sept-Oct 1997 v10 n5 p16). Give a brief overview of the crises facing nonhuman primate populations.
6. Go online to The Jane Goodall Institute (<u>http://www.janegoodall.org/index.html</u>) to find out more about chimpanzee behavior.
7. Go online to the Human Behavior and Evolution Society (<u>http://www.hbes.com/</u>). Follow the link "Intro to the Field" and choose one of the introductory readings. Outline the major tenets of the evolutionary approach to behavioral research.

Multiple Choice Questions

1. As an order, primates
    A. have highly specialized traits.
    B. can be easily defined by one or two traits.
    C. lack traits that define the mammals.
    D. have generalized traits.
    E. have very narrow, or specialized, dietary preferences.

    ANS: D
    PG: 122

2. Which one of the traits listed below is NOT used to define the order *Primates*?
    A. A tendency towards erect posture.
    B. An inflexible, specialized limb structure.
    C. Hands and feet with a high degree of prehensility.
    D. Retention of five digits on the hands and feet.
    E. Generalized dentition.

    ANS: B
    PG: 122-123

3. The presence of five digits on hands and feet is
    A. a primitive mammalian pattern retained to some degree in most primate species.
    B. characteristic only of primates.
    C. characteristic only of apes and humans.
    D. the only truly distinctive primate trait.
    E. none of these

    ANS: A
    PG: 122-124

4. Primates possess _____, whereas other mammals do not.
    A. eye sockets surrounded by a postorbital bar
    B. four different kinds of teeth
    C. the presence of nails rather than claws on most or all digits
    D. behavioral flexibility
    E. A and C only

    ANS: E
    PG: 122-124

5. Primate
    A. teeth are generalized because primates are omnivorous.
    B. teeth are specialized for processing one type of food.
    C. premolars and molars are indistinguishable from those found in carnivores.
    D. tooth form is not correlated with their diet.
    E. none of these

    ANS: A
    PG: 124

6. The primate emphasis on the visual sense is reflected in
    A. the reduction in the size of structures related to the sense of smell.
    B. the presence of color vision in most species.
    C. a more forward facing position of the eyes relative to most other mammals.
    D. all of these
    E. B and C only

    ANS: D
    PG: 124-125

7. The increased period of infant dependency typical of primates
    A. requires more intense and efficient rearing of the offspring.
    B. requires greater parental investment.
    C. provides greater opportunities for the offspring to learn social behaviors.
    D. all of these
    E. A and B only

    ANS: D
    PG: 124-125

8. Traditionally, primate characteristics have been explained as the result of adaptation to _____ environments.
    A. terrestrial
    B. rocky
    C. arboreal
    D. desert
    E. grassland

    ANS: C
    PG: 124-125

9. According to the visual predation hypothesis,
    A. primate characteristics evolved as adaptive advantages in a purely terrestrial environment.
    B. mammalian characteristics evolved as adaptive advantages in a purely arboreal environment.
    C. primate characteristics evolved as adaptive advantages in the shrubby forest undergrowth.
    D. primate characteristics evolved as primates adapted to the highest tiers in the forest canopy.
    E. B and D only

    ANS: C
    PG: 124-125

10. The order *Primates* is traditionally divided into two suborders: _____ and _____.
    A. *Platyrrhine* and *Catarrhine*
    B. *Prosimii* and *Anthropoidea*
    C. *Pongidae* and *Hominidae*
    D. *Cercopithecoidea* and *Hominoidea*
    E. *Pongo* and *Homo*

    ANS: B
    PG: 132-133

11. Which of the following are NOT anthropoids?
    A. New World monkeys
    B. lorises
    C. Old World monkeys
    D. humans
    E. gorillas

    ANS: B
    PG: 132-133

12. Old World monkeys are separated from apes and humans at the level of the _____.
    A. infraorder
    B. genus
    C. superfamily
    D. family
    E. suborder

    ANS: C
    PG: 133

13. Which of the following are prosimians?
    A. baboons
    B. macaques
    C. marmosets
    D. lemurs
    E. gibbons

    ANS: D
    PG: 136-138

14. Some taxonomists have developed an alternate system of classification in which tarsiers, monkeys, apes, and humans are placed together in the suborder
    A. *Prosimii.*
    B. *Lorisoidea.*
    C. *Hominoidea.*
    D. *Haplorhini.*
    E. *Strepsirhini.*

    ANS: D
    PG: 135

15. The tarsier
    A. is unquestionably a prosimian.
    B. is more closely related in some ways to anthropoids than to prosimians.
    C. is a hominid.
    D. is a New World monkey.
    E. is unquestionably an anthropoid.

    ANS: B
    PG: 138

16. Which of the following are not hominoids?
    A. bonobos
    B. gorillas
    C. orangutans
    D. chimpanzees
    E. baboons

    ANS: E
    PG: 143

17. Traditionally, *Pongidae*
    A. is the family name for all the great apes.
    B. used to included modern *Homo sapiens.*
    C. includes Old World monkeys and the great apes.
    D. includes the great apes and the lesser apes only.
    E. includes New World monkeys and the apes.

    ANS: A
    PG: 144

18. Which of the following are **not** apes?
    A. gorillas
    B. orangutans
    C. bonobos
    D. chimpanzees
    E. macaques

    ANS: E
    PG: 144

19. Using all four limbs to support the body during locomotion is called
    A. bipedalism.
    B. quadrupedalism.
    C. vertical clinging and leaping.
    D. brachiation.
    E. semi-brachiation.

    ANS: B
    PG: 132-135

20. Vertical clinging and leaping is a locomotor pattern frequently practiced by some
    A. apes.
    B. prosimians.
    C. terrestrial monkeys.
    D. Old World monkeys.
    E. gibbons.

    ANS: B
    PG: 132

21. Arms that are longer than the legs, and a short stable lumbar spine are traits associated with
    A. brachiation.
    B. vertical clinging and leaping.
    C. arboreal quadrupedalism.
    D. terrestrial quadrupedalism.
    E. full-time bipedalism.

    ANS: A
    PG: 132

22. _____ is seen in some New World Monkeys, but not in any Old World monkeys.
    A. A grasping hand
    B. Quadrupedalism
    C. An arboreal lifestyle
    D. Color vision
    E. A prehensile tail

    ANS: E
    PG: 138

23. Which of the following are capable of brachiation?
    A. gibbons
    B. humans
    C. chimpanzees
    D. all of these
    E. none of these

    ANS: D
    PG: 138,148

24. Comparisons of 97 human and chimpanzee genes indicate that humans and chimpanzees last shared
    a common ancestor about _____ years ago.
    A. 5-6 million
    B. 50-60 million
    C. 2-3 million
    D. 20-30 thousand
    E. none of these

    ANS: A
    PG: 146-148

25. Comparisons of 97 primate genes indicate that humans and chimpanzees last shared a common ancestor about _____ years ago.
    A. 5-6 million
    B. 50-60 million
    C. 2-3 million
    D. 20-30 thousand
    E. none of these

    ANS: E
    PG: 146-148

26. The genus and species designation for the "common" chimpanzee is
    A. *Pan paniscus.*
    B. *Pan gorilla.*
    C. *Pongo paniscus.*
    D. *Pan troglodytes.*
    E. *Pongo troglodytes.*

    ANS: D
    PG: 146

27. The most primitive primates are the
    A. Old World monkeys.
    B. New World monkeys.
    C. tarsiers.
    D. prosimians.
    E. great apes.

    ANS: D
    PG: 136

28. The two major groups of prosimians are the
    A. lemurs and tarsiers.
    B. marmosets and howler monkeys.
    C. lemurs and lorises.
    D. baboons and macaques.
    E. tarsiers and lorises.

    ANS: C
    PG: 136

29. Compared to prosimians, anthropoids generally
    A. have smaller body sizes.
    B. have decreased infant maturation periods.
    C. have smaller brains.
    D. depend less on olfaction and more on vision.
    E. groom less often.

    ANS: D
    PG: 138

30. Monkeys are divided into two major groups:
    A. terrestrial and arboreal forms.
    B. New and Old World species.
    C. large and small-bodied species.
    D. quadrupedal and bipedal.
    E. omnivores and frugivores.

    ANS: B
    PG: 138

31. The smallest of the New World anthropoids are the
    A. marmosets and tamarins.
    B. howler monkeys and baboons.
    C. spider monkeys and capuchin monkeys.
    D. squirrel monkeys and bonobos.
    E. macaques.

    ANS: A
    PG: 138

32. Old World monkeys are found in
    A. Africa and northern Europe.
    B. Mexico and South America.
    C. Africa, southern Asia, and Japan.
    D. India and southern Asia ONLY.
    E. North America and Mexico.

    ANS: C
    PG: 140

33. All Old World monkeys belong to the family
    A. *Ominidae.*
    B. *Cercopithecidae.*
    C. *Callitrichidae.*
    D. *Pongidae.*
    E. *Monkidae.*

    ANS: B
    PG: 140

34. Cercopithecines
    A. are one subfamily of Old World monkeys.
    B. are more generalized than colobines.
    C. include baboons, guenons, and macaques.
    D. have cheek pouches for storing food.
    E. all of these

    ANS: E
    PG: 140

35. Colobines
    A. are found Africa ONLY.
    B. eat only fruit.
    C. eat mostly insects.
    D. are found in Asia ONLY.
    E. are found in Africa and parts of India and Asia.

    ANS: E
    PG: 140

36. Sexual dimorphism
    A. refers to differences between adults and adolescents with regard to sexual behavior.
    B. is particularly pronounced in all primate species.
    C. refers to differences between the sexes with regard to features such as body size.
    D. is more common in arboreal species.
    E. has not been observed in ANY monkey.

    ANS: C
    PG: 142

37. In nonhuman primates, the hormonally initiated period of sexual receptivity is
    A. called sexual dimorphism.
    B. called sexual reciprocity.
    C. typical of males.
    D. called estrus.
    E. C and D only.

    ANS: D
    PG: 147

38. Compared to monkeys, hominoids
    A. generally have larger body sizes and lack a tail.
    B. have a more elongated lower back.
    C. have arms and legs of equal length.
    D. exhibit less complex behavior.
    E. have a shorter period of infant dependency.

    ANS: A
    PG: 143

39. Which are NOT hominoids?
    A. gorillas
    B. humans
    C. orangutans
    D. chimpanzees
    E. baboons

    ANS: E
    PG: 143-148

40. Among the apes, the _____ have the smallest average body sizes.
    A. gibbons and siamangs
    B. bonobos
    C. chimpanzees
    D. macaques
    E. orangutans

    ANS: A
    PG: 143

41. Which of the great apes is found only on the islands of Borneo and Sumatra?
    A. gibbons
    B. gorillas
    C. orangutans
    D. bonobos
    E. chimpanzees

    ANS: C
    PG: 144-146

42. _____ have very large, highly sexually dimorphic body sizes, and live largely solitary lives.
    A. Gorillas
    B. Chimpanzees
    C. Gibbons
    D. Orangutans
    E. none of these

    ANS: D
    PG: 144-146

43. Which are the largest living primates?
    A. orangutans
    B. chimpanzees
    C. gibbons
    D. bonobos
    E. gorillas

    ANS: E
    PG: 144-146

44. Mountain gorilla social groups are usually composed of
    A. one adult male and one adult female, plus their immature offspring.
    B. solitary individuals, except for females with dependent young.
    C. one or two adult males, a few adult females and their immature offspring, plus one or two adult non-breeding, males.
    D. several adults of both sexes and offspring of all ages.
    E. several adult males and only one female and her offspring.

    ANS: C
    PG: 144-146

45. Chimpanzees are found
    A. across forested equatorial Africa as far east as Lake Tanganyika.
    B. in Africa and India.
    C. in open savanna areas of Kenya ONLY.
    D. in the mountainous areas of central Africa ONLY.
    E. in Africa, India and southeast Asia.

    ANS: A
    PG: 146-147

46. Chimpanzees live in groups composed of
    A. one adult male and several females and their young.
    B. several adult males and females plus young of all ages.
    C. one adult male plus one adult female and their young.
    D. several adult females and one adult male and any dependent young.
    E. none of these

    ANS: B
    PG: 146-147

47. Bonobos are
    A. the most thoroughly studied primate species.
    B. in the same genus as the gorilla.
    C. behaviorally indistinguishable from "common" chimpanzees.
    D. in the same genus as the "common" chimpanzee.
    E. almost exclusively arboreal.

    ANS: D
    PG: 147-148

48. In most areas, the single greatest cause of declining numbers of nonhuman primates is
    A. the killing of primates for human consumption.
    B. the trapping of live primates for biomedical research.
    C. habitat loss.
    D. the trapping of live primates for the pet trade.
    E. the overpopulation of nonhuman primate groups.

    ANS: C
    PG: 148-149

True/False Questions

1. Primates are found ONLY in tropical and semitropical habitats of the Old World and North America.

    ANS: False
    PG: 128-129

2. Humans and New World monkeys both have a 2.1.2.3 dental formula.

    ANS: False
    PG: 131

3. The human chromosome 2 appears to be the product of the fusion of two smaller chimpanzee chromosomes.

    ANS: True
    PG: 134

4. The "dental comb" is a specialization found in most of the anthropoid species.

    ANS: False
    PG: 136

5. Although not yet formally accepted, the current genetic evidence is consistent with the classification of humans and all African apes within the same family.

    ANS: True
    PG: 135

6. In the proposed revision of the classification of the primates, the lemurs, lorises, and tarsiers would be placed in the suborder *Strepsirhini*.

    ANS: False
    PG: 136

7. Colobine monkeys specialize in eating mature leaves, and are referred to as "leaf-eating monkeys".

    ANS: True
    PG: 140

8. Many researchers argue that New World monkeys may have originated when they "rafted" over from Africa.

    ANS: True
    PG: 138-140

9. Orangutan adults have a very active locomotion pattern and they frequently brachiate.

    ANS: False
    PG: 144

10. Bonobo communities, like those of chimpanzees, are centered around male-male bonds.

    ANS: False
    PG: 147-148

Short Answer Questions

1. List five traits used to define the order *Primates*.
   (pp. 124-125)

2. Which primate traits are likely to be adaptations to arboreal lifestyles?
   (pp. 127-128)

3. Define three major forms of primate locomotion. Name at least one species associated with each type.
   (pp. 131-132)

4. List five traits that distinguish the prosimians from the anthropoids.
   (pp. 136-142)

5. What traits distinguish Old World monkeys from apes and humans?
   (pp. 140-148)

6. Gibbons are said to be adapted for brachiation. What anatomical features do gibbons possess that enable them to brachiate efficiently?
   (p. 143)

7. Compare chimpanzee and bonobo anatomy and social behavior.
   (pp. 146-148)

Essay Questions

1. What are the main tenets of the visual predation and arboreal theories of primate origins? Discuss the strengths and weaknesses of both.

2. Compare and contrast the social organization of orangutans, gorillas, and common chimpanzees.

3. Discuss the factors that contribute to the depletion of nonhuman primate populations. Which species are most threatened?

CHAPTER 7: PRIMATE BEHAVIOR

Chapter Outline

I. Introduction
a) Animal behavior is a complex phenomenon to study because it has been shaped by evolution through the interaction between environmental and genetic processes.

II. Primate Field Studies
a) In America during the 1920s and 1930s, psychologist Robert Yerkes sent out students to study primates in the field.
b) Jane Goodall began her chimpanzee field studies in 1960, while mountain gorilla studies by Dianne Fossey and orangutan studies by Birute Galdika commenced later.
c) Most of our current knowledge on free-ranging primates comes from studies of species that are primarily terrestrial.
   i)   Others have studied large, provisioned colonies, such as the study of rhesus macaques on Cayo Santiago.
   ii) Much of the data collected concerns life history traits: age at sexual maturity, length of pregnancy, interbirth interval, and life expectancy.

III. The Evolution of Behavior
a) Free-ranging primates are studied within an ecological and evolutionary framework termed behavioral ecology.
   i)   Central to this perspective is the hypothesis that behaviors have evolved through the operation of natural selection.
   ii) Behavior must be viewed as a flexible, complex trait that is influenced by the interaction of genes and the environment.
      (1) Scientists have yet to discover the exact genotype-phenotype interactions that produce specific behavioral traits.
b) **Some factors that influence social structure** include:
   i)   Body size
   ii)   Basal metabolic rate
   iii) Diet
   iv)   Distribution of resources
   v)   Predation
   vi)   Relationships with other nonpredatory species
   vii) Dispersal patterns
   viii) Life Histories
   ix)   Strategies
   x)   Distribution and types of sleeping sites
   xi)   Activity patterns
   xii) Human activities
c) The relationships among these ecological variables have yet to be fully understood.

IV. Sympatric Species
a) These are species that live in the same area whose habitats overlap.
b) **Five Monkey Species in the Kibale Forest, Uganda**
   i)   Struhsaker and Leyland studied sympatric species of monkeys: the black-and-white colobus, the red colobus, the mangabey, the blue monkey, and the redtail monkey.
   ii) The primates varied in average body weight, diet, and social organization.

iii) The authors discovered several important ecological relationships:
  (1) Omnivores move about more than folivores.
  (2) Among the omnivores, body size and group size are inversely related.
  (3) Omnivores are dispersed more widely than folivores.
  (4) Males and females of the same species have different ecological needs and follow different reproductive strategies.

V. Why Be Social?
  a) The disadvantages to group living include increased intragroup competition for resources.
    i) The predation hypothesis implies that the risks of predation must outweigh the costs of sociality.
    ii) Another explanation argues that larger groups can outcompete smaller groups when foraging in the same area.
  b) Solitary foraging is probably related to diet and the distribution of resources.
    i) Solitary feeding reduces competition and helps in predator avoidance in species that rely on concealment.

VI. Primate Social Behavior has evolved as adaptive responses over a period of 50 million years.
  a) **Dominance** hierarchies serve to impose order within primate groups.
    i) Rank or status is measured by access to resources.
    ii) One of the primary benefits of dominance is the increased reproductive success of the individual.
      (1) Not all researchers agree on this point.
    iii) An individual's rank may change throughout their lifetime.
    iv) Males are generally dominant to females in mixed sex groups.
      (1) Males and females maintain separate dominance hierarchies.
    v) Primates learn their position in the dominance hierarchy.
      (1) They also acquire social rank as they play with their age peers.
  b) **Communication** is an act (both intentional and unintentional) that conveys information to another individual.
    i) Primates use a wide variety of gestures, facial expressions, and vocalizations to communicate.
      (1) High-ranking members express dominance to subordinates by the use of mounting behaviors.
      (2) Submission can be indicated by a crouched position or presenting the hindquarters (for baboons), and sometimes by grooming.
      (3) Chimpanzees reassure through holding hands and hugging.
    ii) Displays are elaborate combinations of behavior used to communicate.
      (1) For example, gorillas slap their chest and tear vegetation to threaten.
    iii) Ritualized behaviors are often incorporated into displays.
      (1) For example, mounting is a ritualized behavior because its social purpose is far removed from its biological role in reproduction.
  c) **Aggressive and Affiliative Interactions** are balanced in order to maintain group cohesion.
    i) Conflicts may arise out of resource competition and competition for mates.
      (1) These conflicts are signaled by aggressive behaviors.
      (2) Sometimes, male-male competition for mates results in injury or death.
    ii) Affiliative behaviors serve to minimize violence and defuse dangerous situations.
      (1) Grooming is one of the most important affiliative behaviors.
      (2) Grooming occurs in a variety of contexts; mothers groom infants, males groom sexually reproductive females, and subordinate animals groom dominant animals.
    iii) Reconciliatory behaviors are important in chimpanzee and bonobo societies.
      (1) Bonobos use sex to ensure group cohesion, to restore peace after conflicts, and to relieve intragroup tension.

VII. Reproduction And Reproductive Strategies
   a) Generally, females are sexually receptive to males only when they are in estrus.
   b) Permanent male-female bonds are rare among nonhuman primates.
      i) Savannah baboons form consortships. These are temporary friendships formed between males and females while the female is in estrus.
         (1) Chimpanzees and bonobos also form consortships.
         (2) Bonobo consortships are unusual; males and females continue to mate even when the female is not in estrus.
   c) **Female and male reproductive strategies** may differ from each other.
      i) Primates are exceptionally K-selected.
         (1) They produce relatively few young and invest considerable parental care in their young.
         (2) The mother tends to carry most of the burden of infant care.
      ii) Females spend most of their life pregnant, or lactating, and/or caring for their infant.
         (1) Given the energetic demands of being a female, her strategy is to maximize the available resources.
      iii) Alternately, males attempt to produce as many offspring as possible.
   d) **Sexual selection** refers to a type of natural selection that operates on only one sex within a species.
      i) Sexual selection usually operates on males; either in the guise of male-male competition or female mate choice.
      ii) Monogamous species have reduced male-male competition and therefore usually have reduced levels of sexual dimorphism in canine size and body size.
   e) **Infanticide as a reproductive strategy?**
      i) One explanation of infanticide in Hanuman langurs emphasizes the reproductive benefits to the male performing the behavior.
         (1) Peripheral males often attack social groups, driving out a reproductive male. The new male will sometimes then kill the group's infants.
         (2) This behavior maximizes the new male's reproductive success because the female will begin cycling again (and become sexually receptive to the new male) when her infant is killed.
         (3) Infanticide has also been observed in other monkeys (including baboons), as well as in orangutans, gorillas, and chimpanzees.
      ii) Alternate explanations have been offered to explain infanticide including: resource competition, overcrowding, and inadvertent killing of infants.

VIII. Mothers, Fathers, and Infants
   a) The basic social unit in primates is the female and her infants.
      i) Experiments by the Harlows on macaques indicate that monkeys must learn the rules of social interaction and they need the mother-infant bond for normal psychological and emotional development to proceed.
      ii) Field studies indicate that the mother-infant bond may last throughout life.
      iii) The extension of the mother-infant relationship is alloparenting; this occurs when individuals other than the parent(s) hold, and carry the infant.

Learning Objectives

After reading Chapter 7, the student should be able to:
1. Briefly describe the history of primate field studies and list some of the scientists who initiated pioneering research.
2. Define behavioral ecology and discuss the factors that influence social structure.
3. List the primary generalizations of the Kibale study.
4. Contrast the advantages and disadvantages of primate social groups.

5. Define the types of primate social interactions including dominance, and affiliative and aggressive behaviors.
6. Discuss the various types of primate communication.
7. Differentiate between male and female reproductive strategies and their influence on sex-specific behaviors.
8. Discuss the importance of the mother-infant bond in contributing to the normal social and psychological development of primate infants.

Key Terms and Concepts

Affiliative	p. 168	Life history traits	p. 161
Alloparenting	p. 175	Matrilines	p. 159
Autonomic	p. 166	Metabolism	p. 158
Behavior	p. 155	Philopatric	p. 160
Behavioral ecology	p. 157	Polyandry	p. 173
Communication	p. 166	Reproductive strategies	p. 171
Conspecifics	p. 164	Ritualized behaviors	p. 168
Displays	p. 167	R-selected	p. 171
Dominance hierarchies	p. 165	Sexual selection	p. 171
Free-ranging	p. 156	Social structure	p. 156
Grooming	p. 168	Strategies	p. 161
Home range	p. 163	Sympatric	p. 161
K-selected	p. 171		

Lecture Suggestions and Enrichment Topics

1. It is difficult for students to conceptualize the range of primate behaviors without seeing them. Unless you have a top-quality zoo nearby, observing primate behavior in a zoo setting (with unnatural group sizes and compositions) is not particularly informative for the students. There are a number of good quality videos available that demonstrate primate behavior in the wild; a good choice for a video about chimpanzees is *Among the Wild Chimpanzees*, available through the Jane Goodall Institute (http://www.janegoodall.org).
2. If you have a network connection in your room, you can also use Internet resources to demonstrate primate behaviors. One such site is http://www.emory.edu/LIVING_LINKS/AVLibrary.html where you will find small video clips of chimpanzee behaviors.
3. Links to primates in the news can be found at http://pin.primate.wisc.edu/.

Student Media Exercises

1. From J. Kappelman's *Virtual Laboratories for Physical Anthropology* CD: Students should read Lab 6: *Primate Behavior* and complete Section V: *Lab Exercises*.
2. From J. Kappelman's *Virtual Laboratories for Physical Anthropology* CD: Students should read Lab 6: *Primate Behavior* and complete Section VI: *Self Quiz and Conclusion*.
3. Go online to the Human Behavior and Evolution Society (http://www.hbes.com/). Follow the link "Intro to the Field" and choose one of the introductory readings. Outline the major tenets of the evolutionary approach to behavioral research.
4. Go online to The Jane Goodall Institute (http://www.janegoodall.org/index.html) to find out more about chimpanzee behavior.

Multiple Choice Questions

1. The primary goal of primate field studies is to
   A. collect information for maintaining zoo specimens.
   B. study only monkey species.
   C. study primates whose behavior has been altered by human contact.
   D. collect data on free-ranging animals
   E. none of these

   ANS: D
   PG: 156

2. Studies of free-ranging nonhuman primates
   A. began in the 1800s.
   B. have been done exclusively by American scientists.
   C. are currently conducted by psychologists.
   D. began in the late 1920s and 1930s.
   E. are no more informative than studies of captive primates.

   ANS: D
   PG: 156

3. Most primatologists consider primate behavior to be
   A. influenced by environmental factors.
   B. entirely genetic in origin.
   C. independent of environmental factors.
   D. entirely learned and without any genetic basis.
   E. none of these

   ANS: A
   PG: 157-158

4. _____ is the study of the evolution of behavior, emphasizing the role of ecological factors as agents of natural selection.
   A. Sociobiology
   B. Biological-ecology
   C. Socioecology
   D. Evolutionary ecology
   E. Behavioral ecology

   ANS: E
   PG: 157

5. Behavioral genetics
   A. is the study of how social systems influence disease patterns.
   B. was a theory first proposed by Charles Darwin.
   C. is a theoretical framework that emphasizes the role of natural selection on behavior.
   D. is no longer considered a valid theoretical approach.
   E. emphasizes the role of ecological variables in shaping social behaviors.

   ANS: C
   PG: 157

6. With regards to BMR, it is
    A. the rate at which energy is used by the body during exercise.
    B. the rate at which energy is used by the body at rest.
    C. not correlated with body size.
    D. not an important factor influencing primate social structure.
    E. A and C only

    ANS: B
    PG: 158

7. Of the nonhuman primate social groups listed below, the MOST common form found is
    A. one male, multifemale.
    B. Multimale, multifemale.
    C. monogamous.
    D. polyandry.
    E. solitary.

    ANS: A
    PG: 160

8. Ecological factors influencing primate social behavior include
    A. the distribution of food and water.
    B. the distribution of predators.
    C. the nutritional value of foods.
    D. all of these
    E. A and C only

    ANS: D
    PG: 158-161

9. If females of a given primate group are philopatric, it means that females
    A. only mate once a year.
    B. are dominant over males of the same group.
    C. disperse from their natal group at sexual maturity.
    D. remain in one's natal group as an adult.
    E. A and B only.

    ANS: D
    PG: 160

10. Different species that share the same habitat are said to be
    A. territorial.
    B. sympatric.
    C. diurnal.
    D. dominant.
    E. none of these

    ANS: B
    PG: 161

11. Strategies that increase individual reproductive fitness include
    A. life history strategies.
    B. feeding strategies.
    C. social strategies.
    D. A and B only
    E. all of these

    ANS: E
    PG: 161

12. The five monkey species that share the same habitat in Uganda's Kibale Forest
    A. all had the same type of social grouping.
    B. differ with regard to their group composition and diet.
    C. were always in competition with one another because they all utilized the same resources.
    D. are all leaf-eaters.
    E. regularly killed and ate members of the other groups.

    ANS: B
    PG: 162

13. In the context of social groups, dominance hierarchies
    A. are maintained by females ONLY.
    B. are maintained by males ONLY.
    C. are present in all primate species.
    D. impose a certain amount of order within the group.
    E. have not been studied by primatologists.

    ANS: D
    PG: 165

14. Which of the following statements is/are generally TRUE?
    A. Adult primate males tend to be dominant to females.
    B. Dominant individuals appear to have priority access to desired food items.
    C. Dominant animals may have more frequent access to mating partners.
    D. all of these
    E. A and B only

    ANS: D
    PG: 165-166

15. Some of the deliberate nonhuman primate behaviors that serve as communication include
    A. spoken language.
    B. facial expressions.
    C. gestures.
    D. all of these
    E. B and C only

    ANS: E
    PG: 166-167

16. Chest slapping by gorillas and arm waving by chimpanzees are examples of
    A. reassurance gestures.
    B. submission.
    C. displays.
    D. involuntary behavior.
    E. affiliative behavior.

    ANS: C
    PG: 167

17. Communicative behaviors that have become exaggerated and removed from their original context are said to be
    A. instinctual.
    B. symbolic.
    C. autonomic.
    D. ritualized.
    E. genetically determined.

    ANS: D
    PG: 168

18. The original context of mounting as an expression of dominance in baboons is believed to have been
    A. copulation.
    B. reassurance.
    C. aggression.
    D. threat behaviors.
    E. none of these

    ANS: A
    PG: 168

19. Mounting behavior, as seen in baboons, is a good example of
    A. ritualized behavior.
    B. aggressive behavior.
    C. sexual behavior.
    D. estrus.
    E. none of these

    ANS: A
    PG: 168

20. Amicable behaviors that promote group cohesion are called _____ behaviors.
    A. cultural
    B. philopatric
    C. ritualized
    D. affiliative
    E. autonomic

    ANS: D
    PG: 168

21. For primates, most intragroup aggression takes the form of
    A. fighting.
    B. signals and displays.
    C. throwing of objects.
    D. killing other individuals.
    E. slapping and biting.

    ANS: B
    PG: 167-169

22. In many primate species, _____ have/has a central role in relieving tension and reinforcing social bonds.
    A. play
    B. coalition formation
    C. dominance hierarchies
    D. food sharing
    E. social grooming

    ANS: E
    PG: 169

23. Which of the following is FALSE?
    A. In Old World monkey species, mating occurs only when the female is in estrus.
    B. Among primates, males and females never form close bonds.
    C. Estrus is characterized by some behavioral changes in females.
    D. Bonobo males and females rarely interact.
    E. Chimpanzee males sometimes form consortships with females.

    ANS: B
    PG: 170

24. Permanent male-female bonds are
    A. common among nonhuman primates.
    B. not common among nonhuman primates.
    C. the basis of monogamous pairing typical of ALL nonhuman primate species.
    D. nonexistent in primates.
    E. known only in orangutans.

    ANS: B
    PG: 170

25. In multimale/multifemale groups, males and females
    A. sometimes form friendships and consortships.
    B. never interact except when a female is in estrus.
    C. are usually sexually active throughout the female's estrus cycle.
    D. always interact aggressively.
    E. always avoid one another.

    ANS: A
    PG: 171

26. K-selection refers to
    A. species that produce large numbers of offspring and invest little to no parental care.
    B. species that become extinct after a few generations.
    C. species that produce relatively few offspring but invest increased parental care.
    D. only egg-laying species.
    E. all species except primates.

    ANS: C
    PG: 171

27. Species that produce relatively large numbers of offspring and invest little parental care are said to be
    A. K-selected.
    B. r-selected
    C. p-selected.
    D. alloparental.
    E. sympatric.

    ANS: B
    PG: 171

28. Female primates
    A. spend most of their adult life either pregnant and/or lactating.
    B. assume most of the responsibility for infant care.
    C. have the same nutritional requirements as males.
    D. none of these
    E. A and B only

    ANS: E
    PG: 171

29. When male langurs take over another male's group, they sometimes kill all the young infants. The evolutionary explanation for this behavior is that
    A. it increases the reproductive success of the male.
    B. it causes the infant's mother to cease lactation and resume cycling.
    C. the mother becomes sexually receptive to the new male.
    D. all of these
    E. A and B only

    ANS: D
    PG: 172-173

30. Infanticide by adult males
    A. is rare in primates.
    B. appears to serve no function.
    C. is performed as a means of population control.
    D. is not resisted by females, including the mother.
    E. has been reported for a number of primate species.

    ANS: E
    PG: 172-173

31. A social grouping of two males mated to one female is said to be
    A. monogamous.
    B. polyandrous.
    C. sympatric.
    D. altruistic.
    E. multimale/multifemale.

    ANS: B
    PG: 173

32. The basic primate social unit
    A. is the mother and infant.
    B. is the father and infant.
    C. is the male and female.
    D. are sibling relationships.
    E. none of these

    ANS: A
    PG: 173

33. In laboratory experiments, monkeys raised without mothers
    A. were able to form lasting affectional ties.
    B. displayed completely normal parenting behaviors as adults.
    C. displayed normal sexual behavior.
    D. displayed abnormal social behaviors.
    E. were socially normal as adults, provided they received adequate nourishment.

    ANS: D
    PG: 174

34. Nonhuman primate males
    A. are involved in infant care to some degree in several species.
    A. never display an interest in infants.
    B. contribute as much to infant care as do females in most species.
    C. are usually highly aggressive towards infants.
    D. are never aggressive towards infants.

    ANS: A
    PG: 174-175

35. Alloparenting
    A. is less common in primates than in other mammals.
    B. may help young females to learn proper infant care behaviors.
    C. is defined as helping to care for another individual's infant.
    D. all of these
    E. B and C only

    ANS: E
    PG: 175

36. _____ males assume most of the responsibility for infant care (except for nursing).
   A. Chimpanzee
   B. Baboon
   C. Marmoset and tamarin
   D. Gorilla
   E. A and C only

   ANS: C
   PG: 173

True/False Questions

1. Scientists who use the behavioral ecology approach believe that primate behaviors have evolved through the operation of natural selection.

   ANS: True
   PG: 157

2. Two five kilogram monkeys require the same amount of food as one 10 kilogram monkey.

   ANS: False
   PG: 158

3. Behavioral plasticity refers to the hypothesis that behaviors are genetically determined and are not altered in the face of new environments.

   ANS: False
   PG: 157-158

4. The least common breeding structure among nonhuman primates is the monogamous pair..

   ANS: True
   PG: 160

5. Life history traits are characteristics or developmental stages that typify members of a given species and that affect potential reproductive rates.

   ANS: True
   PG: 161

6. Large primate groups are advantageous because they increase the likelihood of early predator detection.

   ANS: True
   PG: 161

7. Savannah baboons avoid predators by fleeing into trees.

    ANS: True
    PG: 160-161

8. All primate communication is autonomic in nature.

    ANS: False
    PG: 166-167

9. Sexual selection does not seem to be an important factor in the evolution of sexual dimorphism.

    ANS: False
    PG: 171

10. It has been proposed that male Hanuman langurs that commit infanticide are actually reducing their own reproductive success.

    ANS: False
    PG: 171

Short Answer Questions

1. Discuss four factors that affect the social structure of a given species.
   (pp. 158-161)

2. What are dominance hierarchies and what important functions do they serve?
   (pp. 165-166)

3. Discuss the evolutionary explanation of infanticide in Hanuman langurs.
   (p. 172)

4. Contrast autonomic responses and behaviors with intentional behaviors that serve as communication.
   (pp. 166-167)

5. What are the functions of grooming in nonhuman primate groups?
   (p. 168)

6. Define the terms K-selection and r-selection. Are primates K-selected or r-selected?
   (p. 171)

7. Discuss the effects of isolation in infancy and separation from the mother on monkey behavior.
   (pp. 173-174)

8. What is sexual selection and how does it contribute to sexual dimorphism?
   (p. 171)

Essay Questions

1. Discuss the factors that influence social structures in nonhuman primate groups.

2. What are the benefits of large social groups? Cite a few examples.

3. What are the possible advantages of alloparenting, both to the infant and to the alloparent?

4. Defend the proposition that social behaviors can be studied in the context of natural selection.

5. What problems do you think might be associated with the behavioral ecology approach to explaining primate social structures?

CHAPTER 8: PRIMATE MODELS FOR HUMAN BEHAVIORAL EVOLUTION

Chapter Outline

I. Introduction
a) Although there are no primates that display the complete human behavioral repertoire, we can still draw inferences about early human behavior by identifying patterns of behavior shared by humans and nonhuman primates.

II. Human Origins and Behavior
a) Humans and chimpanzees share more than 98% of their DNA, yet they contrast in some aspects of their anatomy and behavior.
    i) Behavioral and anatomical adaptations were selected for as the early hominids spent more time on the ground and began exploiting different types of food resources.
        (1) We need to discover the relationships between life history traits and sociality to unravel the evolutionary history of our lineage.

III. Brain and Body Size
a) The relationship between body and brain size is expressed as the index of encephalization.
    i) Most primates have brain sizes close to their expected values given their body sizes.
    ii) Modern humans are notable because they have a brain size that is much larger than expected for their body weight.
        (1) Early members of the genus *Homo*, as well as Australopithecines were not as encephalized as modern humans.
b) In nonhuman primates, the most rapid period of brain development occurs *either* before or immediately after birth.
    i) Humans are different because their brain growth occurs before *and* after birth, resulting in greater brain expansion during the first year after birth.
    ii) Cross-species generalizations of animals with varying body sizes can only be made when allometric scaling is considered.
c) The social brain hypothesis proposes that primates evolved larger, more complex brains because they live in social groups.
    i) The politics of meat sharing may have also been a prime factor in the evolution of the primate brain.

IV. Language
a) The use of language is a distinctly human trait.
b) Typically, nonhuman animal communication has been described as a system of purely involuntary vocalizations.
    i) However, vervet monkeys are known to use specific vocalizations to refer to snakes, birds of prey, and leopards.
        (1) Vervet communication is restricted to the present, though.
c) Humans use language; sets of arbitrary symbols in their written and spoken communication.
    i) Language has always been thought of as a uniquely human capability.
    ii) Ape language experiments have begun to raise doubts that only humans possess all the attributes necessary for language.
        (1) Apes cannot use speech because they lack the necessary vocal tract anatomy and the language-related structures in the brain.

d) Initial attempts by the Gardners to teach apes to speak failed, so subsequent experiments concentrated on teaching apes to use sign language or various symbols to communicate.
  i) One critique of the ape language experiments was that young chimpanzees had to be taught to use symbols.
    (1) This contrasts with the way in which human children acquire language through exposure.
    (2) One significant finding was that Kanzi, an infant male bonobo, and his younger half–sister both began to spontaneously use the lexigrams they had observed their mother using during her sessions with Savage-Rumbaugh et al.
  ii) Apparently, apes do not acquire and use language in the same way as humans do.
    (1) Also, not all signing apes understand the relationship between symbols and the object, person, or action they are meant to represent.

V. The Evolution of Language
a) The areas of the human brain that are directly involved in the perception and production of speech are usually located on the left side (Wernicke's area in the temporal lobe and Broca's area in the frontal lobe).
  i) Although other species share with humans the association areas necessary to process incoming stimuli, they lack the ability to transform the information into language.
  ii) Recent experiments demonstrate, however, that chimpanzee, bonobo, and gorilla brains have some laterality of Broca's area and they demonstrate a preference for the use of the right hand when gesturing.
    (1) Thus, these hominoids may actually have incipient left hemisphere dominance, a necessary condition for the anatomical basis for speech development.
b) Ape language experiments suggest that the earliest hominids must have had ape-like communicative abilities.
  i) We don't understand why communication became increasingly important in the hominid lineage, and why natural selection acted to enhance our ancestors' ability to use spoken language.
  ii) It is not known whether human-like language capabilities arose around 2 m.y.a., or much later in time as others suggest (around 100,000 to 30,000 years ago).
    (1) The FOXP2 gene is the first gene discovered that influences language development.
      (a) It is a regulatory gene that is found in all mammals, but only in humans does the gene seem to influence language production.

VI. Primate Cultural Behavior
a) Cultural behavior is learned, but whereas humans actively instruct their young, free-ranging primates tend to learn cultural behaviors through observation.
  i) When nonhuman primate infants observe and learn about food items, appropriate behaviors, and how to modify and use objects to achieve certain ends, group-specific or species-specific cultural traditions may emerge.
  ii) Cultural behaviors observed in chimpanzees include tool-use ("termite fishing", leaf sponges, and nut-cracking with stone anvils and hammerstones).
    (1) The use of hammerstones and anvils is restricted to West African chimpanzee groups.
    (2) "Termite fishing" has been observed in central and eastern African groups, but not in the West African groups.
b) The eight criteria for cultural behavior are: innovation, dissemination, standardization, durability, diffusion, tradition, nonsubsistence, and naturalness.
  i) Chimpanzees regularly meet the first six criteria, but occasionally also meet the last two.
  ii) Chimpanzee cultural behaviors are clearly not on par with human cultural behaviors, although they do give us clues as to the possible behavioral capabilities of early hominids.

VII. Aggressive Interactions Between Groups

a) Between-group aggression is used to protect resources by defending a territory. Any area that is defended is defined as a territory.
    i) The home range is that area in which a group stays permanently.
    ii) The core area is the portion of the home range that contains the highest concentration and most reliable resources. Home ranges of adjacent groups may overlap, but core areas do not, since the core area is often defended.
      (1) Not all primates are territorial.

b) Chimpanzees do not display typical territorial behavior, but they tend to be intolerant of unfamiliar chimpanzees.
    i) Male chimpanzees have been observed to patrol borders, the areas of overlap between ranges.
    ii) Border patrols will attack smaller groups of unfamiliar chimpanzees.
    iii) Jane Goodall first recorded these interactions between chimpanzee groups at Gombe in which all seven males and one female of a splinter group were killed in a series of attacks.

c) Unprovoked aggression between groups of conspecifics was previously thought to occur only in humans.
    i) The motivations for this level of conflict are not clear, and chimpanzee conflict is not qualitatively the same as human warfare.
    ii) The fact that both chimpanzees and humans display this behavior may be due to their shared evolutionary heritage.

VIII. Affiliation, Altruism, and Cooperation

a) Affiliative behaviors were previously discussed.

b) **Altruism** is behavior that benefits another while involving some risk to the performer.
    i) The majority of altruistic acts consist of the mother protecting her offspring.
      (1) Primates deviate somewhat from this pattern in that the recipient and the performer of the altruistic acts may not be closely related to each other.
    ii) The evolutionary explanation of altruism focuses on the hypothesis of kin selection.
      (1) Altruistic acts are more likely to be performed if the recipient has a probability of sharing some of the performer's genes. Thus, even if the performer of the altruistic act dies, copies of some of his genes will be passed on and the performer will have increased his (inclusive) fitness.
      (2) Reciprocal altruism has been invoked to explain alliance and coalition formation.

IX. The Primate Continuum

a) Humans tend to view themselves as being separate from the rest of the animals.
    i) Although humans have some unique attributes, they are, in fact, part of a biological continuum.
      (1) The differences that we observe between ourselves and chimpanzees and bonobos are mostly quantitative rather than qualitative.
      (2) Humans, chimpanzees and bonobos all have functionally similar neurological processes, the same need for bonding and close physical contact, the same developmental stages and dependences on learning.
        (a) Chimpanzees and humans also seem to share similar capacities for aggression and cruelty.

b) Many human behaviors seem to be extensions of ape behaviors, so it is important that we recognize our evolutionary connection to our primate heritage when attempting to understand "how we became human".

Learning Objectives

After reading Chapter 8, the student should be able to:
1. Discuss what it "means to be human".
2. Understand the role of allometry in cross-species comparisons.
3. Define language and discuss the evolution of language and the results of ape language experiments.
4. List the criteria for cultural acts in nonhuman species and discuss whether chimpanzees meet these criteria.
5. Discuss between-group aggression in chimpanzees and whether these behavioral tendencies may have been present in our last common ancestor with apes.
6. Discuss the proposed role of kin selection on the evolution of altruistic behaviors.
7. Understand how humans fit into the "biological continuum".

Key Terms and Concepts

Allometry	p. 183	Encephalization	p. 183
Altruism	p. 196	Lateralized	p. 189
Anthropocentric	p. 194	Motor cortex	p. 189
Core area	p. 194	Neocortex	p. 183
Cortex	p. 183	Territory	p. 194

Lecture Suggestions and Enrichment Topics

1. Students tend to be interested in the ape language experiments. Consider showing the video *A Conversation with Koko*, a Nature documentary on Koko the gorilla and interspecies communication. After the video, discuss with your students whether or not the video changed their view of the behavioral and cognitive similarities between humans and apes.
2. Another interesting topic to discuss is nonverbal communication in humans, emphasizing that we share many gestures with nonhuman primates. This topic can generate student participation, and using a video with no sound can be a fun way of demonstrating the importance of gestures, facial expressions, and body posture in human communication. The evolutionary importance of these behaviors and the role of culture are also important subjects for discussions.
3. Discuss the use of medicinal plants by chimpanzees as a model for human attempts to cure or alleviate sickness and pain.

Student Media Exercises

1. In *InfoTrac* search for the article <u>Chimp Culture</u> (Tim Friend, *International Wildlife*, Sept-Oct 2000 pNA). Critique the argument that chimpanzees have regional cultural traditions.
2. In *InfoTrac* do a keyword search on "chimpanzee language" and read a few articles. What do ape language experiments tell us about the origins of human language?
3. Go online to The Jane Goodall Institute (http://www.janegoodall.org/index.html) to find out more about chimpanzee behavior.
4. Go online to the Human Behavior and Evolution Society (http://www.hbes.com/). Follow the link "Intro to the Field" and choose one of the introductory readings. Outline the major tenets of the evolutionary approach to behavioral research.

Multiple Choice Questions

1. Homeobox or regulatory genes
   A. are radically different in each species.
   B. are found only in humans.
   C. cause humans and apes to develop anatomical differences.
   D. are highly conserved throughout all animals.
   E. A and C only

   ANS: D
   PG: 182

2. The human hand is
   A. more derived than that of a chimpanzee.
   B. less derived than that of a chimpanzee.
   C. not similar to the hand of any other primate.
   D. similar to the hand of a cercopithecine monkey.
   E. B and D only

   ANS: E
   PG: 182

3. In the 1970's the prevailing theory emphasized that hominids
   A. initially adapted to a forested environment.
   B. initially adapted to an aquatic environment.
   C. should be modeled as having chimpanzee-like behavior.
   D. initially adapted to a savannah environment.
   E. none of these

   ANS: D
   PG: 183

4. In humans,
   A. proportional brains size is greater than in other primates.
   B. the most rapid period of brain growth occurs for at least the first year after birth.
   C. neurological development accounts for about half of an infant's metabolic output.
   D. all of these
   E. B and C only

   ANS: D
   PG: 183

5. In nonhuman primates, the most rapid period of brain development occurs
   A. several months after birth.
   B. during adolescence.
   C. during the same developmental stages as in humans.
   D. occurs just before birth.
   E. during early adulthood.

   ANS: D
   PG: 183-184

6. When carefully controlled cross-species generalizations regarding animals of differing sizes are made, it is necessary to consider *scaling,* or (more technically)
   A. absolute brain size.
   B. encephalization.
   C. display.
   D. Bergmann's rule.
   E. allometry.

   ANS: E
   PG: 183

7. The social brain hypothesis proposes that primate brains increased in relative size and complexity because
   A. of the demands of social living.
   B. primates need complex brains to be familiar with their home range.
   C. primates often eat food that is difficult to extract (such as underground roots).
   D. A and B only
   E. all of these

   ANS: A
   PG: 185

8. The traditional view of nonhuman communication has been that nonhumans, including primates,
   A. are perfectly capable of conveying information about the external environment or their emotional state.
   B. use symbolic communication.
   C. use language in the same manner as humans.
   D. can convey information about events in the past and future.
   E. communicate information relating to their emotional state ONLY.

   ANS: E
   PG: 186

9. According to the current evidence discussed in the text, which of the following statement is TRUE?
   A. Humans are the only species capable of conveying information pertaining to specific components of the external environment.
   B. Nonhuman primates can communicate any information except that which pertains to their emotional state.
   C. Some nonhuman primates appear to give specific alarm calls that refer to particular categories of predators.
   D. Free-ranging monkeys and apes use symbolic language in the same manner as humans.
   E. Some monkeys communicate about past and future events by means of symbolic gestures.

   ANS: C
   PG: 186-187

10. Vervet monkey vocalizations
    A. are involuntary responses to external stimuli.
    B. are voluntary responses to external stimuli.
    C. refer solely to the emotional state of the individual.
    D. includes information about past and present events.
    E. A and C only

    ANS: B
    PG: 186

11. Human language
    A. uses symbols.
    B. is limited to communicating about the present.
    C. is partly based on the human ability to think symbolically.
    D. all of these
    E. A and C only

    ANS: E
    PG: 189-190

12. Linguistic symbols are said to be _____ because they do not resemble the object or concept they represent.
    A. autonomic
    B. deliberate
    C. arbitrary
    D. closed
    E. innate

    ANS: C
    PG: 187-189

13. Which of the following have been taught to use sign language?
    A. baboons
    B. chimpanzees
    C. macaques
    D. lemurs
    E. all of these

    ANS: B
    PG: 187-188

14. The language experiments with chimpanzees, bonobos, and gorillas indicate that they
    A. lack the ability to communicate symbolically.
    B. can learn to use up to 100 spoken words.
    C. have some ability to use signs to communicate.
    D. have human-like vocal tract anatomies.
    E. think symbolically in the same way humans do.

    ANS: C
    PG: 187-189

15. In humans, language function is
    A. influenced by interconnections between several brain areas.
    B. controlled by only a few cells located in one specific area of the cortex.
    C. controlled only by the same areas that are used in the production of all vocalizations in nonhuman primates.
    D. simply a result of increased brain size.
    E. not related to the reorganization of neurological structures during the course of human evolution.

    ANS: A
    PG: 188-189

16. From an evolutionary perspective, ape language experiments
    A. give us no clues to the origins of human language.
    B. indicate that human language capabilities must have been present in the last common ancestor of hominids and the African apes.
    C. indicate that apes will soon evolve human-like language capabilities.
    D. suggest some clues to the origin of human language.
    E. B and C only

    ANS: D
    PG: 188-189

17. The FOXP2 gene
    A. is unique to humans.
    B. is a gene that influences language development.
    C. produces a protein that regulates the expression of other genes.
    D. B and C only
    E. all of these

    ANS: D
    PG: 191

18. Examples of chimpanzee tool use include
    A. using rocks to crack nuts.
    B. using leaves as sponges.
    C. building temporary shelters when it rains.
    D. all of these
    E. A and B only

    ANS: E
    PG: 191-193

19. Which of the following free-ranging or captive primate species has been observed to use tools?
    A. capuchin monkeys
    B. chimpanzees
    C. bonobos
    D. all of these
    E. B and C only

    ANS: D
    PG: 191-193

20. The fact that chimpanzees sometimes select a stem for eventual use in "termite fishing" and begin stripping its leaves even before the termite mound is in sight, implies
    A. nothing about chimpanzee intelligence.
    B. considerable planning and forethought.
    C. there is a genetic basis for this activity.
    D. that the chimp merely wants to eat the stem without its leaves.
    E. none of these

    ANS: B
    PG: 192

21. Stone tool manufacture
    A. has been observed in East African chimpanzee groups.
    B. has not been observed in free-ranging chimpanzees.
    C. is common among free-ranging bonobos.
    D. has not been observed in any captive nonhuman primate.
    E. none of these

    ANS: B
    PG: 192

22. Primatologists view some chimpanzee behaviors as examples of culture, including
    A. using rocks to crack nuts.
    B. evidence for regional dietary preferences.
    C. "termite fishing".
    D. all of these
    E. B and C only

    ANS: D
    PG: 192-193

23. Primatologists consider chimpanzee "termite fishing" an example of cultural behavior because
    A. adults actively teach their offspring to do it.
    B. it is a learned behavior that continues as a within-group tradition.
    C. it involves tool preparation and use.
    D. all of these
    E. B and C only

    ANS: E
    PG: 192-193

24. Chimpanzee populations
    A. differ from one another with regard to dietary preferences.
    B. all eat exactly the same food items.
    C. show no variation regarding types of tools used.
    D. all use stones to crack hard-shelled nuts.
    E. do not appear to have different cultural traditions.

    ANS: A
    PG: 194

25. Which of the following criteria for culture do chimpanzees meet?
    A. innovation
    B. tradition
    C. dissemination
    D. all of these
    E. A and C only

    ANS: D
    PG: 193

26. When considering cultural behaviors, the term "diffusion" refers to the fact that
    A. a new behavior or activity is invented.
    B. the behavior is acquired through imitation by other individuals.
    C. the behavior spreads from one group to another.
    D. the activity is spread to succeeding generations.
    E. the form of the activity is consistent from one individual to another.

    ANS: C
    PG: 193

27. When considering cultural behaviors, the term "durability" refers to the fact that
    A. a new behavior or activity is invented.
    B. the behavior is acquired through imitation by other individuals.
    C. the pattern is performed without presence of the demonstrator.
    D. the pattern is performed with the demonstrator present.
    E. the form of the activity is consistent from one individual to another.

    ANS: C
    PG: 193

28. When considering cultural behaviors, the term "naturalness" refers to the fact that
    A. the pattern is shown in the absence of direct human influence.
    B. the behavior is acquired through imitation by other individuals.
    C. the pattern is shown in the presence of direct human influence.
    D. the pattern is performed with the demonstrator present.
    E. the form of the activity is consistent from one individual to another.

    ANS: A
    PG: 193

29. When considering cultural behaviors, the term "tradition" refers to the fact that
    A. the pattern is shown in the absence of direct human influence.
    B. the behavior is acquired through imitation by other individuals.
    C. the pattern is shown in the presence of direct human influence.
    D. the pattern is performed with the demonstrator present.
    E. the pattern persists from the innovator's generation to the next generation.

    ANS: E
    PG: 193

30. Physical anthropologists are interested in nonhuman primate tool use because it
    A. is a recently developed behavior.
    B. probably resembles tool use in early hominids.
    C. demonstrates that chimpanzees are on their way to becoming more human.
    D. all of these
    E. none of these

    ANS: B
    PG: 192-194

31. Conspecifics are individuals who are
    A. members of the same species.
    B. members of different species.
    C. partners in coalitions ONLY.
    D. members of a consortship ONLY.
    E. none of these

    ANS: A
    PG: 192-194

32. The core area is that portion of the home range
    A. that contains the highest concentration of resources.
    B. that is frequently defended against intrusion.
    C. where the group is most likely to be found.
    D. all of these
    E. B and C only

    ANS: D
    PG: 194

33. Territorial behavior
    A. has been observed in EVERY primate species.
    B. has been observed in species whose ranges are small enough to permit protection by its residents.
    C. is typical of gibbons.
    D. all of these
    E. B and C only

    ANS: E
    PG: 194

34. Chimpanzee attacks on members of other groups
    A. are definitely motivated by territoriality.
    B. never result in injury.
    C. always occur in the form of displays and nothing more.
    D. can be extremely brutal and result in severe injury or death.
    E. are so rare that only one or two have been observed.

    ANS: D
    PG: 194-196

35. "Border patrols" have been observed in
    A. orangutans.
    B. chimpanzees.
    C. gorillas.
    D. baboons.
    E. none of these

    ANS: B
    PG: 194-196

36. Encounters between male chimpanzees from different groups
    A. are always friendly.
    B. never occur.
    C. are frequently accompanied by some form of aggression.
    D. only occur at Gombe.
    E. none of these

    ANS: C
    PG: 194-196

37. Examples of nonhuman primate altruistic behaviors include:
    A. the adoption of orphaned infants.
    B. females joining forces to protect an infant from an infanticidal male.
    C. one individual coming to the aid of a relative or friend.
    D. all of these
    E. none of these

    ANS: D
    PG: 196

38. The evolutionary explanation of altruism is based on the premise that the
    A. performer's reproductive success is enhanced by the altruistic act.
    B. performer shares some genes with the recipient of the act.
    C. recipient would probably die no matter what the performer did.
    D. all of these
    E. A and B only

    ANS: E
    PG: 196-197

39. To state that humans are part of a biological continuum
    A. means that humans are inherently superior to all other species in every way.
    B. means that no other species is closely related to humans.
    C. means that human neurological processes are unique.
    D. emphasizes the uniqueness of humans in all respects.
    E. means that human are quantitatively rather than qualitatively different from nonhuman primates.

    ANS: E
    PG: 197-198

True/False Questions

1. Primates show a propensity for forming long-term social bonds that include complex alliances and friendships.

   ANS: True
   PG: 181

2. Encephalization is the absolute brain size of a species uncorrected for body size.

   ANS: False
   PG: 183

3. Baboons seem to understand the arrangement of dominance hierarchies within hierarchies.

   ANS: True
   PG: 185

4. Meat is one of the most important components of the chimpanzee diet.

   ANS: False
   PG: 185

5. Vervet monkeys DO NOT use specific vocalizations to refer to predators such as snakes, birds of prey, and leopards.

   ANS: False
   PG: 186

6. Results of ape language experiments leave little doubt that apes can learn to interpret visual signs and use them to communicate.

   ANS: True
   PG: 186-188

7. Association areas of the brain function to integrate information sent from various areas of the brain.

   ANS: True
   PG: 183-184

8. The human capability for language is SOLELY the result of increased brain size through time.

   ANS: False
   PG: 186-187

9. In order to evolve, human language capabilities must have had some selective value in the past.

   ANS: True
   PG: 186-187

10. Captive great apes preferentially use the right hand for gestures.

    ANS: True
    PG: 187

Short Answer Questions

1. How could the homeobox genes have produced the morphological differences between humans and apes?
   (p. 182)

2. Why are paleoanthropologists so concerned with the effects of allometry?
   (p. 183)

3. You text states that the nutrition supplied by meat was not important in the evolution of large brains. What may have been important about meat eating in early hominids?
   (p. 183)

4. Describe the nature of encounters between different groups of male chimpanzees.
   (p. 185)

5. Discuss the probable causes of between-group aggression in chimpanzees.
   (pp. 194-195)

6. Define altruism and discuss the evolutionary explanations of altruistic behaviors.
   (pp. 196-197)

7. Identify and discuss two examples illustrating that humans are part of a biological (and behavioral) continuum with other primate species.
   (pp. 197-198)

Essay Questions

1. Discuss the experimental designs and results of ape language experiments.

2. Discuss the criteria for cultural acts in other species. Which ones do chimpanzees demonstrate?

3. Speculate on the possible cognitive, cultural, and language capabilities of the earliest hominids.

CHAPTER 9: OVERVIEW OF THE FOSSIL PRIMATES

Chapter Outline

I. Introduction
a) This chapter traces primate evolution starting from the earliest fossil evidence of primate-like mammals of the Paleocene up through the hominoid radiation of the Miocene.
   i) Most of the fossil groups discussed in this chapter are not related to any of the living primates and only a few are related to our hominid ancestors.
b) **Background to primate evolution: Late Mesozoic**
   i) Primate origins are not well understood.
   ii) The divergence of the order primates probably began during the Cretaceous period of the Mesozoic Era.
      (1) The living members of the order Primates are closely related to the extinct early primate-like mammals of the order Plesiadapiformes and to the extant members of the orders Scandentia and Dermoptera.
         (a) Most scientists place these four orders into the superorder Archonta.

II. Primate Origins
a) The conventional wisdom is that primate-like mammals first evolved in the early Paleocene. However, new molecular evidence suggests that the LCA between primates and their Archontan relatives was present during the Cretaceous period.
      (1) Combining molecular and morphological evidence yields a divergence time for the LCA of between 55.8 and 90 mya.

III. Paleocene Primate-Like Mammals
a) The plesiadapiforms underwent an adaptive radiation between 64 and 52 mya.
   i) Six families are known from this group, but two genera, *Plesiadapis* and *Carpolestes* are of particular interest to us.
      (1) *Plesiadapis* probably originated in North America and spread into Europe.
         (a) They have rodent-like dentition (but the incisors did not grow continuously) that indicates they had a diet rich in leaves supplemented by fruit.
      (2) *Carpolestes* has features of its postcranial anatomy that indicate adaptations to an arboreal environment.
         (a) A recently discovered skeleton indicates that *Carpolestes* possessed nails rather than claws.
b) **Out of order**
   i) Although *Plesiadapis* and *Carpolestes* share some skeletal characteristics with true primates, cladistic analyses indicate that they should not be placed in the order *Primates*.

IV. Eocene Primates
a) Eocene euprimates (mammals with derived modern primate features) appear nearly simultaneously in North America, Asia, and Europe around 55.8 mya.
   i) However, a close examination of the fossil record indicates that Asia may have been the home of the euprimates.
   ii) The Eocene euprimates are generally divided into two superfamilies: the lemur-like Adapoidea and the tarsier- or galago-like Omomyoidea.
      (1) Both groups are well known from cranial, dental, and postcranial remains from North America, Europe, Asia, and Africa.

b) **Lemur-like adapoids** are represented by more than 35 genera that are divided into 5 geographic families including the notharctids of (primarily) North America, the adapids of Europe, and the amphipithecids of Asia.

    i) Their dental formula is 2.1.4.3.

    ii) *Cantuis,* the earliest notharctid, was probably a diurnal frugivore.

    iii) The adapids appeared in Europe near the end of the Eocene and quickly went extinct.

    iv) The amphipithecids posses anthropoid-like dental traits that are probably homoplasies.

c) **Evolution of true lemurs and lorises**

    i) Ancient adapoids and modern lemurs resemble each other only because modern lemurs retain some ancestral traits.

        (1) Adapoids lack the dental specialization of the lemur's dental comb.

    ii) It is possible that modern lemurs originated on the African mainland because the non-adapoid late Eocene specimen of the genus *Wadilemur* from Egypt may have possessed a dental comb.

        (1) There are numerous large-bodied subfossil lemurs on Madagascar, but few true fossils of lemurs are found there.

d) **Tarsier-like omomyids**

    i) The omomyids are typically divided into three families: one from North America, another from Europe, and the third from Asia.

    ii) European members of this group resemble living tarsiers in a number of ways:

        (1) both have a 1.1.3.3 dental formula,

        (2) both have large orbits,

        (3) both have small snouts.

            (a) However, not everyone agrees on the phylogenetic position of tarsier-like fossils such as *Necrolemur* (from Europe) and *Rooneyia* (from North America).

    iii) The eosimiids, from China and Burma, were once thought to be the ancestors of the anthropoids but they now appear to be the Asian branch of a diverse Eocene radiation of tarsier-like primates.

    iv) **The evolution of true tarsiers** is represented by a meager fossil record.

        (1) Fossils from the middle Eocene of Egypt and China and the late Eocene of Thailand indicate that the tarsier body plan has not changed very much.

        (2) The molecular evidence suggests that the five extant tarsier species diverged in the Miocene.

e) **Eocene and Oligocene early anthropoids**

    i) Anthropoid origins are disputed. Molecular evidence indicates a 77 my time-depth for their origins.

        (1) Fossil anthropoids this old have yet to be discovered.

        (2) Most researchers support an African origin for the anthropoids, while others support an Asian origin.

        (3) The earliest undisputed anthropoid fossil is from the Middle Eocene of Algeria.

    ii) Most of the fossil evidence for early anthropoid origins comes from the Late Eocene and Early Miocene deposits of the Fayum Depression in Egypt.

        (1) *Biretia* is dated to 37 mya and *Catopithecus* is dated to 35 mya.

V. Oligocene Primates

a) Most of the Miocene Old World primate fossil record comes from the Fayum Depression, Egypt.

b) **True anthropoids** of the Oligocene are placed in three families: the oligopithecids, parapithecids, and propliopithecids.

    i) The parapithecid genus *Apidium*, a squirrel-sized arboreal quadruped, is the most abundant of the three Oligocene Fayum families.

ii) *Aegyptopithecus*, a member of the propliopithecid family, is the most significant fossil genus from the Fayum.
  (1) It was about the size of a howler monkey, but with a small brain and a long snout, and it lacks hominoid or Old World monkey derived features.
  (2) *Aegyptopithecus* is generalized enough to be close to the ancestry of both Old World monkeys and hominoids.

c) **Early Platyrrhines: New World anthropoids**
  i) The first New World primates appear about 10 my after the fossil anthropoids of the Fayum.
    (1) The genus *Branisella*, from the late Oligocene of Bolivia, is quite primitive and is unlikely to be related to extant Platyrrhines.
    (2) *Homunculus* is another member of the early platyrrhine radiation. It dates to about 16.5 mya.
  ii) It is thought that the earliest Platyrrhines arrived in South America around 37 to 32 mya.
    (1) Since South America was an island continent until 5 mya, the migration route of the early primates is shrouded in mystery.
      (a) Three migration theories have been proposed: a North American migration, an Antarctic migration, and Atlantic "rafting."
        (i) The most likely scenario involves a combination of rafting and island-hopping across the Atlantic during the Eocene when Africa and South America were closer together and ocean levels were lower than at the present.

VI. **Miocene Primates**
  a) The Miocene was a time during which there was considerable diversification of the primates.
  b) **Monkeying around**
    i) The earliest members of the lineage leading to extant Old World monkeys are in the extinct family Victoriapithecidae from northern and eastern Africa.
      (1) Their appearance at ca. 19 mya predates the split between the colobines and the cercopithecines and they may represent the LCA of all Old World monkeys.
      (2) The ancestral cercopithecines and colobines appeared about 12 mya and the first true colobines appeared ca. 9 mya.
    ii) *Theropithecus* became the dominant cercopithecine genus in East Africa during the Plio-Pleistocene.
      (1) Among the numerous species of the baboon-like *Theropithecus* is, at 225 pounds, the largest monkey that ever lived.
      (2) Most of the *Theropithecus* lineage went extinct during the middle Pleistocene, leaving only one living species, *Theropithecus gelada*, the gelada baboon.
  c) **Aping monkeys**
    i) Continental drift during the Miocene altered climatic patterns and created new migration routes.
      (1) The initial Miocene was warmer than the preceding Oligocene.
      (2) The Arabian Plate "docked" with northeast Africa around 19 mya, allowing African animals direct passage into southwest Asia.
    ii) Molecular analyses indicate that the lineages leading to living monkeys and apes split around 23 mya.
      (1) The first apelike fossil superfamily, the Proconsuloidea, retain numerous monkeylike postcranial features (although they lacked a tail) but are considered dental apes, not true apes, due to the fact that they have Y-5 molars.
        (a) The proconsuloid fossils (dated to 20 to 17 mya) are primarily from East Africa and the various species ranged in size from up to about 220 pounds down to about 8 pounds.
      (2) The Pliopithecoidae date to the early Miocene of Africa and are extremely primitive.
        (a) They successfully moved into Asia and Europe after 19 mya but eventually went extinct during the Pliocene.

d) **Hominoids, the true apes** that are placed in the superfamily Hominaoidea are found in Africa in deposits that date to about 16 mya.
   i) *Kenyapithecus*, a large-bodied terrestrial quadruped and possible knuckle-walker, is the best known early hominoid genus.
   ii) The Miocene hominoids underwent an adaptive radiation shortly after the pliopithecoids left Africa.
      (1) The European forms include a number of derived forms such as *Dryopithecus* and *Ouranopithecus* that are not well understood.
      (2) The Asian forms are the largest and most varied group. The best-known genus is *Sivapithecus*.
         (a) *Sivapithecus* from Turkey and Pakistan has derived facial features that are similar to those of living orangutans.
         (b) *Gigantopithecus*, a descendant of *Sivapithecu*, went extinct around 200 kya. It is known only from 4 mandibles and 1,500 isolated teeth. Estimates place its stature at around 10 feet tall when standing erect (it is presumed to have been a fist-walker) and its weight at more than 900 pounds.
         (c) *Lufengpithecus* (from southern China) may represent a previously unidentified extinct sixth great ape. This approximately 110 pound ape may be a distant relative of *Sivapithecus*.
e) **Evolution of the extant hominoids**
   i) **Hylobatids: the lesser apes** split from the great ape lineage around 15 to 18 mya.
      (1) The molecular evidence indicates that the radiation of the extant hylobatids occurred around 10.5 mya, but their fossil record is meager.
         (a) The pliopithecoids have been eliminated as possible hylobatid ancestors.
   ii) **Pongids: the great apes** also have a meager fossil record because there is a gap in the African hominoid fossil record between 13 and 9.5 mya.
      (1) *Ouranopithecus* from Greece has been suggested as a possible ancestor to the extant African apes.
      (2) *Samburupithecus,* a Miocene African hominoid represented by a few teeth and a fragmentary maxilla, shows similarities to the gorilla.
      (3) The fossil record of the chimpanzee dates back only 500 ky; the only chimpanzee fossils (a few teeth) found to date are from Kenya near Lake Baringo.
      (4) Based on the molecular evidence, the orangutan lineage probably split from the other great apes around 14 mya. Many argue that orangutans are descendants of *Sivapithecus* but not all researchers agree on that point.

Learning Objectives

After reading Chapter 9, the student should be able to:
1. Discuss the nature of the Paleocene primate-like mammals.
2. Discuss the evidence for the evolution of the earliest euprimates, including the evolution of the tarsiers, lemurs, and lorises.
3. Discuss the fossil evidence for the evolution of the true anthropoids.
4. Discuss the fossil evidence for the origins of the Platyrrhines and include the models for their entry into South America.
5. Discuss the evolution and dispersal of the Miocene apelike primates.
6. Discuss the molecular and fossil evidence for the evolution of the true hominoids.

Key Terms and Concepts

Archonta	p. 203	Orthograde	p. 203
Bilophodonty	p. 212	Paleoprimatologist	p. 213
Dental ape	p. 223	Postcranial	p. 207
Dental Formula	p. 210	Sagittal crest	p. 225
Endocast	p. 214	Sister group	p. 221
Euprimate	p. 209	Subfossil	p. 212
Island hop	p. 219	Y-5 molars	p. 223
Last common ancestor (LCA)	p. 207	Zygomatic	p. 225

Lecture Suggestions and Enrichment Topics

1. If you have an internet connection available, go to the Interactive Anthropology sub-section of the Physical Anthropology section of the Wadsworth Resource Center and do the primate evolution drag and drop exercises together as a class.
2. Remind students that although the Cenozoic is often referred to as the "Age of the Mammals" mammalian evolutionary roots actually extend back into the Mesozoic. Details of Mesozoic life forms can be found on the University of California Museum of Paleontology website (http://www.ucmp.berkeley.edu/mesozoic/mesozoic.html).
3. Remind students that global changes in the environment are a crucial force in macroevolution. With this in mind, prepare a short lecture on Paleocene, Eocene, Oligocene and Miocene climates and their effects on primate ecology and evolution. Helpful information can be found on the Paleomap website (http://www.scotese.com/climate.htm).

Student Media Exercises

1. From J. Kappelman's *Virtual Laboratories for Physical Anthropology* CD: Students should complete Lab 7, Section II: *Geological Record,* to help them understand the geologic time scale and dating methods.
2. From J. Kappelman's *Virtual Laboratories for Physical Anthropology* CD: Students should complete Lab 7, Section IV: *Fossil Primates,* to help them understand the Paleocene through Miocene primate fossil record.
3. From J. Kappelman's *Virtual Laboratories for Physical Anthropology* CD: Students should complete Lab 7, *Lab Exercise,* to help them understand the phylogenetic relationships of the Miocene hominoids.
4. Log on to Wadsworth's *Primate Evolution Module* (http://www.wadsworth.com/ anthropology_d/ special_features/primate_evolution/) and answer the *Questions for Review*.
5. In *InfoTrac* search for the article Wyoming's Garden of Eden (Kenneth D. Rose, *Natural History*, April 2001 v110 i3 p55). Answer the following questions: What are some of the Eocene vertebrate fossils found in Wyoming? During which epoch are the first primate fossils found?

Multiple Choice Questions

1. During which of the following epochs did primate-like mammals (65.5 m.y.a.) appear?
    A. Pleistocene
    B. Holocene
    C. Miocene
    D. Paleocene
    E. Pliocene

    ANS: D
    PG: 206

2. During which of the following epochs did the first true primates, Prosimians (55.8 m.y.a.) appear?
    A. Holocene
    B. Eocene
    C. Miocene
    D. Paleocene
    E. Pliocene

    ANS: B
    PG: 206

3. During which of the following epochs did the first monkeys, apes, and human-like creatures (23 m.y.a.) appear?
    A. Holocene
    B. Eocene
    C. Miocene
    D. Paleocene
    E. Pliocene

    ANS: C
    PG: 206

4. Which are the two main families of Paleocene primate-like mammals?
    A. Plesiadapids & carpolestids
    B. Carpolestids & sahelanthropus
    C. *Australopithecus* & plesiadapids
    D. Adapoids & plesiadapids
    E. None of the above

    ANS: A
    PG: 207

5. Which of the following is true about plesiadapids?
    A. Originated in North America
    B. Mouse to rat size
    C. Large incisors
    D. Both A & C
    E. All are correct.

    ANS: D
    PG: 207

6. Which of the following is true about carpolestids?
   A. Mouse to rat sized
   B. Specialized dental traits.
   C. A *Carpolestes* was discovered in Wyoming recently.
   D. Postcranial anatomy reveals many traits adapted to highly arboreal environment.
   E. All are correct.

   ANS: E
   PG: 207

7. In Eocene primates (known as euprimates) the recognizable and modern derived primate traits are:
   A. Forward facing eyes.
   B. Opposable big toes.
   C. Claws instead of nails
   D. All are correct.
   E. Only A & B are correct.

   ANS: E
   PG: 209

8. Which are the two main branches of euprimates, grouped into superfamilies?
   A. Omomyodea
   B. Carpolestids
   C. Adapoidea
   D. Both A & B
   E. Both A & C

   ANS: E
   PG: 210

9. Which of the following is not true about lemur-like adapoids?
   A. They are the best known of the Eocene prosimians.
   B. They have a primitive dental formula (2.1.4.3).
   C. Most prominent families are the notharctids, adapids, amphipithecids.
   D. Can only be found in Africa.
   E. All are correct.

   ANS: D
   PG: 210

10. In the study of true lemurs' and lorises' evolution which of these factors took place?
    A. The existence of an African loris in Egypt supports the idea that lemurs were from Africa.
    B. It is believed that lemurs colonized Madagascar by rafting over the Mozambique Channel.
    C. Lemurs were bats during early stages and flew to Madagascar from Africa.
    D. All are correct.
    E. Only A & B.

    ANS: E
    PG: 211-212

11. The best know of the giant lemurs
    A. Was named *Megaladapis* and weighed 170 pounds.
    B. Probably became extinct due to deforestation caused by human farming.
    C. Was built more like a gorilla than a lemur
    D. All are correct
    E. Only A & B.

    ANS: D
    PG: 212

12. Which is true about the tarsier-like omomyoids?
    A. They have a tarsier-like dental formula (1:1:3:3).
    B. They have small orbits and large snouts.
    C. Includes the Texan *Rooneyia*.
    D. All are true
    E. Only A & C

    ANS: E
    PG: 213

13. Which of the following is/are not general prosimian characteristics?
    A. Grooming claw
    B. Dental comb
    C. Eye sockets not completely enclosed in bone
    D. Fusion of the two sides of the mandible to form one bone
    E. Smaller brain size relative to body size.

    ANS: D
    PG: 215

14. Which of the following is/are not general anthropoid characteristics?
    A. Nails instead of claws on all digits.
    B. Back of eye socket formed by bony plate.
    C. Shorter snouts with greater emphasis on smell
    D. Larger brain
    E. All of the above are correct.

    ANS: E
    PG: 215

15. The most complete remains of an early African anthropoid is a new species of *Biretia*:
    A. Dated to 37 m.y.a.
    B. Weighs under a pound
    C. Was a nocturnal primate based on its large orbits
    D. All are correct.
    E. Only A & B.

    ANS: D
    PG: 215

16. Why is the Egyptian site of Fayum relevant to Oligocene primates?
    A. It is where the vast majority of Old World primate fossils from this period were found.
    B. It was the only part of the world where any primates have been found.
    C. It is the site where written records of primate existence were found.
    D. Archaeologists love to excavate this site due to its beautiful climate.
    E. All are correct.

    ANS: A
    PG: 215

17. The early primates of the Oligocene are placed into which three families?
    A. Oligopithecids, parapithecids, & propliopithecids.
    B. Parapithecids, adapids, & oligopithecids
    C. Lemurcids, parapithecids, & propliopithecids
    D. *Rooneyia*, oligopithecids, & adapids
    E. None of the above.

    ANS: A
    PG: 216

18. Which is true about *Apidium*?
    A. The most abundant of Oligocene fossils of parapithecid family.
    B. Unusually large sexual dimorphism.
    C. Teeth suggest a diet composed of fruits and some seeds.
    D. All are correct.
    E. Only A & C.

    ANS: D
    PG: 216

19. Which is true about *Aegyptopithecus*?
    A. It is part of the propliopithecid family.
    B. Weighed over 50 pounds.
    C. Proposed ancestor of Old World monkeys and hominoids.
    D. All are correct.
    E. Only A & C.

    ANS: E
    PG: 217

20. *Branisella* and *Homunculus* both represent different side branches from the clade of living New World monkeys. What else is known about these early platyrrhines?
    A. Both were found in South America.
    B. They give us specific insights to modern day platyrrhines.
    C. Migrated from the Old World to South America about 37 m.y.a.
    D. All are correct.
    E. Only A & C.

    ANS: E
    PG: 217-218

21. Identify which of the following is not a New World monkey characteristic:
    A. Sideways facing nostrils.
    B. Dental formula of 2.1.3.3.
    C. Tube-like ear hole.
    D. Grasping tail.
    E. Distribution: Mexico & South America.

    ANS: C
    PG: 219

22. Identify which of the following is not a Old World monkey characteristic:
    A. Downward facing nostrils.
    B. Dental formula of 2.1.3.3.
    C. Tube-like ear hole.
    D. Ischial callosities.
    E. Distribution: Africa, southern Asia & Japan.

    ANS: B
    PG: 219

23. _____ is an extinct family that represents the earliest member of the lineage leading to present-day Old World Monkeys.
    A. Victoriapithecus
    B. *Aegypithecus.*
    C. *Macaca.*
    D. *Proconsul.*
    E. None of these

    ANS: A
    PG: 221

24. *Cercopithecines*:
    A. Include baboons and macaques.
    B. Are members of *Victoriapithecus.*
    C. Include tarsiers.
    D. Are a group of New World Monkeys.
    E. All are correct.

    ANS: A
    PG: 221

25. _____ are often called the cheek-pouch monkeys, because of hamster-like pockets in their mouths that allow them to store food.
    A. Macaques
    B. Rhesus monkeys
    C. Baboons
    D. All are correct.
    E. Only A & B.

    ANS: D
    PG: 221

26. Which of the following is true about the East African baboon-like *Theropithecus*?
    A. Dietary niche was almost exclusively grasses.
    B. Contained some notable fossil specimens, like a 225-pound monkey.
    C. The only extant (still living) species is the Gelada.
    D. All are correct.
    E. Only A & C.

    ANS: D
    PG: 221

27. During the Miocene, the drifting of _____ and _____ away from Antarctica
    significantly altered ocean currents.
    A. Southeast Asia and Australia
    B. South America and Australia
    C. South America and Africa
    D. Australia and Africa
    E. None of the above.

    ANS: B
    PG: 223

28. Y-5 molar
    A. Are molars that have the 4 cusps positioned in 2 parallel rows or lobes.
    B. Have 5 cusps with grooves running between them.
    C. Is characteristic of all primates.
    D. All are correct
    E. Both B & C.

    ANS: B
    PG: 223

29. Proconsulids ranged in size from that of a male orangutan (165-220 pounds) in _____ to the
    tiny _____, which was probably the smallest ape ever known, weighing less than 7 pounds.
    A. *Proconsul & Micropithecus.*
    B. *Micropithecus & Ouranopithecus.*
    C. *Aegypithecus & Proconsul.*
    D. *Dryopithecus & Ouranopithecus.*
    E. *Ouranopithecus & Micropithecus.*

    ANS: A
    PG: 223

30. *Proconsul*
    A. Lived in Africa from 20-17 m.y.a.
    B. Was a fruit-eating, ape-like creature.
    C. Ranged greatly in size from 10 to 150 pounds.
    D. All of the above.
    E. A and B only

    ANS: D
    PG: 223

31. *Pliopithecus*, the best-known pliopithecoid from Europe, had which characteristics?
    A. Robust features of the mandible and a sagittal crest.
    B. Diet consisted of relatively tough foods, mostly leaves.
    C. Locomotion mainly terrestrial, knuckle-walking.
    D. All of the above.
    E. A and B only.

    ANS: E
    PG: 224

32. Which of the following is not a general characteristic of Old World Monkeys?
    A. Broad nose and palate.
    B. Smaller brain (in absolute terms and relative to body weight).
    C. Shorter arms.
    D. Longer torso.
    E. Tail.

    ANS: A
    PG: 224

33. Which of the following is not a characteristic of Great Apes?
    A. Narrow nose and palate
    B. Y-5 molars.
    C. Larger average body size.
    D. Shorter torso.
    E. Longer arms.

    ANS: A
    PG: 224

34. The best known of the first true apes (Hominoidea) appeared in Africa during the middle Miocene approximately 16 m.y.a.
    A. *Pliopithecus*
    B. *Proconsul*
    C. *Kenyapithecus*
    D. *Aegyptopithecus*
    E. Omomyoids

    ANS C
    PG: 224

35. Which of the following hominoids resulted from a European radiation around 16 m.y.a?
    A. *Dryopithecus* from southern France and northern Spain.
    B. *Ouranopithecus* found in Greece.
    C. *Proconsul* from Italy.
    D. All are correct.
    E. Only A & B.

    ANS: E
    PG: 225

36. Which of the following is/are true about the Asian radiation of hominoids?
    A. Geographically dispersed from Turkey in the west to China in the east.
    B. Includes *Sivapithecus*, a large hominid of 70 to 150 pounds.
    C. Includes a late Miocene a hominoid descendant, known as *Gigantopithecus*.
    D. All of the above
    E. A and B only

    ANS: D
    PG: 225

37. Which is/are the distinct great ape lineage(s) in Asia?
    A. *Gigantopithecus*
    B. *Pongo*
    C. *Lufengpithecus*
    D. All of the above
    E. Only A & C.

    ANS: C
    PG: 229

True/False Questions

1. In the study of primate fossils is to bridge the gap between prosimians and hominids.

    ANS: False
    PG: 203

2. The emergence of the first hominoids dates back about 23 million years ago during the Miocene.

    ANS: True
    PG: 203

3. The abbreviation LCA stand for "Last Common Ape."

    ANS: False
    PG: 207

4. The presence of nails in *Carpolestes* is likely due to homoplasy rather than a shared derived characteristics.

    ANS: True
    PG: 209

5. The term "euprimate" refers to the primate-like primitive species that preceded plesiadapids.

    ANS: False
    PG: 209

6. At the beginning of the Eocene epoch, North America and Europe were connected and they shared many species in common.

ANS: True
PG: 210

7. The term "subfossil" refers to a fossil of a more primitive species.

ANS: False
PG: 212

8. A paleoprimatologist is someone who specializes in the study of modern nonhuman primates.

ANS: False
PG: 213

9. Early platyrrhines or New World anthropoid fossils are found in the late Oligocene of Brazil. And are placed into the genus *Branisella*.

ANS: False
PG: 217

10. The most likely scenario for the arrival of platyrrhines ot South America involves floating across the Atlantic Ocean on rafts made of naturally forming mats of vegetation.

ANS: True
PG: 219

11. During the late Miocene, Allied soldiers dug trenches in Greece in World War I and found various fossils of *Ouranopithecus*.

ANS: True
PG: 224

12. After flourishing from more than 8.5 million years, *Giganto* went extinct during the late Miocene period due human predation and/or environmental change.

ANS: False
PG: 229

Short Answer Questions

1. Describe the early evolution of prosimians, including their characteristics and family tree. (pp. 207-214)

2. Describe the evolution of anthropoids, including the characteristics of New vs. Old World Monkeys. (pp. 214-221)

3. Why is it difficult to distinguish the earliest members of the primate order from other placental mammals? (pp. 207- 214)

4. What are some of the ways in which monkeys are thought to have colonized the New World and what evidence exists to support this theory? (pp.218-220)

5. Where is the Fayum Depression and how it is significant in primate evolution? (pp. 219-225)

Essay Questions

1. Give an overview of the evolution of primates according to the epochs and their characteristics. Construct a family tree of the various families of primates and their ancestor/descendant relationships.

2. Describe the importance of molecular anthropology for paleoprimatology. Explain how both of these work together to reconstruct the evolutionary history of primates and give examples of their research.

3. Describe the theories of primate migration to the New World, list the evidence used to support this theory, including its weaknesses.

4. Describe *Gigantopithecus*, how it lived, its region, diet and locomotion; how did paleoanthropologists learn of it, and what happened to it?

CHAPTER 10: PALEOANTHROPOLOGY: RECONSTRUCTING EARLY HOMINID BEHAVIOR AND ECOLOGY

Chapter Outline

I. **Introduction**
   a) Definite hominid fossil material has been found in Africa that dates to just after 5 mya.
      i) The hominid nature of these remains is indicated because of the way they behaved.
      ii) Hominid behavioral adaptations are the focus of this chapter.

II. **Definition of a Hominid**
   a) Hominid origins date to the end of the Miocene.
   b) Hominids have been variously defined as having: a large brain, bipedal locomotion, and/or tool-making behavior.
      i) It is clear that these characteristics did not evolve simultaneously. The phenomenon of different physiological systems evolving at different rates is called mosaic evolution.
   c) **Biocultural evolution: the human capacity for culture**
      i) The most distinctive feature of humans is our dependence on culture.
         (1) Human culture is an adaptive strategy that includes cognitive, political, social, and economic aspects as well as the capacity to make and use tools.
      ii) The earliest hominids of 7-5 mya did not regularly manufacture stone tools.
         (1) They probably had the tool-making capabilities of living chimpanzees.
            (a) Stone tools appear in the archaeological record about 2.5 mya.
         (2) By 7 to 6 mya, hominids had developed bipedalism.
      iii) The dynamics between neuronal reorganization, tool use, changing social organization, and communication form the core of biocultural evolution.

III. **The Strategy of Paleoanthropology**
   a) Paleoanthropology, the study of ancient humans, is a multidisciplinary approach that includes geologists, archaeologists, physical anthropologists, and paleoecologists.
      i) Paleoanthropologists must synthesize information regarding:
         (1) Dating of the site.
         (2) The paleoecology of the site.
         (3) Any archaeological traces of behavior.
         (4) Any anatomical evidence from hominid remains.
      ii) The ultimate goal is to "flesh out" the hominids to produce a more complete and accurate understanding of human evolution.

IV. **Paleoanthropology in Action-Olduvai Gorge**
   a) Olduvai Gorge, located on the eastern branch of the Great Rift Valley of Africa, has yielded an immense quantity of high-quality data on early hominid behavior.
   b) Olduvai has a well-documented sequence of geological, paleontological, archeological, and hominid remains that span the last 2 million years.
      i) The earliest hominid site dates to about 1.85 mya, and is accompanied by the Oldowan tool industry.
      ii) The most famous hominid fossil from Olduvai is probably the *Zinjanthropus* skull, discovered by Mary Leakey in 1959.

V. Dating Methods

a) The two types of dating methods are relative dating and chronometric, or absolute, dating.
   i) One relative dating method is based on stratigraphy.
      (1) The law of superposition states that (in an undisturbed deposit) a lower layer is older than a higher layer.
   ii) Another relative dating method is fluorine analysis.
      (1) Groundwater contains fluorine, and the longer a bone is in a deposit; the more fluorine will accumulate during the fossilization process.
      (2) The fluorine method can only be used to compare bones found at the same location.
   iii) Chronometric methods are based on the phenomenon of the radioactive decay of unstable isotopes.
      (1) Depending on the half-life of the isotope used, the time range for this method varies from the age of the earth (billions of years) to less than 1,000 years.
         (a) Paleoanthropologists use the K/Ar method extensively to determine the age of volcanic deposits (and therefore the associated fossils) in East Africa.
            (i) The $^{40}Ar/^{39}Ar$ method can be used on smaller samples and provides more accurate results.
         (b) The C-14 method is used on organic materials and has a useful time-range of 75,000 to less than 1,000 years.
         (c) Thermoluminescence dates can be obtained from burnt flints.

b) **Applications of dating methods: examples from Olduvai**
   i) Olduvai has several reliable K/Ar dates for the underlying basalt and the tuffs in Bed I, and the Zinj site has been dated to $1.79 \pm .3$ mya
      (1) K/Ar dates must be cross-checked, since all dates have errors associated with them.
         (a) Cross-checking with different methods lends confidence to the results because each method has a different source of error.
      (2) One important cross-check is to use the fission-track method.
      (3) Another way of cross-checking is to use paleomagnetism.
         (a) With this technique, the orientation of magnetic sediments is checked to determine whether they were deposited during a period of normal or reversed magnetism.
      (4) Biostratigraphy, or faunal correlation, is another cross-check.
         (a) This technique matches faunal remains, such as pigs, elephants, rodents, and antelopes at the site in question with the known evolutionary sequences of the same faunal species.

VI. Excavations at Olduvai

a) There are three broadly defined site types present at Olduvai.
   i) "Butchering" localities.
      (1) These are areas one or a few large mammals associated with archaeological traces.
   ii) Quarry localities.
      (1) These are areas where hominids obtained stone and initially fashioned stone tools.
   iii) Multipurpose localities ("campsites").
      (1) These are general-purpose areas where hominids carried out daily activities.
      (2) The exact nature of the activities carried out at these sites is not fully understood.
         (a) Initially, they were interpreted as true campsites. Alternately, the accumulations could have been produced by nonhominids, or the accumulations could be the result of hominid gathering and scavenging activities.

VII. Experimental Archaeology
    a) Archaeologists try to reconstruct prehistoric techniques of tool-making, butchering, and other activities in order to answer fundamental questions about hominid behavior.
        i) **Stone tool (lithic) technology** is the most commonly preserved aspect of hominid cultural behavior.
            (1) Initially, archaeologists thought that the Oldowan industry consisted of deliberately fashioned cores and flakes.
                (a) Richard Potts believes that only the flakes were being deliberately produced, and the "core tools" were merely byproducts of flake manufacture.
            (2) Flakes can be removed from cores by direct percussion and/or pressure flaking.
                (a) The nodules found in Bed I at Olduvai (1.85-1.2 mya) have been unifacially flaked by using direct percussion.
                (b) Later, in Bed IV (400,000 ya), most tools are flaked bifacially with direct percussion, but they could only have been produced with a "soft" hammer, most likely a piece of bone or antler.
                (c) The microliths found in the upper beds (17,000 ya) must be produced using the pressure flaking method in which a pointed piece of bone, antler, or wood is pressed firmly against the stone.
            (3) Microwear analysis is performed by observing stone tools under high magnification to detect patterns of polish and striations characteristic of tool use on various materials such as bone or wood, as well as the way the tools were used (such as cutting versus scraping).
                (a) Tools observed under a scanning electron microscope may reveal the presence of the phytoliths of the different species of plants on which the tool was used.
        ii) **The analysis of bone** is undertaken to determine how humans and natural forces affect bone.
            (1) Taphonomy is the branch of paleoecology concerned with the influence of natural forces on bone deposition and preservation.
                (a) Research such as observing human butchering practices, or analyzing scavenger bone accumulations is conducted to determine the extent to which these factors can account for the composition of bone accumulations at hominid sites.
                (b) Another research concern is to determine the effects of natural forces, such as running water, on patterns of bone accumulations.
            (2) Bones may also be examined for evidence of hominid activity in the form of cut marks.

VIII. Reconstruction of Early Hominid Environments and Behavior
    a) The behavioral interpretation of archaeological and skeletal evidence is speculative and not as amenable to rigorous testing as are the original data.
        i) Nevertheless, behavioral and environmental reconstructions (or scenarios) give us a broader view of evolution and adaptation.
            (1) **Environmental explanations for hominid origins** focus on the environment as a major factor in evolution.
                (a) It is possible to oversimplify the complex interactions between the organism and the environment by making sweeping generalities about environmental determinism.
                (b) There may have been major ecological changes occurring in Africa at or around the same time that hominids were evolving (i.e. a trend towards cooler, drier, and more seasonal environments).
                    (i) However, the causal connection between environmental change and the initial hominoid/hominid transition has not yet been convincingly demonstrated.

(2) **Changing environments and later hominid diversifications**
    (a) The evolutionary pulse theory proposes a causal connection between periods of increased aridity in South and East Africa and the evolution of new species of hominids.
        (i) Recent detailed analysis indicates that there is little support for this theory.
(3) **Why did hominids become bipedal?**
    (a) The shift to bipedality is the fundamental hominid adaptive shift.
    (b) Hominids are adapted to a more mixed and open-country habitat than are the chimpanzees, yet no other mixed to open-country adapted mammals are full-time bipeds.
        (i) There can be no simple environmentally-driven explanation for the shift to full-time bipedalism.
        (ii) Jolly's seed-eating hypothesis proposes that early hominids, like living gelada baboons, were highly dependent on eating seeds and nuts but they stood upright while feeding.
            1. Fossil evidence indicates that the dental adaptations predicted by Jolly's hypothesis are not restricted only to the early hominids.
        (iii) Lovejoy has devised a scenario in which hominids are tied to a "home base" that requires female provisioning by pair-bonded males.
            1. The skeletal evidence suggests early hominids were not pair-bonded because they are highly sexually dimorphic. A recent study, however, questions the high level of sexual dimorphism in early hominids.
        (iv) Falk has proposed the "radiator theory" which proposes a link between bipedalism and brain expansion.
            1. Falk argues that the hominids that exploited the hot savannah evolved a venous drainage system that better cooled the brain. This particular venous drainage pattern also removed the constraints for encephalization because it efficiently cooled larger brains too.
            2. This hypothesis does not explain the origins of bipedalism, nor does it explain *why* brain size increased in the genus *Homo*.

Learning Objectives

After reading Chapter 10, the student should be able to:
1. Discuss the definition of a hominid, integrating the concept of biocultural evolution.
2. Understand the strategy of paleoanthropology in regards to reconstructing human biocultural evolution.
3. Discuss the nature of the data gathered from Olduvai Gorge and how it is incorporated into evolutionary scenarios.
4. Define the various dating methods mentioned in the text.
5. Discuss the scope of experimental archaeology.
6. Discuss the methods and assumptions used in reconstructing early hominid environments and behavior.
7. Detail the various hypotheses concerning the evolution of bipedalism.

Key Terms and Concepts

Lecture Suggestions and Enrichment Topics

1. Many students have difficulty with the concept of mosaic evolution. It is beneficial to spend some extra time talking about the fact that not all hominid characteristics evolved at the same time. This can also lead into a discussion of how one determines when we "became" human. Should we consider Australopithecines to be human, despite their small cranial capacities? Or should we only consider members of the genus *Homo* to be humans? Besides, what criteria should we use to assign fossils to the genus *Homo*? The point to be made is that "becoming human" was a process of adding different components at different times (e.g. bipedalism, tool use, brain expansion), so defining when our ancestors crossed the threshold into "humanness" is somewhat arbitrary.

2. Invariably, a student will mention Elaine Morgan's Aquatic Ape Theory of human origins, so you better be prepared to respond. The core of the "theory" is that competition for food forced a lineage of proto-hominids to live in the coastal regions of Africa and hunt for food in shallow water. Reduced body hair is therefore a selected trait that enabled them to swim faster, giving them a reproductive advantage. Discussing this theory can also help to clarify evolutionary concepts. For example, in the aquatic ape theory, the diving reflex is considered a recently evolved trait. However, it is clearly an ancestral trait, and offers no support for the hypothesis that humans have recent aquatic ancestry. Additionally, the rest of our anatomy, such as our hands, is clearly adapted for climbing and manipulation.

Student Media Exercises

1. From J. Kappelman's *Virtual Laboratories for Physical Anthropology* CD: Students should complete the Lab 11: *The Archaeological Record*.
2. From J. Kappelman's *Virtual Laboratories for Physical Anthropology* CD: Students should complete the Lab 9: *The Evolution of Bipedalism*.
3. In *InfoTrac* search for the article <u>The naked and the bipedal</u> (Tim Folger. *Discover*, Nov 1993 v14 n11 p34). Answer the following questions: What are the advantages of bipedalism with respect to thermal stress? What are the possible evolutionary connections between bipedalism and large brains and naked skin?
4. In *InfoTrac* do a keyword search on "fission-track". What specific geologic questions are being answered with this method?
5. Follow the link <u>http://www.clarku.edu/~piltdown/map_prim_suspects/primarysuspects_lvl1.html</u> to find out more information about the principal players in the Piltdown story.

Multiple Choice Questions

1. Hominids have been variably defined as having
    A. a large brain.
    B. toolmaking abilities.
    C. adaptations for bipedalism.
    D. all of these
    E. A and C only

    ANS: D
    PG: 235-236

2. For humans, culture is an adaptive strategy involving
    A. cognitive components.
    B. political components.
    C. economic components.
    D. B and C only
    E. all of these

    ANS: E
    PG: 236-237

3. The earliest hominid tools thus far discovered are made of
    A. bone.
    B. stone.
    C. metal.
    D. wood.
    E. ivory.

    ANS: B
    PG: 236, 240

4. Before hominids made stone tools, they probably
    A. used sticks.
    B. had weapons made of metal.
    C. made tools from ivory.
    D. used pottery.
    E. A and D only

    ANS: A
    PG: 236-237

5. Paleoanthropology is
    A. defined as the study of ancient humans.
    B. practiced by archaeologists ONLY.
    C. concerned with fossilized skeletal remains ONLY.
    D. defined as the study of fossilized non-primate mammals.
    E. practiced by physical anthropologists ONLY.

    ANS: A
    PG: 239

6. Hominid fossil sites can be identified by a number of methods including
    A. aerial photography.
    B. satellite photography.
    C. geological surveys.
    D. all of these
    E. A and B only

    ANS: D
    PG: 239

7. The earliest recognizable stone tools are approximately _____ years old.
    A. 500,000
    B. 7-8 million
    C. 2.5 million
    D. 10,000
    E. 1 million

    ANS: C
    PG: 239-241

8. Team-members at an early hominid site gather various information such as
    A. ecological data.
    B. geological data
    C. faunal data.
    D. all of these
    E. none of these

    ANS: D
    PG: 239-241

9. The environmental setting where an archeological trace is found is called the
    A. sediment.
    B. category.
    C. geomorphology.
    D. context.
    E. palynology.

    ANS: D
    PG: 239-241

10. Paleoecological research
    A. attempts to reconstruct ancient environmental settings.
    B. is of little use to paleoanthropology.
    C. concentrates on hominid remains ONLY.
    D. concentrates on evidence of non-hominid faunal materials ONLY.
    E. is not concerned with plant materials.

    ANS: A
    PG: 239-241

11. The task of interpreting various sources of information such as the dating, paleoecology, and evidence of hominid remains at a site is the responsibility of the
    A. archaeologist.
    B. taphonomist.
    C. cultural anthropologist.
    D. palynologist.
    E. physical anthropologist.

    ANS: E
    PG: 239-241

12. Which of the following sites has yielded the most information about early hominid behavior?
    A. Hadar
    B. Olduvai Gorge
    C. the Potwar Plateau
    D. Omo
    E. Lake Turkana

    ANS: B
    PG: 241

13. The present climatic environment at Olduvai Gorge
    A. does NOT resemble the region's climatic environment during the previous 2 million years.
    B. is similar to the region's climatic environment during the previous 2 million years.
    C. is a semi-tropical rainforest.
    D. would never have provided a suitable habitat for hominids.
    E. B and C only

    ANS: B
    PG: 241

14. Olduvai Gorge
    A. was discovered in 1992.
    B. is located in Ethiopia.
    C. is where Louis and Mary Leakey conducted their search for hominid fossils.
    D. has NOT produced any hominid fossils.
    E. has NOT produced any evidence of hominid tools.

    ANS: C
    PG: 241

15. Fossilized remains of non-hominid species at Olduvai Gorge
    A. include fish, birds, and antelopes.
    B. provide important information regarding the ecological conditions of early human habitats.
    C. may provide some information about hominid diets if they are found in association with hominid artifacts.
    D. all of these
    E. A and B only

    ANS: D
    PG: 241-242

16. *Zinjanthropus*
    A. was discovered by Mary Leakey.
    B. is the name of a tool tradition at Olduvai Gorge.
    C. was the name given to the first early hominid discovered in Olduvai Gorge.
    D. is now included in the genus *Homo*.
    E. A and C only

    ANS: E
    PG: 242

17. Relative dating techniques
    A. can provide exact dates of fossil material.
    B. are always accurate to within 500 years.
    C. were used to date the *Zinjanthropus* cranium to 2.8 million years ago.
    D. all of these
    E. none of these

    ANS: E
    PG: 243

18. Dating methods indicating that something is older or more recent than something else
    A. are called chronometric dating methods.
    B. are called absolute dating methods.
    C. include the K/Ar method.
    D. never require stratigraphic information.
    E. are called relative dating methods.

    ANS: E
    PG: 242

19. The dating method that uses the principle that undisturbed underlying geologic deposits are older than overlying geologic deposits is called
    A. stratigraphic dating.
    B. paleomagnetism.
    C. carbon-14 dating.
    D. K/Ar dating.
    E. fluorine analysis.

    ANS: A
    PG: 242-243

20. Fluorine analysis can only be used on
    A. volcanic rock.
    B. fossilized plants.
    C. bone.
    D. sedimentary rock.
    E. petrified wood.

    ANS: C
    PG: 243

21. The Piltdown hoax was revealed in the 1950s through the application of
    A. carbon –14 dating.
    B. fluorine analysis.
    C. stratigraphic dating.
    D. potassium-argon dating.
    E. biostratigraphy.

    ANS: B
    PG: 243

22. _____ make the best samples for the K/Ar and ^{40}Ar/^{39}AR dating methods.
    A. Bones
    B. Stone tools
    C. Ostrich shells
    D. Teeth
    E. Volcanic rocks

    ANS: E
    PG: 243

23. _____ is a radiometric dating method popular with archaeologists that can be used to date
    materials up to 75,000 years old.
    A. Carbon-14
    B. Paleomagnetism
    C. Dendrochronology
    D. K/Ar
    E. Biostratigraphy

    ANS: A
    PG: 243

24. If an isotope has a half-life of 4 billion years, then in 4 billion years
    A. all of the original amount will have decayed.
    B. ¼ of the original amount will still remain.
    C. ½ of the original amount will still be present.
    D. all of the original amount will still be present.
    E. none of these

    ANS: C
    PG: 243

25. Chronometric dating (or more specifically, radiometric) techniques
    A. are based on the phenomenon of radioactive isotope decay rates.
    B. can be used to determine the absolute age of geological formations and some organic materials.
    C. include the K/Ar and carbon-14 methods.
    D. all of these
    E. A and C only

    ANS: D
    PG: 242-243

26. The K/Ar method is most appropriate for dating
    A. the actual fossils within rock.
    B. charcoal.
    C. volcanic rock.
    D. pottery fragments.
    E. anything that once was living.

    ANS: C
    PG: 243

27. Potassium-40 (^{40}K)
    A. decays to the gas, argon-40 (^{40}Ar).
    B. decays to carbon-14.
    C. has a half-life of 1.25 billion years.
    D. all of these
    E. A and C only

    ANS: E
    PG: 243

28. Which of the following would be best suited to the carbon-14 dating technique?
    A. Materials more than 100,000 years old
    B. Volcanic rock
    C. Sedimentary rock
    D. Metals
    E. Certain organic materials less than 75,000 years old

    ANS: E
    PG: 242-244

29. The ± portion of a chronometric date indicates
    A. the number of different techniques used.
    B. the total number of samples used.
    C. one standard deviation confidence intervals for the mean date obtained from the samples.
    D. all of these
    E. none of these

    ANS: C
    PG: 244

30. The Bed I site at Olduvai Gorge is about _____ years old.
    A. 3 million
    B. 500,000
    C. 2.5 million
    D. 5 million
    E. 1.8 million

    ANS: E
    PG: 245

31. The various methods used to cross-check K/Ar dates include
    A. paleomagnetism.
    B. fission-track dating.
    C. biostratigraphy.
    D. A and B only
    E. all of these

    ANS: E
    PG: 245

32. _____ relies on identifying changes in the orientation of the earth's geomagnetic poles.
    A. Stratigraphy
    B. Dendrochronology
    C. Fluorine analysis
    D. Biostratigraphy
    E. Paleomagnetism

    ANS: E
    PG: 245

33. If two sites both contain fossil remains of the same extinct animal species (such as pigs or elephants), and there is a K/Ar date for one site, we can infer that the other site has a similar age using
    A. dendrochronology.
    B. paleomagnetism.
    C. biostratigraphic dating.
    D. radiometric dating.
    E. chronometric dating.

    ANS: C
    PG: 245-246

34. Different site-types found at Olduvai Gorge include
    A. butchery localities.
    B. living localities.
    C. multipurpose localities.
    D. all of these
    E. A and C only

    ANS: E
    PG: 246-247

35. Butchering localities at Olduvai Gorge
    A. all contain the butchered remains of 20 or more elephants.
    B. provide clear evidence of how the animals were killed.
    C. consist of the fossilized remains of one or a few animals.
    D. definitely demonstrate that hominids were successfully hunting large animals by 1.75 million years ago.
    E. indicate that fire was used to cook meat.

    ANS: C
    PG: 246

36. Archaeologist Lewis Binford argues that the stone tool and bone remains at Olduvai Gorge
    A. are ALL the result of hominid activities.
    B. are ALL the result of nonhominid activities.
    C. are in part the result of hominid activities.
    D. have been put there by unscrupulous paleoanthropologists.
    E. none of these

    ANS: C
    PG: 248

37. New biochemical analyses of South African hominid teeth indicate they were
    A. eating meat ONLY.
    B. eating grass products or the meat or marrow of animals who ate grass products.
    C. exploiting more heavily forested regions of their environments.
    D. exploiting more open regions of their environments.
    E. B and D only

    ANS: E
    PG: 249

38. Experimental archaeologists have attempted to learn more about stone tools by
    A. replicating stone tool manufacturing methods.
    B. using stone tools to butcher an elephant.
    C. cutting down trees with stone axes.
    D. A and B only
    E. all of these

    ANS: E
    PG: 251

39. Stable carbon isotope analyses
    A. are performed on fossil plants.
    B. are performed on bones.
    C. are performed on teeth.
    D. B and C only
    E. none of these

    ANS: D
    PG: 252-253

40. For most of the Miocene, Africa was
    A. very cold and dry.
    B. warm, but with a few periods of intense cold that produced glaciers.
    C. very sparsely forested.
    D. generally tropical and heavily forested.
    E. A and C only

    ANS: D
    PG: 252-253

41. The hypothesis that the evolution of African hominids was significantly influenced by increased aridity at various times during the Pliocene and early Pleistocene is called the
    A. punctuated equilibrium theory.
    B. aridity cycle theory.
    C. radiator theory.
    D. stable isotope theory.
    E. evolutionary pulse theory.

    ANS: E
    PG: 253

42. The hypothesis to explain why hominids became bipedal include
    A. carrying objects.
    B. seed and nut gathering.
    C. long-distance walking.
    D. visual surveillance.
    E. all of these

    ANS: E
    PG: 256

43. Jolly's seed-eating hypothesis
    A. is considered the best supported hypothesis explaining the origins of hominid bipedalism.
    B. is based on the ecology of African apes.
    C. is based on the ecology of gelada baboons.
    D. is based on the ecology of modern human hunter-gatherers.
    E. A and C only

    ANS: C
    PG: 255-257

44. Lovejoy's male provisioning scenario
    A. is now the best supported explanation for the evolution of bipedalism.
    B. has not been significantly critiqued by paleoanthropologists.
    C. is entirely consistent with the hominid fossil record.
    D. is entirely consistent with the archaeological record.
    E. none of these

    ANS: E
    PG: 257-258

True/False Questions

1. Hominid emergence is characterized by the simultaneous appearance of bipedalism, toolmaking behavior, and a large brain.

    ANS: False
    PG: 236-237

2. The earliest members of the hominid lineage, dating back to 7-5 m.y.a. may be referred to as protohominids.

    ANS: True
    PG: 236-237

3. Because organic materials such as sticks and bones are usually well preserved in the archaeological record, we have good evidence of the earliest stages of hominid cultural modifications.

    ANS: False
    PG: 236-237

4. Taphonomy is the study of how bones and other materials come to be buried in the earth and preserved as fossils.

    ANS: True
    PG: 239-241

5. Although excavations at Olduvai Gorge have yielded abundant archaeological traces, no hominid remains have ever been found there.

    ANS: False
    PG: 241-242

6. The $^{40}Ar/^{39}Ar$ dating method may be used on very small samples of volcanic rock, including single crystals.

    ANS: True
    PG: 243

7. A "core" refers to a stone that has been reduced by flake removal.

    ANS: True
    PG: 249-250

8. Detailed examinations of bone can reveal evidence of butchering and bone breaking by hominids.

    ANS: True
    PG: 251-252

9. Environmental determinism refers to a detailed and multifaceted, explanation of the role of the environment in evolutionary change.

    ANS: False
    PG: 252

10. Falk's "radiator theory" was proposed as an explanation of the origins of bipedalism in protohominids.

    ANS: False
    PG: 257

Short Answer Questions

1. First define what makes a hominid a hominid, and then discuss which aspects of your definition can be assessed in the fossil and/or archaeological record.
(pp. 235-236)

2. Define the term *mosaic evolution*. Discuss three different anatomical or behavioral hominid traits that demonstrate the nature of mosaic evolution.
(p. 236, and Figure 10-1)

3. Explain the basis of fluorine analysis. What type(s) of material is/are appropriate for fluorine analysis and how accurately can this method date material? Are their any special limitations to this technique? What is the most famous application of fluorine analysis?
(pp. 242-245)

4. Define the term *half-life* and discuss how the length of an isotope's half-life relates to the useful time-range of chronometric dating techniques.
(p. 243)

5. What is the nature of the evidence for the presence of hominids at Olduvai Gorge? What three different site types have been identified there?
(pp. 246-248)

6. How has experimental archaeology contributed to our knowledge of hominid behavioral patterns?
(pp. 248-249)

7. Compare two different hypotheses that attempt to explain the origins of hominid bipedalism. How secure do you think the evidence is to verify *either* view?
(pp. 255-259)

8. What is the "radiator theory"?
(p. 257)

Essay Questions

1. You are a paleoanthropologist planning an excavation at a possible hominid site in East Africa. Make a list of the other team members (i.e. their field of knowledge) you require in order to gather as much data at the site as possible.

2. Why are the Olduvai Gorge localities so important to paleoanthropological research?

3. Explain the differences between relative and chronometric (absolute) dating techniques. Give an example of each; include the type of material on which each is used, as well as their useful time-ranges.

CHAPTER 11: HOMINID ORIGINS IN AFRICA

Chapter Outline

I. Introduction
   a) This chapter concerns the Plio-Pleistocene hominid fossil record.
      i) The Plio-Pleistocene spans the time period from 5-1 mya.
         (1) Some of the earliest hominids may date to the end of the Miocene.
         (2) All of the early hominids are confined to Africa.

II. The Bipedal Adaptation
   a) Among living primates, only hominids have habitual, obligate, and efficient bipedalism.
   b) There are numerous modifications of the basic primate quadrupedal body-plan.
      i) The most dramatic modifications are in the pelvis. In quadrupeds, the two *ossa coxae* are elongated and oriented approximately parallel to the spine (i.e. dorsally). In bipeds, the *ossa coxae* are shorter and broader, and oriented more towards the side (i.e. laterally).
         (1) The more basin-like shape of the bipedal pelvis alters the function of the *gluteus maximus* muscle, increasing its ability to extend the thigh, an important movement in running and climbing.
      ii) Other modifications for bipedalism include:
         (1) repositioning of the foramen magnum,
         (2) increased spinal curvature,
         (3) lengthening of the hind limb,
         (4) inward angling of the femur,
         (5) development of the longitudinal arch in the foot,
         (6) realignment of the big toe.
   c) All the major structural modifications for bipedalism are present in the early hominid skeletons from Africa.
      i) Some new South African hominid fossils that include the ankle and the big toe indicate the heel and form of the longitudinal arch were adapted for bipedalism, while the big toe appears to be adapted for grasping.
         (1) This (plus interpretations of fossil foot remains from Olduvai Gorge and Hadar) suggests to some that early hominids, though bipedal, were not necessarily obligate bipeds.

III. Early Hominids from Africa (Pre-*Australopithecus* finds)
   a) The earliest hominids are all from Africa.
      i) The stratigraphy of the East African sites is well defined and gives us the clearest picture of hominid chronological relationships.
      ii) The fossils from South Africa are embedded in rock matrix, are difficult to recover, and have complex stratigraphic and chronological relationships.
         (1) Nevertheless, one of the most complete early hominid skeletons is being excavated at Sterkfontein cave.
   b) The **earliest traces** of hominid evolution were thought to date to between 3 and 4 million years ago in 1999, but now the earliest traces may date to 7 million years ago.
      i) In **Central Africa**, A nearly complete cranium from Toros-Menalla was discovered in 2001 and has been assigned the name *Sahelanthropus tchadensis*.
         (1) The braincase is small (320-380 cm^3) but it has huge browridges combined with a sagittal crest and large muscle attachments in the rear.
            (a) The face does not protrude, unlike other early hominids, and this is a key derived feature linking it to later hominids such as early members of the genus *Homo*.
            (b) There are no postcranial elements, so its locomotor capabilities are unknown.
            (c) In sum, the hominid status of *Sahelanthropus* is insecure, and some have argued it is actually an ape.

ii) **East Africa** has some other important discoveries.
  (1) The Tugen Hills area is located near Lake Baringo, Kenya. The fossils found here have been named *Orrorin tugenensis* and they date to about 6 mya
    (a) There are some dental remains and some relatively complete lower limb bones. The limb bones are argued to indicate adaptations for bipedalism.
  (2) Fragmentary, late Miocene (5.8-5.2 mya) fossils discovered in 1997 through 2001 in the Middle Awash (Ethiopia) consist of mostly teeth, a jaw fragment, and some pieces of the limbs.
    (a) The morphology of the toe bone is suggestive of bipedalism.
    (b) The morphology of these remains is similar to previously discovered remains from the Middle Awash that are assigned to *Ardipithecus ramidus*.
iii) *Ardipithecus* **from Aramis (Ethiopia)**
  (1) Fossil remains of perhaps 50 individuals from Aramis (Ethiopia) were excavated between 1992 and 1995 and date to about 4.4 mya
    (a) Indications of bipedal adaptations include a partial cranium with an anteriorly placed foramen magnum and a humerus lacking weight-bearing morphology.
    (b) Obligate bipedalism is suggested by the initial interpretation of a 40% complete skeleton that is yet to be fully described.
    (c) There are a number of primitive aspects too: the cranial base is flat and the molars have thin enamel caps.
      (i) The remains are so primitive that they have been assigned to *Ardipithecus ramidus,* a new genus and species.
      (ii) Interestingly, environmental reconstructions of early hominid locales (i.e. Tugen Hills, the early Middle Awash sites, and Aramis) indicate a more heavily forested environment than at most of the later hominid sites.

IV. *Australopithecus/Paranthropus* **from East Africa**
  a) East African fossil remains assigned to the genus *Australopithecus* (or in some cases, *Paranthropus*) date from 4.2 to 1.4 mya
    i) The genus *Homo* appears near the end of this time span.
  b) The earliest *Australopithecus* remains come from Allia Bay, Kanapoi, and the Middle Awash (4.2-3.9 mya).
    i) The limb remains are indicative of bipedality, and the molars have characteristically thick enamel caps.
    ii) They retain primitive characteristics such as large canines and a sectorial lower first premolar.
      (1) They are slightly more primitive than later australopithecines, so they are assigned to a different species, *anamensis*.
  c) Later, more complete remains of *Australopithecus* come from Hadar, Ethiopia and Laetoli, Tanzania.
    i) Laetoli is also the site where 3.7–3.5 my old fossilized hominid footprints have been found.
    ii) The "Lucy" skeleton (*A. afarensis*), discovered in 1974, is one of the most famous specimens from Hadar. Another famous collection of specimens representing at least 13 individuals (also *A. afarensis*) was discovered in 1975. The Hadar material dates to 3.9-3.0 mya
  d) *Australopithecus afarensis* **from Laetoli and Hadar**
    i) The material from Laetoli and Hadar (fragmentary remains of 60-100 individuals) constitutes the largest and best-studied assemblage of early hominids.
    ii) Except for *A. anamensis*, *A. afarensis* is the most primitive member of its genus.
      (1) The canines are large, the lower first premolar is semisectorial, the tooth rows are parallel, there is a compound crest on the back, and the cranial base is primitive.
      (2) The cranial capacity averages about 420 cm^3.

(3) The postcranial remains indicate that the upper limbs, relative to the lower limbs, are longer than expected when compared to modern human proportions.

    (a) Stature estimates indicate *A. afarensis* was short, ranging from 3'6" to about 5' tall.

    (b) If we accept that the taller individuals are male, then *A. afarensis* has a large degree of sexual dimorphism in body size- though this conclusion has been recently disputed.

(4) Despite the many primitive dental and cranial traits, it is clear that *A. afarensis* is a hominid because it was a biped when on the ground (although *A. afarensis* may have retained significant climbing capabilities).

    iii) An almost complete 3.3 my old infant *A. afarensis* skeleton from Dikika, Ethiopia was discovered in 2000 announced in 2006.

        (1) It appears to be a 3 year old female. This specimen should tell us a lot about australopithecine developmental biology.

e) **Another East African hominid**, contemporaneous with *A. afarensis* (at 3.5 mya), was discovered at Lake Turkana in 1999.

    i) The 400-500 cm^3 cranium has a flat face and small molars. This is not an *A. afarensis* pattern, so it has been given a new genus name, *Kenyanthropus*.

f) **Later East African finds** include specimens that date to after 3 mya and are primarily from East and West Lake Turkana and Olduvai Gorge.

    i) These finds include later members of *Australopithecus* as well as the earliest members of *Paranthropus*.

g) ***Australopithecus* and *Paranthropus* from Olduvai and Lake Turkana**, representing two different genera and up to six different species, are later in time and more derived than *A. afarensis*.

    i) Traditionally, these australopithecines are divided into "robust" and "gracile" species, emphasizing the different craniodental adaptations of the two groups, but now many people think that the "robust" australopithecines should be included in their own genus, *Paranthropus*.

        (1) The virtually complete cranium of the 2.5 m.y. old WT 17000 (*Paranthropus aethiopicus*) from West Lake Turkana is the earliest trace of the "robust" forms in East Africa.

            (a) Its mix of primitive and derived traits places it between *A. afarensis* and the later "robust" australopithecines.

        (2) These later "robust" australopithecines are found at Olduvai and Koobi Fora starting around 2 mya

            (a) They have small crania (510-530 cm^3) and large, broad faces with massive molars, and males have a sagittal crest.

            (b) The "Zinj" fossil (now *P. boisei*) was the first of these specimens to be found.

V. Early *Homo*

a) Fossils from Olduvai and Koobi Fora, assigned to the genus *Homo*, are contemporaneous with East African *Paranthropus*.

    i) Additionally, a temporal fragment from Lake Baringo (at 2.4 mya) and a mandible from Hadar (at 2.3 mya) are both probably from early *Homo*.

    ii) Louis Leakey and his colleagues created the species *habilis* for material discovered at Olduvai Gorge in the 1960s that range in time from 1.85 to 1.6 mya. Not all paleoanthropologists accept the taxon as valid.

        (1) The validity of *Homo habilis* has been further questioned with the discovery of early *Homo* material from Koobi Fora (e.g. ER 1470), suggesting to some that more than one species of early *Homo* were present in East Africa by 2.4 mya.

b) **Redefining the genus *Homo*?**
   i) Recently, Bernard Wood and Mark Collard suggest that the early forms of the genus *Homo* should be placed into the genus *Australopithecus*.
      (1) This interpretation is controversial, yet it is not to be unexpected given the morphological variation of the specimens assigned to *Homo*.

VI. South African Sites
a) The **earliest discoveries** came in 1924 when Raymond Dart discovered the Taung specimen.
   i) He argued it was more hominid-like than hominoid-like, based on the forward position of the foramen magnum, the more vertical orientation of the forehead, the small size of the milk canines, and the presence of large, broad permanent molars.
      (1) Dart published his findings in *Nature*, calling the specimen *Australopithecus africanus*.
      (2) Many scientists didn't accept Dart's conclusions, in part because most scientists believed at the time that the origins of humans lay in Asia, not Africa.
b) **Further discoveries of South African hominids** came after Dart enlisted the aid of Robert Broom to search for more fossils.
   i) More australopithecine remains were found at Sterkfontein in 1936 and later at Swartkrans.
      (1) By 1949, five hominid sites had been found and the remains representing at least 30 individuals recovered.
      (2) One of the most remarkable finds at Sterkfontein was that of a virtually complete australopithecine skeleton discovered in 1998.
         (a) Analysis of the foot bones indicates retained arboreal capabilities.

VII. Review of Hominids from South Africa
a) The South African and East African hominids are broadly similar, but there are enough distinctive features that warrant separating them at the species level.
   i) *Paranthropus*
      (1) These forms are similar to those found in East Africa. They have small cranial capacities, large broad faces, and very large molars and premolars.
      (2) Most researchers agree that these hominids have distinctive enough dental proportions and facial architecture to be designated a separate species (*P. robustus*).
      (3) All "robust" species are adapted to a diet of hard food items such as seeds and nuts.
   ii) *Australopithecus*
      (1) The *Paranthropus* lineage is present in both East and South Africa, but *A. africanus* is present only in South Africa.
      (2) *A. africanus* is also small-brained but not as large-toothed as *Paranthropus*.
      (3) There seem to be no significant differences in body size between the *Paranthropus* and *Australopithecus*.
   iii) **Early *Homo* in South Africa**
      (1) Traces of early members of the genus *Homo* have been found at Sterkfontein, Swartkrans, and perhaps Drimolen. There is still considerable disagreement as to whether specimens from South Africa such as Stw 53 belong in the species *habilis*.

VIII. Geology and Dating Problems in South Africa
a) The South African hominid sites have complex geologic contexts.
   i) Hominid remains are found in limestone cliffs, caves, fissures, and sinkholes mixed with other fossils in conglomerated blocks of sand, pebble, and stone, called breccia.
      (1) None of the hominid sites appear to be primary hominid localities, although Dart thought differently. He proposed the osteodontokeratic culture complex because he thought the australopithecines were responsible for the stone, bone, and animal horn accumulations.

ii) The dating of the South African sites has been difficult, especially since there are no volcanic deposits.
    (1) Faunal sequencing suggests that Swartkrans formed about 1 mya, Taung formed about 2 mya, and Sterkfontein formed about 3 mya.
    (2) Paleomagnetic dates are somewhat ambiguous, so most researchers argue that all the South African hominid sites are younger than the East African sites yielding *A. afarensis*.

IX. Interpretations: What Does It All Mean?

a) Assigning the numerous genus and species names to fossil hominids is an attempt to make biological sense out of the tremendous morphological variation present in the samples.

b) When we make genus level distinctions, such as *Australopithecus* vs. *Homo*, we are saying that any two species within one genus (such as *Australopithecus*) are more similar to each other than they are to any one member of another genus (such as *Homo*).
    i) Assigning fossil species to a particular species is one of the last analytical steps.
    ii) Phylogenetic interpretations necessarily follow after classifications have been proposed.

c) **Continuing Uncertainties-Taxonomic Issues**
    i) There is always ongoing debate about Plio-Pleistocene hominid taxonomies. Among the issues are:
        (1) Determining the hominid status of the *Sahelanthropus*, *Ardipithecus*, and *Orrorin* specimens.
        (2) Determining the number of genera present.
        (3) Determining the number of species present in the material assigned to early genus *Homo*.

d) **Seeing the bigger picture**
    i) In order to avoid the complex phylogenetic arguments, it is helpful to divide up the Plio-Pleistocene hominid material into four "sets".
        (1) Set I: Pre-*Australopithecus*/basal hominids (7.0-4.4 mya). These are the earliest and most primitive of the hominid remains that have been assigned to *Sahelanthropus*, *Orrorin*, and *Ardipithecus*.
        (2) Set II: *Australopithecus*/*Paranthropus*
            (a) Subset A: The early (4.2-3.0 mya), primitive members of the genus *Australopithecus* (*afarensis* and *anamensis*).
            (b) Subset B: The later (2.5-1.4 mya), more derived members of the genus *Paranthropus* that come from both South and East African sites.
        (3) Set III: Fossils assigned to the genus *Homo* present in East and South Africa between 2.4-1.8 mya.
    ii) Several phylogenies have been proposed which reflect different views of human evolution.

X. Seeing the Very Big Picture: Adaptive Patterns of Early African Hominids

a) The early hominid species had restricted ranges and genetic drift and natural selection could have caused rapid speciation.

b) The early hominids relied on varying degrees of arboreality.

c) There is little evidence of increasing body size or increased encephalization over time (with the exception of some early *Homo* specimens).

d) The early hominids had ape-like developmental rates.

Learning Objectives

After reading Chapter 11, the student should be able to:
1. Discuss the major skeletal adaptations for full-time bipedalism.
2. Discuss the fossil evidence for Pre-*Australopithecus* discoveries.
3. List the Plio-Pleistocene hominids in chronological order.
4. Identify the geographic location and the names of the major early hominid fossil sites in East and South Africa.

5. List the morphological traits that characterize the different Plio-Pleistocene hominid species, with special attention to the morphology of *A. afarensis*.
6. Contrast the morphology of the earliest members of the genus *Homo* from the morphology of the genus *Australopithecus*.
7. Contrast the geological context of the East versus the South African hominid sites and discuss how it affects the reliability of the dates for these sites.
8. Discuss the history of the South African fossil hominid discoveries.
9. Describe the depositional history of the South African hominid fossil sites.
10. Outline the taxonomic issues discussed in the text.
11. Discuss the adaptive patterns of the Early African hominids.

Key Terms and Concepts

Aramis	p. 271	Morphological	p. 263
Australopithecine	p. 274	Plio-Pleistocene	p. 263
Australopithecus	p. 271	Postcranial	p. 269
Australopithecus africanus	p. 283	Robust	p. 279
Endocast	p. 282	Sagittal crest	p. 279
Gracile	p. 279	Sectorial	p. 272
Homo habilis	p. 280	Sterkfontein	p. 265
Line of weight transmission	p. 265	Swartkrans	p. 284
Megadont	p. 285		

Lecture Suggestions and Enrichment Topics

1. If students with fundamentalist Christian views of human origins haven't challenged the scientific view of human evolution by now, they may begin to do so. You can choose to mention creationist arguments against evolution in your lectures or wait until someone mentions these arguments when posing a question. Nevertheless, it pays to be prepared with some responses. A good critique of creationist arguments can be found on the web at http://www.talkorigins.org/origins/faqs-creationists.html.
2. Stress to your students that Darwin, without the benefit of the hominid fossil record, predicted that the common ancestor of apes and humans would be found in Africa. This demonstrates the power of scientific reasoning and the strength of evolutionary theory. Also stress the mix of ape-like and human-like morphologies found in the earliest hominids, a condition predicted by evolutionary theory.
3. In order to impress students with the great quantity of early hominid materials discovered over the past 30 years, you could bring in an anthropology text from the early 1970s and contrast the amount information presented about the Plio-Pleistocene hominids in the older text with the amount presented in this text.

Student Media Exercises

1. From J. Kappelman's *Virtual Laboratories for Physical Anthropology* CD: Students should complete the Lab 8: *The Australopithecines*.
2. Have students go to the Interactive Anthropology sub-section of the Physical Anthropology section of the Wadsworth Anthropology Resource Center and complete the exercise *Drag and Drop the Plio-Pleistocene Hominid Sites to the Correct Place on the Timeline*.
3. Have students go to the Interactive Anthropology sub-section of the Physical Anthropology section of the Wadsworth Anthropology Resource Center and complete the exercise *Drag and Drop the Plio-Pleistocene Hominids to the Correct Place on the Timeline*.

4. Have students go to the Interactive Anthropology sub-section of the Physical Anthropology section of the Wadsworth Anthropology Resource Center and complete the exercise *Identify the Plio-Pleistocene Hominids.*

5. In *InfoTrac* search for the article <u>Hunting the first hominid</u> (Pat Shipman, *American Scientist*, Jan-Feb 2002 v90 p25). Based on the discussion of hominid traits, describe what the earliest hominid might look like. Are any of these features present in the *Ororrin* or *Ardipithecus* fossil remains?

6. Log on to the Talk Origins Archive and follow the link http://www.talkorigins.org/faqs/knee-joint.html. Read the article and then answer these questions: What claim do creationists make regarding the finding of "Lucy's" knee joint? What are creationists trying to show with this claim? What is the source of their confusion regarding this claim? How many creationists repeated the erroneous claim?

Multiple Choice Questions

1. Current evidence indicates that the earliest primates were diverging from the other placental mammals by the
   A. Miocene.
   B. Quaternary.
   C. Oligocene.
   D. Paleocene.
   E. Eocene.

   ANS: D
   PG: 263

2. Anatomical changes in hominids that are indicative of habitual bipedal locomotion include
   A. feet with opposable big toes for grasping.
   B. shortening and broadening of the pelvis.
   C. increased length of arms relative to legs.
   D. increased length of the spine.
   E. all of these

   ANS: B
   PG: 266-267

3. Fossil evidence for hominid foot structure has come from
   A. Sterkfontein.
   B. Olduvai Gorge.
   C. Hadar.
   D. B and C only.
   E. all of these

   ANS: E
   PG: 266-267

4. Paleoanthropologists who have studied the fossil remains of hominid feet from South Africa believe
    A. they indicate obligate quadrupedalism.
    B. they indicate the big toe could have aided the foot in grasping.
    C. they are adapted for bipedalism.
    D. they indicate the big toe could NOT have aided the foot in grasping.
    E. B and C only

    ANS: E
    PG: 268

5. The oldest POSSIBLE hominid found to date has been given the genus name
    A. *Australopithecus.*
    B. *Sahelanthropus.*
    C. *Zinjanthropus.*
    D. *Ardipithecus.*
    E. *Orrorin.*

    ANS: B
    PG: 268-269

6. *Sahelanthropus* was discovered in
    A. South Africa.
    B. East Africa.
    C. the Rift Valley.
    D. Central Africa.
    E. none of these

    ANS: D
    PG: 269

7. *Sahelanthropus* has an unusual combination of characteristics, including
    A. a small braincase and huge browridges.
    B. a large braincase and huge browridges.
    C. a small braincase and small muscle attachments in the rear of the cranium.
    D. a small vertical face and small browridges.
    E. none of these

    ANS: A
    PG: 269

8. Recently discovered remains from the Tugen Hills, dated to about 6 million years ago have been placed in the genus
    A. *Sahelanthropus.*
    B. *Australopithecus.*
    C. *Paranthropus.*
    D. *Ardipithecus.*
    E. *Orrorin.*

    ANS: E
    PG: 269-271

9. The late Miocene remains of around five possible hominids, assigned to the genus *Ardipithecus*, were discovered
    A. at Hadar.
    B. at Laetoli.
    C. in South Africa.
    D. in the Middle Awash.
    E. none of these

    ANS: D
    PG: 271

10. Sectorial premolars
    A. are characteristic of *A. anamensis*.
    B. are found on the lower jaw.
    C. are considered a primitive trait.
    D. function as shearing surfaces with the upper canines.
    E. all of these

    ANS: E
    PG: 272-273

11. The fossil skeleton known as "Lucy" belongs to the species
    A. *africanus*.
    B. *aethiopicus*.
    C. *habilis*.
    D. *boisei*.
    E. *afarensis*.

    ANS: E
    PG: 272

12. *Australopithecus afarensis*
    A. is the largest well-studied collection of early hominids.
    B. is the oldest hominid discovered to date.
    C. is the smallest least-studied collection of early hominids.
    D. is only found in South Africa.
    E. C and D only

    ANS: A
    PG: 274

13. Which of the following hominids has the most primitive (ancestral) traits?
    A. *Homo habilis*
    B. *Australopithecus africanus*
    C. *Australopithecus robustus*
    D. *Australopithecus boisei*
    E. *Australopithecus afarensis*

    ANS: E
    PG: 274-275

14. The hominid fossils from Laetoli and Hadar are classified by most researchers as
    A. *Australopithecus africanus.*
    B. *Homo afarensis.*
    C. *Homo habilis.*
    D. *Australopithecus robustus.*
    E. *Australopithecus afarensis.*

    ANS: E
    PG: 274-275

15. The cranium of a hominid contemporary with *A. afarensis* that was discovered in 1999 at Lake Turkana has been given the genus designation
    A. *Ardipithecus.*
    B. *Kenyanthropus.*
    C. *Orrorin.*
    D. *Australopithecus.*
    E. none of these

    ANS: B
    PG: 277

16. The "robust" australopithecines
    A. were twice the size of "gracile" australopithecines.
    B. overlap in body size with the "gracile australopithecines.
    C. were not appreciably different in any way from the "gracile" australopithecines.
    D. had small molars.
    E. have come from East African sites only.

    ANS: B
    PG: 278-279

17. The oldest "robust" australopithecine fossil
    A. is dated to 1.8 m.y.a.
    B. was discovered at West Lake Turkana.
    C. is nicknamed the "black skull."
    D. B and C only
    E. none of these

    ANS: D
    PG: 278-279

18. The hominid fossil from Olduvai, originally named *Zinjanthropus*, is
    A. now called *Australopithecus boisei.*
    B. actually *Homo habilis.*
    C. now considered to be an *Australopithecus afarensis* specimen.
    D. considered to be a "gracile" australopithecine.
    E. now called *Australopithecus africanus.*

    ANS: A
    PG: 279

19. A sagittal crest is
    A. only present in some nonhuman primates.
    B. a characteristic of some "robust" australopithecines.
    C. a raised ridge of bone running along the midline of the cranium for the attachment of muscles.
    D. not present in any hominid fossils.
    E. B and C only

    ANS: E
    PG: 279

20. _____ was contemporaneous with australopithecines but had a significantly larger brain.
    A. *A. afarensis*
    B. *Aegyptopithecus*
    C. *Homo habilis*
    D. *A. africanus*
    E. *Ardipithecus*

    ANS: C
    PG: 280

21. The best documented remains of early genus *Homo* have been found at
    A. Hadar.
    B. Koobi Fora.
    C. Olduvai Gorge.
    D. Aramis.
    E. B and C only

    ANS: E
    PG: 280

22. By using the designation *Homo habilis* Louis Leakey was implying
    A. there were at least two hominid lineages present at Olduvai Gorge.
    B. the *Homo* lineage was distinct from the australopithecines.
    C. that *Homo habilis* was more closely related to modern humans than were the australopithecines.
    D. all of these
    E. B and C only

    ANS: D
    PG: 280-282

23. Regarding the fossil material termed "early *Homo*",
    A. some scholars think there may actually be more than one species present.
    B. there is definitely only one species.
    C. it is certain that one species, *Homo habilis*, evolved directly into *Homo sapiens*.
    D. all the individuals appear to be about the same size.
    E. there is almost no anatomical variation among in these specimens.

    ANS: A
    PG: 280-282

24. The very first australopithecine fossil was discovered in
    A. South Africa.
    B. the 1920s.
    C. East Africa.
    D. none of these
    E. A and B only

    ANS: E
    PG: 282

25. The first person to describe and classify an australopithecine fossil was
    A. Robert Broom.
    B. Donald Johanson.
    C. Raymond Dart.
    D. Mary Leakey.
    E. Louis Leakey.

    ANS: C
    PG: 282

26. What feature(s) convinced Raymond Dart that the Taung child was not an ape?
    A. The position of the foramen magnum, which indicated an erect posture.
    B. The fact that the deciduous canine teeth were quite small.
    C. The shape and orientation of the forehead.
    D. all of these
    E. none of these

    ANS: D
    PG: 283

27. The taxonomic designation Raymond Dart assigned to the Taung fossil was
    A. *Australopithecus boisei.*
    B. *Australopithecus afarensis.*
    C. *Australopithecus africanus.*
    D. *Homo habilis.*
    E. *Australopithecus robustus.*

    ANS: C
    PG: 283

28. In order to substantiate Raymond Dart's assertion that the Taung child was indeed a hominid, who subsequently found additional (adult) australopithecine fossils?
    A. Arthur Keith
    B. Robert Broom
    C. Louis Leakey
    D. Grafton Elliot Smith
    E. W. E. Le Gros Clark

    ANS: B
    PG: 283

29. The most complete South African hominid skeleton was discovered in 1998 at the site of
    A. Hadar.
    B. Taung.
    C. Swartkrans.
    D. Olduvai Gorge.
    E. Sterkfontein.

    ANS: E
    PG: 284

30. The geological context of fossil hominid materials in South Africa
    A. is more complicated than in East Africa.
    B. is less complicated than in East Africa.
    C. permits precise dating of South African material.
    D. makes it much easier to date material from South Africa compared to East Africa.
    E. is precisely the same as East African sites.

    ANS: A
    PG: 286

31. South African hominid fossils are found imbedded in a cement-like conglomerate of sand, soil and gravel called
    A. paleoglom.
    B. granite.
    C. breccia.
    D. sandstone.
    E. volcanic rock.

    ANS: C
    PG: 286

32. The osteodontokeratic culture complex
    A. was proposed by Raymond Dart.
    B. is a tool assemblage composed of stone tools.
    C. refers to the proposed use of horn, bone and teeth as tools.
    D. is considered to be a real culture complex by all researchers.
    E. A and C only

    ANS: E
    PG: 286-288

33. The task of interpreting early hominid evolution
    A. is still not complete.
    B. does not require a chronological framework.
    C. does not require assigning taxonomic names to fossil materials.
    D. B and C only
    E. all of these

    ANS: A
    PG: 289

34. Concerning the taxonomy of the Pliocene hominids:
    A. the evolutionary picture is becoming clearer.
    B. the evolutionary picture is becoming more complex.
    C. there is increasing certainty as to genus and species assignment.
    D. there is little to no disagreement between paleoanthropologists as to their phylogenetic affinities.
    E. A, C, and D only

    ANS: B
    PG: 288-289

35. The earliest hominids have varied combinations of features. For example, *Sahelanthropus* has
    A. a very primitive looking braincase (in the back).
    B. chimpanzee-looking teeth.
    C. a hominid-looking face and teeth.
    D. A and B only
    E. A and C only

    ANS: E
    PG: 290

36. The earliest hominids have varied combinations of features. For example, *Ororrin* has
    A. a very primitive looking braincase (in the back).
    B. chimpanzee-looking teeth.
    C. a hominid-looking face and teeth.
    D. A and B only
    E. A and C only

    ANS: B
    PG: 290

37. Concerning the adaptive patterns of early hominids: there is little evidence for trends of increasing body size and encephalization in any lineages except
    A. *Homo*
    B. *Ardipithecus*
    C. *Paranthropus*
    D. pre-*Australopithecus*
    E. C and D only

    ANS: A
    PG: 292

True/False Questions

1. Unfortunately, except for the footprints at Laetoli, there is no evidence of early hominid foot structure.

    ANS: False
    PG: 268

2. The fossils assigned to the genus and species *Orrorin tugenensis* are universally agreed to be hominids.

    ANS: False
    PG: 269

3. The *Ardipithecus ramidus* hominids have highly derived dental features including heavily enameled molars that resemble those of *A. boisei*.

    ANS: False
    PG: 271

4. The *A. afarensis* hand, wrist, and foot bones are indistinguishable from those of modern humans.

    ANS: False
    PG: 276

5. If not for the fact that the *Kenyanthropus* specimen was found in South Africa, it would have been called *A. afarensis*, since the two are contemporaneous and virtually indistinguishable from each other.

    ANS: False
    PG: 277

6. Just as in East Africa, the South African sites are securely dated by chronometric techniques.

    ANS: False
    PG: 277

Short Answer Questions

1. Provide an overview of the hominid line using a chronological framework.
   (pp. 288-290)

2. Describe the suite of skeletal changes that are required for a shift from quadrupedalism to obligate bipedal locomotion.
   (pp. 263-267)

3. What is the fossil evidence for bipedal locomotion in the early hominids?
   (p. 265)

4. Where and when are the earliest possible hominid remains found?
   (pp. 268-269)

5. Where and when are the first definite hominid remains found? Explain why we know they are definitely hominids.
   (pp. 271-277)

6. Contrast the craniodental traits of *A. afarensis* with those of *A. boisei* and *A. robustus*.
   (pp. 274-275, 278, 285)

7. Where and when are the fossils assigned to *Homo habilis* found? Are there any reasons to suspect that there is more than one species of hominids present in the sample?
   (pp. 279-280)

8. There was opposition from some members of the scientific community to Raymond Dart's assessment of the Taung child as hominid. Why was this so and how was Dart eventually proven correct?
   (pp. 282-284)

Essay Questions

1. Create a chronology of South and East African Plio-Pleistocene hominids. Begin with the oldest possible hominids and continue up to about 1.8 m.y.a. Be sure to include genus and species names, associated dates, and geographic locations.

2. Using the information from the previous question, construct your own Plio-Pleistocene hominid phylogeny. Defend your phylogeny.

3. The text organizes the Plio-Pleistocene hominids into "sets" in order to make general statements regarding dates and morphology. Describe these "sets". Include the species, dates, and morphological traits characteristic of each "set".

CHAPTER 12: THE EARLIEST DISPERSAL OF THE GENUS *HOMO: HOMO erectus* AND CONTEMPORARIES

Chapter Outline

I. Introduction

    a) All the early hominids are found exclusively in Africa.

    b) Starting around two million years ago a new and significantly different hominid, *H erectus*, dispersed out of Africa.

II. The Life and Times of *Homo erectus*

    a) The oldest *H. erectus* specimens are from East Africa and are about 1.8 my old.

        i) They exploited diverse environments, used Oldowan tools, and scavenged and ate meat.

    b) Their initial dispersal out of Africa is documented at Dmanisi in the Republic of Georgia (1.7 mya).

        i) The next earliest sites are in Java at about 1.6 mya.

    c) *H. erectus* is recognized as a new grade of hominid because it demonstrates changes in skeletal robusticity, limb proportions, and body size relative to earlier hominids.

III. The Morphology of *Homo erectus*

    a) **Body size**

        i) The postcranial skeleton of *H. erectus* was not well known until the discovery of the Nariokotome skeleton in 1984.

            (1) From this specimen and other remains it is now estimated that their average adult stature was about 5'6".

            (2) The skeleton of *H. erectus* is also more robust than that of previous hominids.

    b) **Brain size**

        i) *H. erectus*, with a mean cranial capacity of 900 cm^3, had a larger brain than early *Homo*.

            (1) This is an increase of 40% over the small-bodied group of early *Homo*, and a 25% increase over the larger-bodied group of early *Homo*.

            (2) However, when the larger body size of *H. erectus* is considered, *H. erectus* seems to have been no more encephalized than the larger-bodied sample of early *Homo*.

    c) **Cranial shape**

        i) The *H. erectus* cranium has a distinctively shaped, long and low, heavily built cranium.

            (1) The cranial bones are thick, the supraorbital tori are large, and there is a distinct nuchal torus.

IV. Who Were the Earliest African Emigrants?

    a) The best-dated *H. erectus* remains in East Africa are 1.8 mya old, and the dispersal of *H. erectus* out of Africa is thought to have occurred around that time for the following reasons:

        i) Radiometric dates from Java indicate the presence of *H. erectus* at 1.8 to 1.6 mya

        ii) The Dmanisi fossils from the former Soviet Republic of Georgia are dated to more than 1.7 mya

            (1) The newest cranium, discovered in 2002, is that of an edentulous adult male.

            (2) All four Dmanisi crania have small cranial capacities and in one specimen (2700) the browridge is less robust and thinner than normal.

            (3) Stature estimates for two individuals indicate they were small, just over 4 ½ feet tall.

            (4) The skeletal and archaeological remains beg the question of whether hominids really required large brains, robust bodies, and sophisticated stone tools for the dispersal out of Africa.

V. Historical Overview of *Homo erectus* Discoveries

a) **Java**

    i) Eugene Dubois, a Dutch anatomist, discovered the first *H. erectus* fossils in Java in 1891.

        (1) He initially looked for the "missing-link" in Sumatra in 1887, but never found any hominid remains there.

        (2) In 1890, he began exploring the deposits around the Solo River, near the town of Trinil, Java.

            (a) A 900-cm^3 skullcap was found in 1891, and a femur that Dubois claimed belonged to the same individual was found the next year.

                (i) Many now believe the femur belongs to a modern human.

            (b) In 1894 he published his findings, calling the remains *Pithecanthropus erectus*.

                (i) His analysis was not well received, and controversies continued until the discovery of the hominids from Peking (Beijing).

                (ii) Dubois did not accept the mainstream analyses indicating that the Chinese and Javanese materials were similar to each other.

b) ***Homo erectus* from Java**

    i) Presently, *H. erectus* fossils have been found at 6 sites, including Trinil, Modjokerto, Sangiran, and Ngandong.

    ii) The chronological framework for the Javanese fossils is unclear due to the complex geology of the sites.

        (1) One Modjokerto specimen has been dated to 1.8 mya

        (2) One fossil from the Sangiran site has been dated to 1.6 mya

        (3) The Ngandong remains have been recently dated to between 50 kya and 25 kya, making them contemporaneous with modern *H sapiens* elsewhere in the Old World.

c) **Peking (Beijing)**

    i) A Swedish geologist initially investigated a fossil-bearing site near the village of Zhoukoudian in 1921.

        (1) Pei Wenshong (a Chinese geologist) took over excavations in 1929 and found a skullcap.

        (2) Davidson Black (an anatomist) removed the fossil from its limestone matrix and he declared it was a hominid.

        (3) Franz Weidenreich (an anatomist) took over from Black.

            (a) In 1933, Japan invaded China and all the fossils found at Zhoukoudian were entrusted to the U.S. Marines to be shipped to the United States. The fossils were lost during transport.

            (b) Fortunately, Weidenreich left China in 1941 and had prepared excellent casts, taken photographs, and made drawings of all the fossils.

d) **Zhoukoudian *Homo erectus***

    i) To date the mostly fragmentary remains of 14 skullcaps, 6 facial bones, 15 mandibles, 122 isolated teeth, 38 teeth rooted in jaws, 3 humeri, 1 clavicle, 1 lunate, 7 femura, and 1 tibia have been recovered from Zhoukoudian.

        (1) The Zhoukoudian fossil remains possess typical *H. erectus* features such as large supraorbital tori, a nuchal torus, a sagittal ridge, shoveled incisors, and a low position for the maximum breadth of the skull.

    ii) The **cultural remains** include over 100,000 artifacts recovered from layers representing 250,000 years of intermittent occupation.

        (1) The most common tools are chopper and chopping tools, but scrapers, points, burins, and awls are present. There is some evidence for technological evolution through time.

        (2) The traditional interpretation of the evidence from Zhoukoudian indicates that *H. erectus* was a hunter-gatherer and possibly used fire.

(3) Some unsettled questions include:

    (a) Do the cultural remains at Zhoukoudian represent evidence of hominid habitation, or do they really represent the activities of carnivores?

    (b) Are the "ash layers", cited as evidence for the use of fire, really ash, or are they naturally accumulated organic residues?

    (c) Was Zhoukoudian cave an easily accessible habitation site, or was it only accessible through a vertical shaft?

e) **Other Chinese sites** provide clues to the morphology and earliest appearance of *H. erectus* in China.

  i) The earliest cultural evidence of *H erectus* in China is 1.66 mya the site of Majuangou.

  ii) The partial cranium from the Lantian site at perhaps 1.15 mya appears to be the earliest skeletal evidence for *H. erectus* in China.

  iii) The two approximately 580-800 k years old Yunxian crania, though crushed and covered with a calcareous matrix, may become central to clarifying the course of hominid evolution in China.

  iv) The remains of several individuals from Hexian are probably the youngest specimens of *erectus* in China, but their age is disputed.

f) **East Africa**

  i) **Olduvai**

    (1) Louis Leakey discovered a 1.4 m.y. old *H. erectus* skull, OH 9, in Upper Bed II in 1960.

      (a) It has the largest cranial capacity of all African *H. erectus* specimens (1,067 cm^3), as well as the largest browridges of any known hominid.

      (b) As is typical of most African *H. erectus* specimens, the cranial bones are thin.

  ii) **East Turkana**

    (1) Discovered in 1974 and dating to 1.8 mya, ER 3733 is an almost complete *H. erectus* skull.

    (2) Few tools have been found in East Turkana, but there is evidence for the introduction of the Acheulian tradition at about 1.4 mya.

  iii) **West Turkana**

    (1) WT 15000, the most complete *H. erectus* skeleton ever found, was discovered in 1984.

      (a) The fossil is dated to about 1.6 mya.

      (b) The fossil is complete enough to determine the stature at 5'3" and the skeletal age of 12 years. At maturity, this male *H. erectus* would have been over 6' tall.

  iv) **Bouri**

    (1) A mostly complete 1 my old cranium of *H. erectus* was discovered recently at the Bouri locale in the Middle Awash. Significantly, the cranium resembles Asian *H. erectus* specimens and lends credence to the argument that African and Asian specimens are not separate species.

g) **Summary of East African *H. erectus***

  i) Compared to samples from Java and China, East African *H. erectus* samples generally have thinner cranial bones and less strongly buttressed crania.

    (1) Some argue that these differences warrant a separate species designation, *H ergaster*.

h) **Europe**

  i) It was previously thought that hominids did not inhabit Europe until after 400 kya, but hat view is changing.

    (a) The Dmanisi material is dated at 1.8-1.7 mya.

    (2) All other European hominid fossils are about 1 my later than Dmanisi. This includes Ceprano and the early material from Atapuerca.

      (a) The Ceprano skull appears to be *H. erectus,* but the material from Atapuerca has been assigned to a different species by Spanish researchers.

    (3) The more abundant fossil material that appears after 400 kya is generally referred to as premodern *H. sapiens*, though the taxonomic status of these specimens is in flux.

VI. Technological Trends in *Homo erectus*
   a) One change in the tool kit is the introduction of the biface that enabled knappers to produce more efficient tool with sharper, straighter edges.
   b) New excavations in China, where numerous 800 k year old bifaces have been found, are challenging the long-held notion that Acheulian technologies are not found in Eastern Europe and most of Asia.
   c) Although there is widespread evidence for animal butchery by *H erectus*, there is still disagreement as to whether *H. erectus* was primarily a scavenger or a consistent hunter.
      i) *H. erectus* also relied on extensive gathering of wild plants, tubers, and fruits.

VII. Seeing the Big Picture: Interpretation of *Homo erectus*
   a) The Dmanisi cranial remains indicate that the first emigrants out of Africa retained some early *Homo*-like features and had only basic stone tools.
      i) These remains also demonstrate that this population had considerable intraspecific variation, begging the question as to whether *H ergaster* is a valid species.
   b) The new Bouri discovery deals another blow to the *erectus/ergaster* distinction.
   c) The separate species designation for the material from the Gran Dolina is tentative.

Learning Objectives

After reading Chapter 12, the student should be able to:
1. Discuss the features of *H. erectus* that make it a new grade of hominid.
2. Describe the morphology and geographical distribution of *H. erectus*.
3. Discuss the evidence relating to the dispersal of *H. erectus* out of Africa.
4. Detail the history of *H erectus* discoveries in Java and China.
5. Discuss the cultural remains and other materials pertaining to the *H erectus* lifestyle at Zhoukoudian. The student should also mention the alternate interpretations of Zhoukoudian regarding its status as a hominid habitation site.
6. List *H. erectus* sites and important fossil discoveries from East Africa, with particular reference to WT 15000.
7. List the dates assigned to *H. erectus* in East Africa, Java, Asia, and Europe
8. Discuss the fossil discoveries from Europe and focus on their taxonomic status.
9. Discuss the technological trends evident in *H. erectus* archaeological sites.
10. Review the current interpretation of *H. erectus*.

Key Terms and Concepts

Acheulian	p. 303
Dmanisi	p. 297
Grade	p. 297
Nariokotome	p. 300
Pleistocene	p. 304
Zhoukoudian	p. 304

Lecture Suggestions and Enrichment Topics

1. Emphasize that *H. erectus* existed for over 1.5 million years, making it the most successful hominid species known. Point out the relatively short time that modern *H. sapiens* has been around compared to *H. erectus*.
2. Don't let students forget that as *H. erectus* populations expanded out of Africa, the evolutionary forces that you talked about previously (natural selection, gene flow, founder effect, genetic drift, mutation) were still at work in these populations. Emphasize that it is not surprising that we see some geographic differences among *H. erectus* populations, because populations are becoming more

widespread and encountering different environments and therefore, different evolutionary pressures. It is important to keep stressing these concepts as you continue onto archaic *H sapiens* and theories regarding the origins of modern humans.

3. Remind students at the beginning of your lecture that although the name *H. erectus* implies the discovery of the first upright walking hominid, this is far from the case. You might take a few minutes to review the time scale for the origins of bipedalism and note that *erectus* was discovered before we had knowledge of the African hominids.

Student Media Exercises

1. Have students go to the Interactive Anthropology sub-section of the Archaeology section of the Wadsworth Anthropology Resource Center and complete the exercise *Drag and Drop the Homo erectus Sites to the Correct Place on the Map* of Europe and Africa.

2. Have students go to the Interactive Anthropology sub-section of the Archaeology section of the Wadsworth Anthropology Resource Center and complete the exercise *Drag and Drop the Homo erectus Sites to the Correct Place on the Map* of Asia.

3. Have students go to the Meet the Scientist sub-section of the Physical Anthropology section of the Wadsworth Anthropology Resource Center and complete the study questions for *Dr. Josep Gibert Clols: Early Man in Spain*.

4. In *InfoTrac* do a keyword search on "Dmanisi" and read the articles and abstracts that are retrieved. What claims were made about the importance of the first hominid fossils found there? Have these claims been substantiated by more recent hominid fossil finds?

5. In *InfoTrac* search for the article *Homo erectus* shows staying power on Java (Bruce Bower, *Science News*, Dec 14, 1996 v150 n24 p373). Read the article and answer the following questions: What were the prior age estimates for *Homo erectus* in Java? Given the new dates for *Homo erectus* in Java, what are the implications for theories of modern human origins?

6. Go online to the University of Burgos' website on Atapuerca (http://www.atapuerca.com). Explore the website and list three reasons why paleoanthropologists consider this to be one of the most important hominid sites outside of Africa.

Multiple Choice Questions

1. In the 1950s, the genera *Sinanthropus* and *Pithecanthropus* were included in a single species of the genus
   A. *Australopithecus.*
   B. *Ardipithecus.*
   C. *Paranthropus.*
   D. *Homo.*
   E. none of these

   ANS: D
   PG: 297

2. The oldest, most securely dated *Homo erectus* fossils are from
   A. Europe.
   B. North Africa.
   C. East Africa.
   D. China.
   E. India.

   ANS: C
   PG: 297

3. Definite *Homo erectus* fossil remains have been found in
   A. South America.
   B. North America.
   C. Mexico.
   D. Spain.
   E. none of these

   ANS: E
   PG: 303-313

4. Current evidence indicates that _____ was the first hominid to migrate out of Africa.
   A. *A. africanus*
   B. *A. boisei*
   C. *A. robustus*
   D. *H. habilis*
   E. *H. erectus*

   ANS: E
   PG: 297

5. The discoveries of what we now refer to as *Homo erectus* go back to the _____ century.
   A. 17th
   B. 16th
   C. 19th
   D. 20th
   E. none of these

   ANS: C
   PG: 297

6. The original genus name for *Homo erectus* from northern China was
   A. *Pithecanthropus.*
   B. *Carsonanthropus.*
   C. *Erectanthropus.*
   D. *Chinanthropus.*
   E. *Sinanthropus.*

   ANS: E
   PG: 297

7. Of the hominid sites listed below, which one/s has/have fossil material that is the earliest possible evidence for *Homo erectus* (strictly defined) in Europe?
   A. Gran Dolina (Atapuerca)
   B. Ceprano
   C. Ubeidiya
   D. Boxgrove
   E. all of these

   ANS: B
   PG: 313

8. Which of the following statements is FALSE?
    A. Several definite *Homo erectus* fossils have been discovered in France.
    B. Earlier *Homo erectus* populations had a smaller cranial capacity than later populations.
    C. Thick cranial and postcranial bones characterize most *Homo erectus* specimens.
    D. *Homo erectus* appears to have been less encephalized than *Homo sapiens*.
    E. *Homo erectus* was most likely the first hominid to live outside of Africa.

    ANS: A
    PG: 312-313

9. The average cranial capacity of *H. erectus* is
    A. the same as for early *Homo*.
    B. approximately 900 cubic centimeters.
    C. the same as that for modern humans.
    D. the same as for *Australopithecus*.
    E. approximately 700 cubic centimeters.

    ANS: B
    PG: 300

10. The estimated cranial capacities for *Homo erectus* ranges from
    A. 450 to 800 cubic centimeters.
    B. 750 to 1,250 cubic centimeters.
    C. 1,000 to 2,000 cubic centimeters.
    D. 1,250 to 1,600 cubic centimeters.
    E. 300 to 700 cubic centimeters.

    ANS: B
    PG: 300

11. *Homo erectus* differs most distinctly from modern humans in
    A. the postcranial skeleton.
    B. the way they walked.
    C. height.
    D. cranial shape.
    E. all of these

    ANS: D
    PG: 300-301

12. In general, the cranium of *Homo erectus*
    A. has a high vertical forehead.
    B. is composed of delicate, thin bone.
    C. has no brow ridges.
    D. is virtually identical to that of modern humans.
    E. none of these

    ANS: E
    PG: 301

13. The original genus name assigned to what we now call *Homo erectus* from Java is
    A. *Sinanthropus.*
    B. *Zinjanthropus.*
    C. *Dryopithecus.*
    D. *Pithecanthropus.*
    E. *Paranthropus.*

    ANS: D
    PG: 304

14. Who made the first discovery of what we now call *Homo erectus* fossil remains?
    A. Eugene Dubois
    B. Franz Weidenreich
    C. Louis Leakey
    D. Raymond Dart
    E. Mary Leakey

    ANS: A
    PG: 304

15. The date for the *Homo erectus* fossil from Modjokerto, Java
    A. has been established with certainty.
    B. has been difficult to establish due to the complicated geological setting.
    C. has recently been reported to be as early as 1.8 million years old.
    D. none of these
    E. B and C only

    ANS: E
    PG: 304

16. The date for the *Homo erectus* specimen from Ngandong, Java
    A. has been established with certainty.
    B. has recently been reported to be as early as 1.8 million years old.
    C. has recently been reported to be as young as 50,000 to 25,000 years old.
    D. none of these
    E. A and B only

    ANS: C
    PG: 304

17. All the original *Homo erectus* fossils discovered at Zhoukoudian during the 1920s and 1930s
    A. are now housed in a museum in Beijing.
    B. disappeared during World War II.
    C. are kept in a small museum near Zhoukoudian.
    D. were destroyed in a fire in the 1970s.
    E. are available for study at Cambridge University.

    ANS: B
    PG: 305

18. Fossil remains of 40 or more *Homo erectus* individuals and thousands of artifacts have been found at
    A. Sangiran.
    B. Zhoukoudian.
    C. Olduvai.
    D. Trinil.
    E. Lantian.

    ANS: B
    PG: 305

19. Evidence from Zhoukoudian suggests that *Homo erectus*
    A. lived there continuously for over 250,000 years.
    B. were settled agriculturalists.
    C. intermittently occupied the area.
    D. built wooden structures.
    E. kept domesticated animals.

    ANS: C
    PG: 305

20. Of the sites listed below, which one is the *Homo erectus* site that provides the longest record of habitation?
    A. Trinil
    B. Swartkrans
    C. Zhoukoudian
    D. West Turkana
    E. none of these

    ANS: C
    PG: 305

21. Analysis of the stone artifacts from Zhoukoudian indicate that the tools from
    A. the Final Stage are large and crudely made.
    B. the Earliest Stage are made from flint and fine-grained quartz.
    C. all stages are identical to each other.
    D. the Middle Stage are heavier and larger than the previous stage.
    E. the Final Stage are small and the tool materials are of better quality than the previous stages.

    ANS: E
    PG: 305

22. At Zhoukoudian, there is some evidence that *Homo erectus*
    A. killed deer and horses.
    B. ate berries and seeds.
    C. used fire, but not everyone agrees on this point.
    D. all of these
    E. A and C only

    ANS: D
    PG: 305-3108

23. The *Homo erectus* remains at Zhoukoudian indicate that
    A. the majority of these people lived to be 50 or 60 years old.
    B. infant and childhood mortality were high.
    C. they buried their dead.
    D. they used fishing nets.
    E. none of these

    ANS: B
    PG: 305-308

24. The oldest *Homo erectus* fossils from China are (possibly) about _____ years old.
    A. 300,000
    B. 1.52 million
    C. 500,000
    D. 1.15 million
    E. 800,000 to 450,000

    ANS: D
    PG: 308-309

25. Which of the following site/sites is/are in China?
    A. Yunxian
    B. Hexian
    C. Longtandong
    D. Chenjiawo
    E. all of these

    ANS: E
    PG: 308-309

26. The oldest *Homo erectus* remains from East and West Lake Turkana are _____ years old.
    A. 2.5 - 3.5 million
    B. 500,000 - 200,000
    C. 800,000
    D. 5.5 million
    E. 1.8 - 1.6 million

    ANS: E
    PG: 310

27. The almost complete skeleton of a male *Homo erectus* with an approximate age at death of 12 years was found at
    A. Olduvai.
    B. Lantian.
    C. West Turkana.
    D. Zhoukoudian.
    E. Trinil.

    ANS: C
    PG: 310

28. The Nariokotome *Homo erectus* specimen
    A. was discovered at Olduvai Gorge.
    B. is estimated to have been about 65 years old at death.
    C. is a young female.
    D. would have reached an adult height of around 6 feet.
    E. C and D only

    ANS: D
    PG: 310

29. The most complete *Homo erectus* skeleton found to date
    A. is properly known as WT 15000.
    B. was discovered at West Turkana.
    C. is that of a 12 year old male.
    D. all of these
    E. none of these

    ANS: D
    PG: 310

30. The earliest occupation of North Africa by *Homo erectus*, as evidenced by the remains from Ternifine, dates to about
    A. 700,000 years ago.
    B. 1.5 million years ago.
    C. 500,000 years ago.
    D. 250,000 years ago.
    E. None of these, because *Homo erectus* never occupied North Africa.

    ANS: A
    PG: 310-312

31. The term *Homo ergaster*
    A. is sometimes used to refer to African *Homo erectus* specimens.
    B. is sometimes used to refer to Asian *Homo erectus* specimens.
    C. is fully accepted by all paleoanthropologists.
    D. was initially proposed by Eugene Dubois.
    E. B and C only

    ANS: A
    PG: 316-317

32. The Dmanisi site is located in
    A. North Africa.
    B. South Africa.
    C. Java.
    D. Europe.
    E. none of these

    ANS: D
    PG: 312

33. The fossil remains from Dmanisi
    A. are essentially indistinguishable from modern *Homo sapiens*.
    B. bear some similarities to early *Homo* specimens from Africa.
    C. bear some similarities to *Homo erectus* specimens.
    D. have cranial capacities that exceed 1,500 cubic centimeters.
    E. B and C only

    ANS: E
    PG: 302-303

34. The fossil remains from Dmanisi indicate that
    A. large brains were required to migrate out of Africa.
    B. complex stone tools were required to migrate out of Africa.
    C. large brains were NOT required to migrate out of Africa.
    D. A and B only
    E. B and C only

    ANS: C
    PG: 302-303

35. Bifacially flaked tools characterize the _____ stone tool industry.
    A. Oldowan
    B. Acheulian
    C. Shewlian
    D. Osteodontokeratic
    E. none of these

    ANS: B
    PG: 314

36. The Acheulian tool industry is found in
    A. Africa.
    B. western Europe.
    C. southwest Asia.
    D. B and C only
    E. all of these

    ANS: E
    PG: 314-316

37. Evidence for animal butchering is
    A. lacking in *Homo erectus* sites.
    B. found only in African *Homo erectus* sites.
    C. found only in Asian *Homo erectus* sites.
    D. widespread in *Homo erectus* sites.
    E. found only at Dmanisi.

    ANS: D
    PG: 314-316

True/False Questions

1. *Homo erectus* is the first hominid for which we have evidence of wide geographical dispersion.

   ANS: True
   PG: 297

2. Raymond Dart made the initial discovery of *Homo erectus* on the island of Java.

   ANS: False
   PG: 304

3. Given the newest dates for the Ngandong *Homo erectus* material on Java, it is possible that *Homo erectus* could have existed contemporaneously with *Homo sapiens*.

   ANS: True
   PG: 304

4. New evidence from Zhoukoudian cave has substantiated the long held notion that *Homo erectus* used controlled fire.

   ANS: False
   PG: 305-307

5. The Asian *Homo erectus* crania from both China and Java are so different from each other that most researchers have suggested that they be separated into two different species.

   ANS: False
   PG: 308-309

6. An analysis of the WT 15000 specimen suggests it would only have been about 4 feet tall at maturity.

   ANS: False
   PG: 310

7. Despite numerous excavations, the only early stone tools that have been found in China are those from Zhoukoudian.

   ANS: False
   PG: 314

8. The Acheulian biface or "hand axe" is a basic tool of the Acheulian tradition.

   ANS: True
   PG: 314

9. One clear technological trend evident in the Middle Pleistocene archaeological record is that early bifaces are elegant-appearing pear-shaped implements, whereas later bifaces are cruder with deep flake-removal scars.

   ANS: False
   PG: 314-316

Short Answer Questions

1. Compare the cranium and brain size of *Homo erectus* to that of modern *Homo sapiens*. (pp. 300-302)

2. Review the history of *Homo erectus* discoveries in Java and China (specifically Zhoukoudian). (pp. 304-309)

3. Although Zhoukoudian is the most famous *Homo erectus* site in China, there are other sites. Name two of these sites and give their dates. (pp. 305-309)

4. Is there any evidence to suggest that *Homo erectus* evolved outside of Africa? (pp. 310-312)

5. How could *Homo erectus* have benefited from using fire? Is there evidence to suggest that *Homo erectus* actually did use fire? (pp. 314-316)

6. Is there any evidence to suggest the Zhoukoudian was NOT a hominid habitation site? (pp. 305-309)

Essay Questions

1. Discuss the recently published early dates for *Homo erectus* in Java and their implication for the evolution and dispersal of *Homo erectus*.

2. What have scientists been able to ascertain about the *Homo erectus* lifestyle at Zhoukoudian? Be sure to include any disagreements within the scientific community. What is the nature of the evidence?

3. Discuss the fossil finds at Dmanisi in terms of their morphology and in terms of the information they provide about the dispersal of hominids out of Africa

4. Compare the cranial capacity, cranial and postcranial morphology, stature, and cultural behavior (including the types of stone tools they used) of *Homo erectus* to that of earlier hominids, including early *Homo*.

5. What suggestions have been made regarding the hunting capabilities of *Homo erectus*? How have these views changed in recent years and why? Discuss the limitations of these types of archaeological inferences.

CHAPTER 13: PREMODERN HUMANS

Chapter Outline

I. Introduction

    a) *Homo erectus* was a new grade of human. The hominids that appeared after *H. erectus* were not quite like fully modern people, so they are referred to as "premodern humans."

II. When, Where, and What

    a) **The Pleistocene** was a time that saw numerous glacial advances and retreats.

        i) There were at least 15 major and 50 minor glacial advances in Europe.

        ii) The hominids living in Europe and northern Asia were most affected by these climatic oscillations.

        iii) As ice sheets expanded, the more northern areas of Europe and Asia became uninhabitable. As the climate warmed, migration routes such as the one from Central into Western Europe would have reopened.

    b) **Dispersal of Middle Pleistocene humans**

        i) Middle Pleistocene hominids were dispersed throughout the Old World and Europe became more permanently and densely populated.

    c) **Middle Pleistocene hominids: terminology**

        i) With the exception of Asia, where *H. erectus* and premodern hominids may have coexisted, premodern humans appear after *H. erectus*.

        ii) The major morphological changes relative to *Homo erectus* are an increase in brain size, a more globular cranial vault, a more vertical nose, and a reduction in the angulation of the occipit.

        iii) There is considerable disagreement on the taxonomy of these hominids.

            (1) *Homo heidelbergensis* is used for premodern Middle Pleistocene fossils from Africa and Europe.

III. Pre-Modern Humans of the Middle Pleistocene

    a) **Africa**

        i) The two most important specimens come from Bodo and Broken Hill. All other 8 African specimens resemble Bodo and Broken Hill in morphology.

        ii) Importantly, there is no evidence that the Neandertal morphology ever evolved in Africa.

    b) **Europe**

        i) **Europe**

            (1) The earliest occurrence of *H. heidelbergensis* may be the remains from the Gran Dolina at *ca.* 850 kya. However, their taxonomic status is disputed.

            (2) Other later premodern humans retain many *H. erectus* traits.

               (a) These include Steinheim, Swanscombe, and Arago.

            (3) Fossils that date to the latter half of the Middle Pleistocene, such as those from Atapuerca (the Sima de los Huesos), show some Neandertal traits, and their lineage probably gave rise to the Neandertals.

               (i) The remains from the Sima de los Huesos (300 kya) have arched browridges and a projecting midface similar to that of Neandertals.

        ii) **Asia**

            (1) Specimens from **China,** argue Chinese paleoanthropologists, indicate a great degree of genetic continuity from earlier Chinese *H. erectus* populations.

               (a) Some Chinese researchers hold the controversial view that modern Chinese evolved from a separate Chinese *H. erectus* lineage.

            (2) The most complete late Middle or early Upper Pleistocene skull from China is the Dali specimen. The cranial capacity of the Jinniushan partial skeleton (dated to about 200 kya) is fairly large, at about 1,260 cm^3, and the cranial walls are thin.

            (3) There is considerable controversy regarding the classification of Asian specimens.

IV. A Review of Middle Pleistocene Evolution

a) Middle Pleistocene human fossils from Africa and Europe resemble each other more than either resembles the pre-human fossils from Asia.

    i) Thus, the African and European materials are generally referred to as *Homo heidelbergensis*.

b) Chinese paleoanthropologists argue that contemporary fossils from Asia, such as Jinniushan, should be considered early members of *Homo sapiens*.

c) The African premodern humans are argued to have evolved into modern humans, the European premoderns into Neandertals, whereas the Chinese premodern humans may have gone extinct.

V. Middle Pleistocene Culture

a) During the later Middle Pleistocene premodern humans in Africa and Europe invented the Levallois technique, which may reflect their increased cognitive abilities relative to *H. erectus*.

    i) There is considerable intraregional diversity in stone tool assemblages. It is unclear whether this is because different cultural traditions coexisted side-by-side, whether dissimilar assemblages represent different activities carried out there, or whether there was differential stone resource availability.

b) Premodern humans increased their use of cave sites, there is some evidence for the controlled use of fire, and there is also evidence for temporary shelters being built.

c) Numerous resources such as fruits, vegetables and bird eggs were utilized for food, as was fish.

    i) Premodern humans were probably not the accomplished hunters as was once previously thought, given new archaeological reconstructions at Terra Amata, Torralba and Ambrona.

        (1) There is better evidence for a type of hunting at the site of La Cotte de Saint-Brelade, where the remains of mammoths and wooly rhinoceros are found in association with stone flakes. It is likely that these animals were killed by hominids driving them off nearby cliffs.

        (2) Three six foot long wooden spears, dating to around 400 kya, were found at the site of Schöningen. It is argued that these are throwing spears that were used for hunting large animals.

VI. Neandertals: Premodern humans of the Late Pleistocene

a) Neandertals lived for about 100 k.y. in Europe and western Asia. They have been at the center of controversies regarding the origins of modern humans ever since their 1856 discovery by workmen quarrying in limestone caves in Germany's Neander Valley.

b) Neandertal remains are as old as 130 kya and their evolutionary roots stretch back to ca. 500 kya in western Europe; but we usually think of Neandertals as living during the last glaciation (starting 75 kya).

    i) Specimens from western Europe are often called *classic* Neandertals because they tend to be more robust than the rest of the Neandertal sample.

    ii) Neandertals had large brains (1,520 cm^3 average) that may be partially explained by their large body size and need for metabolic efficiency in colder climates.

        (1) The Neandertal cranium is large, long, and low with an occipital bun. The forehead is more vertical than in *H. erectus*, the brow ridges are arched rather than straight, and the face projects distinctly forward.

        (2) The postcranial skeleton is robust and the muscle markings are indicative of powerful musculature. Neandertals have short limbs, a feature that has been interpreted as the product of cold adaptation.

c) **Western Europe**
   i) One of the most important Neandertal discoveries comes from La Chapelle in France.
      (1) French anatomist M. Boule incorrectly reconstructed the Neandertal as bent-kneed.
      (2) La Chapelle is often depicted as the typical Neandertal when in fact he is extremely robust, even for a Neandertal.
   ii) The 100 kya to 120 kya French site of Moula-Guercy has 78 broken hominid bone fragments that have been interpreted as the best evidence for Neandertal cannibalism.
   iii) The more recent remains from St. Césaire in southwestern France are dated to 35 kya and are associated with an Upper Paleolithic tool industry, the Chatelperronian.
   iv) Zafarraya Cave in southern Spain has yielded a few Neandertal fragments, and it dates to about 29 kya (6 k.y.a after St. Césaire).
      (1) Radiocarbon dates for the Neandertal levels at Vindija Cave, Croatia (central Europe), are also quite young at 28 kya to 29 kya
      (2) The late dates for St. Césaire, Zafarraya, and Vindija indicate Neandertals and modern *H. sapiens* could have coexisted for several thousand years. The exact nature of their interactions, if any, is the subject of intense debate.
d) **Central Europe** is a region with a number of important Neandertal sites.
   i) Krapina, Croatia, is a site dating to the last Interglacial (130 – 110 kya) with the earliest intentional burials and perhaps the earliest appearance of "classic" Neandertal features.
   ii) Vindija cave, near Krapina, has 35 Neandertal specimens dating from 42 kya to 28 kya
      (1) Some believe the morphology of these fossils indicates *in situ* evolution from Neandertals to early modern humans in central Europe.
e) **Western Asia** is another region with a number of important Neandertal sites.
   i) The important sites from **Israel** include Tabun (dating to 120 to 110 kya) and Kebara (dating to about 60 kya).
   ii) The site of Shanidar, **Iraq**, has the remains of nine individuals, four of whom were intentionally buried.
      (1) The Shanidar 1 specimen is the skeleton of a 30 to 45 year old male who has a healed fracture on the left side of the head, a withered right arm and shoulder (in fact, the bones of the lower arm and hand are missing), and (among other pathologies) a healed fracture of the right foot. His survival of these injuries has been cited as evidence for compassion among Neandertals.
f) **Central Asia**
   i) Located in **Uzbekistan**, the site of Teshik-Tash has the remains of an intentionally buried 9-year-old male, and may represent the easternmost Neandertal locality.
      (1) A recent analysis, however, indicates that Teshik-Tash is an early modern human.

VII. **Culture of Neandertals**
a) Neandertals are primarily associated with a Middle Paleolithic stone tool industry called the Mousterian.
   i) Neandertal **technology** improved on the Levallois technique by inventing a technique in which numerous flakes could be produced from the same core. These flakes were then retouched into forms such as scrapers, points, and knives.
      (1) Neandertals rarely used bone tools.
   ii) Evidence for Neandertal **settlements** is found in open sites, caves, and rock shelters.
      (1) There is some evidence for shelters (in the form of an oval-shaped concentration of mammoth bones at the site of Moldova, in the Ukraine).
      (2) Settlements were probably temporary and short-term in duration.

iii) Neandertal **subsistence** included hunting, and their sites contain abundant remains of animal bones.
    (1) Neandertals may not have been as efficient at hunting as later Upper Paleolithic humans.
        (a) They lacked long-distance weaponry, and an analysis of Neandertal skeletal fractures is consistent with up-close hunting methods.
        (b) Neandertals must have worn clothing, but there is no evidence of sewing equipment.
    (2) Neandertal **symbolic behavior** most likely included articulate speech, but whether they had the same language capacities as modern *H. sapiens* is the subject of debate and current scientific inquiry.
        (a) Upper Paleolithic humans are hypothesized to have possessed some sort of behavioral advantage over Neandertals; whether this was superior language capability, technological superiority, or increased subsistence efficiency is not clear.
iv) Neandertal **burials** are intentional. This cultural practice is evident in sites located in Europe and western Asia (Kebara), but contemporary hominids in Africa did not treat their dead in the same way.
    (1) After 35 kya in Europe, burial practices associated with modern *H. sapiens* become more complex.
    (2) Neandertals had a preference for placing the body in a flexed position (this position is found in 16 of the 20 best-documented burials).
    (3) Most of the assertions of symbolic treatment of the dead are questionable, and only 14 of 33 Neandertal burials studied have definite associations of stone tools and/or animal bones with the dead.

VIII. Genetic Evidence
a) The mtDNA from 12 Neandertal specimens, ranging from 32 to 50 kya, has been extracted and partially sequenced.
b) Parts of their nuclear DNA have also been sequenced.
    i) These results indicate Neandertal mtDNA is more different from contemporary *Homo sapiens* populations than these latter populations are from each other, and that the Neandertal and modern human lineages must have separated from each other between 700 kya and 500 kya
        (1) The interpretation of the genetic evidence is still controversial, but those researchers working on Neandertal DNA sequencing argue that they should be considered a separate species, *H. neanderthalensis*.

IX. Trends of Human Evolution: Understanding the Pre-Modern Hominids
a) Many paleoanthropologists suggest that there could be several species present in the premodern human fossils.
    i) Extreme lumpers prefer to call all the fossils *Homo sapiens*.
    ii) Splitters generally recognize two species (*H. heidelbergensis* and *H. neanderthalensis*) and some even recognize a third species (*Homo helmei*).
b) The naming of multiple species based on fossil remains is not necessarily meant to represent actual biological species; rather the practice of splitting emphasizes the complex interactions of evolving populations.
    i) The problematic Neandertals are morphologically distinct, but their status as a separate species of humans is unclear.

Learning Objectives

After reading Chapter 13, the student should be able to:

1. Discuss the morphology and geographic and temporal distributions of early premodern *Homo sapiens*.
2. Contrast the evolutionary trajectories of premodern *Homo sapiens* in Africa, Asia, and Europe, emphasizing the evidence that Neandertals evolved in Europe.
3. Discuss Middle Pleistocene cultural innovations, emphasizing tool technologies and hunting capabilities.
4. Contrast the Neandertal morphological complex with that of earlier premodern *H. sapiens*.
5. Detail the temporal and geographic distribution of the Neandertals.
6. Discuss the culture of Neandertals, including their technology, settlement patterns, subsistence behaviors, and symbolic behaviors.
7. List the cultural contrasts between Neandertals and Upper Paleolithic humans.
8. Critically review the taxonomic issues surrounding Pleistocene humans, including both genetic and fossil evidence.

Key Terms and Concepts

Chatelperronian	p. 337
Flexed	p. 335
Glaciations	p. 323
Interglacials	p. 323
Late Pleistocene	p. 323
Middle Pleistocene	p. 323
Mousterian	p. 339
Upper Paleolithic	p. 336

Lecture Suggestions and Enrichment Topics

1. Remind students that the richest human fossil and archaeological records are in Europe and western Asia, so we know more about Neandertal morphology and behavior than any other premodern human population. However, this doesn't mean that other regions of the world are any less important. This fact tends to get lost during discussions about Neandertals, even to the point that students think that only Neandertals existed during the Late Pleistocene.
2. Our current interpretation of Late Pleistocene fossil and archeological evidence is conditioned by the long history of (good and bad) research on the subject of early humans. Emphasize to students that our view of Neandertals has changed considerably since their initial discovery. The book *Neandertals: Changing the Image of Mankind,* by Trinkaus and Shipman, is an excellent source on the history of research on Neandertals.
3. The term "cave-man" is synonymous with "Neandertal" in the mind of most students. Remind them of two facts: 1) Neandertals (and other Middle and Late Pleistocene humans) used rock shelters and open-air sites, in addition to caves; 2) Upper Paleolithic modern humans also used caves, as well as rock shelters and open-air sites.
4. Another area of interest is the degree to which the Neandertals were capable of fully articulate speech. You could assign additional readings by Lieberman, Crelin, and Laitman to illustrate the approaches these authors have taken to address this issue. Another interesting approach is the one taken by Kay, Cartmill, and Balow (using the size of the hypoglossal canal). Point out that the only Pleistocene hominid hyoid bone belongs to the Kebara Neandertal, and it is virtually indistinguishable from a modern human hyoid bone.

Student Media Exercises

1. From J. Kappelman's *Virtual Laboratories for Physical Anthropology* CD: Students should complete the Lab 11: *The Archaeological Record.*

2. From J. Kappelman's *Virtual Laboratories for Physical Anthropology* CD: Students should complete Lab 10: *Fossil Hominids of the Genus Homo.*

3. In *InfoTrac* search for the article Tools underfoot: human trampling as an agent of lithic artifact edge modification (Sally McBrearty; Laura Bishop; Thomas Plummer; Robert Dewar; Nicholas Conard. *American Antiquity*, Jan 1998 v63 n1 p108). This article is an example of experimental archaeology. Why would archaeologists be concerned about the effects of trampling of stone flakes? Does this kind of experiment help us to interpret the archaeological record?

4. In *InfoTrac* search for the article Neandertal neck bone sparks cross talk (Bruce Bower. *Science News*, April 24, 1993 v143 n17 p262). Answer the following questions: What is the hyoid bone? How many Neandertal hyoid bones had been found before the Kebara discovery? What was the impact of this finding on the debate over Neandertal language capabilities?

5. Go online to the Proceedings of the National Academy of Sciences website (http://www.pnas.org/). You can search back issues and abstracts without a subscription. These short articles announce new and significant scientific research. Search for "Neanderthal" (some journals use Neanderthal while others use Neandertal) and read some of the original research articles that strike you as interesting.

Multiple Choice Questions

1. The earliest member of our own species are frequently referred to as
   A. pre-modern *Homo sapiens.*
   B. anatomically modern *Homo sapiens.*
   C. late *Homo erectus.*
   D. *Homo habilis.*
   E. none of these

   ANS: A
   PG: 323

2. The term "pre-modern *Homo sapiens*"
   A. refers to forms that were transitional from *Homo habilis* to *Homo erectus.*
   B. is another term for *Homo erectus.*
   C. refers only to Neandertals.
   D. refers to forms that display some derived features of *Homo sapiens* but retain some *Homo erectus* features.
   E. refers to forms that are completely modern in appearance but lived 400,000 years ago.

   ANS: D
   PG: 325

3. Compared to *Homo erectus*, the cranium of pre-modern *Homo sapiens*
   A. has a less vertical forehead.
   B. has a more angled occipital region.
   C. has a smaller average cranial capacity.
   D. A and C only
   E. none of these

   ANS: E
   PG: 325

4. Pre-modern *Homo sapiens* fossils are found in
    A. North America.
    B. Europe and elsewhere in the Old World.
    C. Australia only.
    D. South America.
    E. A and D only

    ANS: B
    PG: 325

5. In Africa, early pre-modern *Homo sapiens* appeared around _____ years ago.
    A. 200,000
    B. 400,000
    C. 100,000
    D. 600,000
    E. 35,000

    ANS: D
    PG: 326

6. Some pre-modern *Homo sapiens* and *Homo erectus* specimens share traits such as
    A. a large face.
    B. the lack of a supraorbital torus.
    C. the presence of a chin.
    D. thin cranial bones.
    E. none of these

    ANS: A
    PG: 325

7. Which of the following statements regarding pre-modern *Homo sapiens* is TRUE?
    A. There is no controversy concerning the taxonomic status of many pre-modern specimens.
    B. The dating of pre-modern specimens is always precise.
    C. Most pre-modern specimens have some *Homo erectus* traits, so evaluating their taxonomic status is complicated.
    D. There is only one hypothesis regarding their species designation.
    E. Most fossils are complete and are therefore easily analyzed.

    ANS: C
    PG: 326-330, 343-348

8. In Africa, pre-modern *Homo sapiens* fossils have been found in
    A. Ethiopia.
    B. South Africa.
    C. Zambia.
    D. all of these
    E. A and B only

    ANS: D
    PG: 326

9. Pre-modern *Homo sapiens* fossil sites include
   A. Swanscombe.
   B. Steinheim.
   C. Laetoli.
   D. all of these
   E. A and B only

   ANS: E
   PG: 327

10. Which of the following pre-modern *Homo sapiens* crania shows possible evidence of cannibalism in the form of cut marks?
   A. Broken Hill
   B. Tabun
   C. Bodo
   D. La Chapelle
   E. Swanscombe

   ANS: C
   PG: 326

11. Which of the following sites, dated to approximately 300,000 years ago, has yielded a sample representing about 32 pre-modern *Homo sapiens* individuals?
   A. Ehringsdorf
   B. Atapuerca
   C. Steinheim
   D. Swanscombe
   E. Petralona

   ANS: B
   PG: 327

12. The tool technology of pre-modern *Homo sapiens* in the Middle Pleistocene (in Europe and Southwest Asia)
   A. differed considerably from the Acheulian tools of *Homo erectus*.
   B. continued to be the Acheulian tradition.
   C. incorporated the use of bone and antler for the first time.
   D. is termed the Oldowan.
   E. involved the use of finely made, bifacially flaked blades and points.

   ANS: B
   PG: 330-331

13. In Africa, Neandertal fossils have been found at
   A. Olduvai Gorge.
   B. Broken Hill.
   C. Laetoli.
   D. all of these
   E. none of these

   ANS: E
   PG: 332-339

14. During the Middle Pleistocene, pre-modern *Homo sapiens*
    A. occupied open-air campsites.
    B. may have increased their use of caves.
    C. are believed by many researchers to have used fire.
    D. all of these
    E. A and C only

    ANS: D
    PG: 330-331

15. During the Middle Pleistocene, there is evidence that temporary shelters were built by
    A. *Australopithecus*.
    B. pre-modern *Homo sapiens*.
    C. *Paranthropus*.
    D. *Homo erectus*.
    E. *Homo habilis*.

    ANS: B
    PG: 330-332

16. Neandertals are classified in the text
    A. as Upper Pleistocene pre-modern humans.
    B. as *H. erectus neanderthalensis*.
    C. as *H. sapiens neanderthalensis*.
    D. A and C only
    E. all of these

    ANS: D
    PG: 332

17. Upper Pleistocene pre-modern *Homo sapiens* from Europe and western Asia are called
    A. *Homo sapiens sapiens*.
    B. anatomically modern humans.
    C. Neandertals.
    D. *Homo ergaster*.
    E. late *Homo erectus*.

    ANS: C
    PG: 332

18. The majority of Neandertal fossils have been found in
    A. South America.
    B. Asia.
    C. India.
    D. Africa.
    E. Europe.

    ANS: E
    PG: 332

19. The evolutionary roots of Neandertals reach as far back as _____ years ago.
    A. 100,000
    B. 300,000
    C. 65,000
    D. 10,000
    E. 130,000

    ANS: B
    PG: 332

20. Neandertal brain size
    A. was smaller, on average, than that of modern humans.
    B. was larger, on average, than that of modern humans.
    C. was smaller, on average, than that of *Homo erectus*.
    D. averaged about 2,500 cm^3.
    E. averaged about 1,100 cm^3.

    ANS: B
    PG: 335

21. The average Neandertal was
    A. more robust than modern humans.
    B. tall and gracile.
    C. less robust than modern humans.
    D. very small-brained.
    E. none of these

    ANS: A
    PG: 335

22. Neandertal crania are characterized by
    A. small, flat faces.
    B. the absence of brow ridges.
    C. a rounded, smooth occipital area like that seen in modern humans.
    D. a vertical forehead like that seen in modern humans.
    E. a projecting midface.

    ANS: E
    PG: 335

23. Some Neandertal physical characteristics may have arisen as adaptations to a _____ environment.
    A. humid
    B. hot
    C. cold
    D. tropical
    E. high altitude

    ANS: C
    PG: 335

24. Where have Neandertal skeletal remains NOT been found?
    A. Israel
    B. France
    C. Iraq
    D. Germany
    E. China

    ANS: E
    PG: 334-339

25. The La Chapelle-aux-Saints skeleton
    A. is a Neandertal.
    B. was probably a deliberate burial.
    C. is that of an older male.
    D. all of these
    E. A and B only

    ANS: D
    PG: 335

26. The French Neandertal site of St. Césaire dates to _____ years ago.
    A. 75,000
    B. 50,000
    C. 100,000
    D. 35,000
    E. 65,000

    ANS: D
    PG: 336

27. The Neandertal site in southern France that has evidence of cannibalism is
    A. Atapuerca.
    B. Zafarraya.
    C. La Chapelle-aux-Saints.
    D. Bodo.
    E. Moula-Guercy.

    ANS: E
    PG: 336

28. There is some evidence to suggest that Neandertals
    A. made temporary shelters.
    B. buried their dead.
    C. were capable of symbolic behavior.
    D. occasionally engaged in cannibalism.
    E. all of these

    ANS: E
    PG: 336, 339, 340-342

29. The Neandertal site in Croatia which has produced nonhuman faunal remains, artifacts, and some hominid remains is
    A. La Chapelle-aux-Saints.
    B. Krapina.
    C. Shanidar.
    D. Arago Cave.
    E. Broken Hill.

    ANS: B
    PG: 337

30. Shanidar cave is located in
    A. Israel.
    B. France.
    C. Germany.
    D. Croatia.
    E. Iraq.

    ANS: E
    PG: 339

31. The skeleton of a 30 to 45 year old male with a healed fracture to the face, right arm and right leg was found at the site of
    A. Amud.
    B. Shanidar.
    C. Tabun.
    D. Qafzeh.
    E. Krapina.

    ANS: B
    PG: 339

32. The stone tool technology most often associated with the Neandertals is termed
    A. Acheulian.
    B. Mousterian.
    C. Middle Paleolithic.
    D. Upper Paleolithic.
    E. B and C only

    ANS: E
    PG: 339-340

33. The Mousterian stone tool tradition
    A. was developed by *Homo erectus*.
    B. is associated with Neandertals ONLY.
    C. is found in Asia ONLY.
    D. is found in Western Europe ONLY.
    E. none of these

    ANS: E
    PG: 339-340

34. Neandertal subsistence was based on
    A. mastodon hunting.
    B. hunting and gathering.
    C. intense agriculture.
    D. fishing ONLY.
    E. herding domesticated animals.

    ANS: B
    PG: 340-341

35. Compared to the Upper Paleolithic, Mousterian
    A. burials are more complex, usually containing hundreds of tools.
    B. burials usually contain several individuals, precisely oriented relative to each other.
    C. tools are usually more sophisticated.
    D. tools are made of materials transported (traded) over long distances.
    E. none of these

    ANS: E
    PG: 339-343

36. Neandertal art consists of
    A. large painted depictions found in caves.
    B. elaborately carved full-sized sculptures.
    C. large base-relief carvings on rock faces.
    D. "Venus" figurines.
    E. none of these

    ANS: E
    PG: 341-342

37. The first evidence of deliberate burial of the dead is associated with
    A. *Homo erectus.*
    B. *Homo habilis.*
    C. Neandertals.
    D. early pre-modern *Homo sapiens* from Africa.
    E. anatomically modern *Homo sapiens.*

    ANS: C
    PG: 342-343

38. Supposed grave goods found in Neandertal burials
    A. have been cited as evidence for Neandertal symbolic behavior.
    B. include stone tools.
    C. include animal bones.
    D. all of these
    E. A and B only

    ANS: D
    PG: 342-343

39. The genetic evidence from Neandertal remains is in the form of
    A. ribosomal information.
    B. nuclear DNA.
    C. mtDNA.
    D. all of these
    E. A and B only

    ANS: C
    PG: 343

40. The genetic analysis of Neandertal fossils indicates they were
    A. identical to *Homo erectus* samples.
    B. identical to *Homo sapiens* samples.
    C. most similar to chimpanzee samples.
    D. about three times as different from modern *Homo sapiens* samples as they are from each other.
    E. so different from other hominids that they should be placed in a different family than *Homo sapiens*.

    ANS: D
    PG: 343

41. One interpretation of the genetic evidence is that the split of the Neandertal lineage from the modern human lineage
    A. never occurred.
    B. occurred between 2 million and 1 million years ago.
    C. occurred between 290,000 and 150,000 years ago.
    D. occurred between 690,000 and 550,000 years ago.
    E. none of these

    ANS: D
    PG: 343

42. The Middle Pleistocene humans are
    A. morphologically diverse and broadly dispersed throughout time and space.
    B. morphologically diverse but NOT broadly dispersed throughout time and space.
    C. morphologically similar and broadly dispersed throughout time and space.
    D. morphologically similar and NOT broadly dispersed throughout time and space.
    E. none of these

    ANS: A
    PG: 344

43. Additional species of Middle Pleistocene humans suggested by some experts (and mentioned in the text) include
    A. *ergaster.*
    B. *helmi..*
    C. *heidelbergensis.*
    D. all of these
    E. A and B only

    ANS: D
    PG: 344-347

44. The sum of the genetic, fossil, and archaeological evidence suggests that Neandertals
    A. are closely related to modern humans.
    B. are a fully separate biological species.
    C. were probably incapable of fertilely interbreeding with modern humans.
    D. B and C only
    E. all of these

    ANS: A
    PG: 344-347

True/False Questions

1. The main effect of fluctuating climates in Africa during the Pleistocene was to change rainfall patterns.

    ANS: True
    PG: 324

2. *Homo heidelbergensis* refers to finds from China dating to between 850,000 and 200,000 years ago.

    ANS: False
    PG: 325

3. Chinese archaeologists point out that Chinese pre-modern *H. sapiens* specimens show no indications of genetic continuity with modern *H. sapiens* from China.

    ANS: False
    PG: 327-330

4. The Gran Dolina human remains are definitely from *Homo erectus*.

    ANS: False
    PG: 326-327

5. An interesting fact regarding the site called the Sima de los Huesos is that carnivore and human remains are generally found in different locations.

    ANS: True
    PG: 327-330

6. The pre-modern human fossils from Africa and Europe are more similar to each other than they are to the hominids from Asia.

    ANS: True
    PG: 330

7. Pre-modern *Homo sapiens* was probably able to control fire, since there is evidence of hearths at several sites, including Bilzingsleben.

    ANS: True
    PG: 330-332

8. No hypotheses have been proposed to explain the fact that different stone tool industries coexisted in some areas for long periods during the Middle Pleistocene.

   ANS: False
   PG: 330-331

9. The evolutionary roots of Neandertals are shrouded in mystery because there are no fossils from Europe that predate Neandertals.

   ANS: False
   PG: 332

10. The Chatelperronian tool industry is associated with Neandertals, and may be the product of cultural diffusion from modern *H. sapiens*.

    ANS: True
    PG: 335

Short Answer Questions

1. Do the early pre-modern *Homo sapiens* fossils most resemble *Homo erectus* or *Homo sapiens* in morphology? Be sure to defend your answer by discussing specific traits.
   (p. 325)

2. Contrast the morphology of the earliest European pre-modern *Homo sapiens* with that of later European pre-modern *Homo sapiens* such as Neandertals.
   (pp. 325, 335-337)

3. Discuss the evidence that pre-modern *Homo sapiens* built temporary shelters and used fire.
   (pp. 330-332)

4. What is known about the hunting capabilities of Middle Pleistocene humans?
   (pp. 330-332)

5. Discuss the geographic distribution and temporal span of Neandertals.
   (pp. 332-339)

6. Describe the cranial and postcranial anatomy of Neandertal skeletons.
   (pp. 332-335)

7. Describe the injuries and pathologies evident in the Shanidar I skeleton. What, if anything, does this tell us about Neandertal lifestyle and/or cultural behavior?
   (pp. 338-339)

8. Discuss four cultural contrasts between Neandertals and Upper Paleolithic modern humans.
   (p. 341; Table 13-1)

Essay Questions

1. Describe what is known about Middle Pleistocene culture. Include information about technology, settlement, and subsistence.

2. Why do some paleoanthropologists classify Neandertals as *Homo neanderthalensis*? What are the biological and phylogenetic implications of this designation?

3. What is known of Mousterian technology, subsistence, settlements, and symbolic behavior?

4. Discuss the evolutionary trends in the genus *Homo*. Start with the transition from early *Homo* to *Homo erectus* and end with the Neandertals. Be sure to include the temporal and geographic distributions of the various species of *Homo*.

5. Construct two plausible alternate phylogenies for the genus *Homo*. Next, defend each of the phylogenies.

CHAPTER 14: THE ORIGIN AND DISPERSAL OF MODERN HUMANS

Chapter Outline

I. Introduction
   a) Modern *Homo sapiens* evolved in Africa around 200 kya and then dispersed to the rest of the Old World and Australia and then later into the Americas.
      i) These first modern humans are clearly the descendents of the previously discussed premodern humans.
   b) The primary questions that need to be addressed are:
      i) When did modern humans first appear?
      ii) Where did the transition take place?
      iii) What was the pace of the evolutionary change?
      iv) How did the dispersal of modern humans to other areas of the world take place?

II. Approaches to Understanding Modern Human Origins
   a) **The complete replacement model (Recent African Evolution)**
      i) Developed by Christopher Stringer and Peter Andrews, this model proposes that anatomically modern populations arose in Africa about 200 kya, dispersed from Africa, replacing premodern populations in Asia and Europe.
         (1) This model assumes that the origin of modern humans was a speciation event, so there could be no modern human/premodern human admixture.
         (2) Stringer argues that even if interbreeding could have taken place, very little actually occurred.
         (3) The mtDNA analyses of recent human populations that tend to support this model have met with criticism for their methods and conclusions.
            (a) Analyses of the Y chromosome indicate humans are much less genetically variable than other primates, thus supporting the replacement hypothesis.
            (b) Also, ancient mtDNA studies (of Neandertals) support the replacement scenario.
   b) **Partial replacement models** are various perspectives that emphasize that modern humans dispersed out of Africa, but that there was considerable interbreeding among the dispersing modern humans and preexisting regional premodern populations.
   c) **The Regional continuity model (Multiregional Evolution)**
      i) This model, defended by Milford Wolpoff and others, proposes that premodern forms throughout the Old World evolved into modern humans.
         (1) The earliest modern *H. sapiens* did not arise exclusively in Africa, as postulated by the complete replacement model.
         (2) Gene flow between geographically widespread populations prevented speciation.

III. The Earliest Discoveries of Modern Humans
   a) **Africa**
      i) Fully anatomically modern forms dating to 120 – 80 kya come from Klasies River Mouth and Border Cave in South Africa, and Omo Kabish 1, in Ethiopia.
         (1) Not all paleoanthropologists agree that these are the oldest forms of modern humans because of problems with dating and differing interpretations of the specimens.
      ii) Fossils from **Herto**, Ethiopia, were announced in 2003 (but discovered in 1997).
         (1) The cranial remains are definitely from *Homo sapiens* and have been securely dated to 160 to 154 kya.
         (2) They have been placed in a new subspecies, *H. s. idaltu*, to emphasize the fact that they are on the verge of modernity.
         (3) These fossils are the most conclusive evidence to date of an African origin for modern humans.

b) **The Near East**
   i) The sites of Skhūl (115 kya) and Qafzeh Caves (100 kya) in Israel have yielded the combined remains of about 30 individuals of modern morphology (although some specimens retain premodern features).
      (1) If the dates for the Neandertal site of Tabun are 120 kya, then Neandertals may slightly predate modern humans in this region, but there is still considerable chronological overlap between these two different forms. This is a problem for proponents of the regional continuity model.
c) **Asia**
   i) Of the six localities in China that have modern human remains, the most important are Zhoukoudian (Upper Cave) and Ordos in Mongolia.
      (1) The Upper Cave remains are between 18 ky and 10 ky old, and the Ordos material, at 50 kya, may be the oldest modern human material from China.
   ii) If the Jinniushan skeleton proves to be as early as 200 kya it would push the appearance of modern human morphology in Asia back to the same time-frame as in Africa.
      (1) Many Chinese paleoanthropologists argue for continuity from *H. erectus* to modern humans in China.
d) **Australia**
   i) Modern humans already inhabited Sahul, the area including New Guinea and Australia, by at least 50 kya.
   ii) Since Australia was separated from Indonesia by deep water even during glacial times, it is not known how humans reached Australia, although they presumably used some sort of boat.
   iii) The earliest occupations, judging by the archaeological evidence, date to about 55 kya.
      (1) The earliest skeletal evidence is from Lake Mungo in southeastern Australia. Radiocarbon dates and the archaeological context indicate an age of 30 to 25 kya ESR and U-S dates indicate an age of 60 kya.
         (a) The mtDNA was extracted from the Lake Mungo remains and the initial report indicated that an ancient mtDNA lineage was found. This result has been criticized, and it is not clear if the result is valid.
e) **Central Europe**
   i) The earliest anatomically modern human remains in Europe, dated to 35 kya, are from Oase Cave, Romania.
      (1) The material includes the cranial remains of three robust, but anatomically modern individuals.
      (2) Modern human specimens from Mladeč in the Czech Republic date to about 33 kya.
      (3) After 28 kya, modern humans were widely dispersed in Central and Western Europe.
f) **Western Europe**
   i) Historically, fossils from this area of the Old World have received the greatest amount of attention when considering theories of modern human origins.
   ii) The best-known sample of western European *H. sapiens* is from the site of Cro-Magnon.
      (1) These fossils (the remains of 8 individuals associated with an Aurignacian tool assemblage) were discovered in 1868 and date to 30 kya.
      (2) Of the three male crania, Cro-Magnon I is the most modern looking.
   iii) A newly discovered child's skeleton from the Lagar Velho site in Portugal, dated to 24.5 kya, is argued by Duarte, Trinkaus, and colleagues to display a suite of traits indicative of past admixture of Neandertals and modern humans.

IV. Something New And Different
   i) By 25 kya, modern humans had dispersed throughout the Old World.
      (1) There may have been a late surviving population of *erectus*-like humans on the island of Flores, Indonesia.
      (2) The remains of nine individuals, dated to as late as 13 kya, were discovered in Liang Bua Cave in 2004.
         (a) The more complete female adult skeleton (LB1) is barely three feet tall with a cranial capacity of only 380 cm^3.
            (i) Their unique morphology earned them a new species designation: *Homo floresiensis*.
         (b) Some have suggested that LB1 is actually a microcephalic modern human.
         (c) Others, such as U.C. Berkeley anthropologist Gary Richards, argues that the Flores individuals are not pathological, but have unusually small body and brain sizes due to microevolutionary adaptations to their island habitat.

V. Technology and Art in the Upper Paleolithic
   a) In **Europe**, the Upper Paleolithic began about 40 kya and this cultural period is divided into 5 different industries: Chatelperronian, Aurignacian, Gravettian, Solutrean, and Magdalenian.
      i) Starting about 30 kya, there was a warming trend that produced tundra and steppe throughout much of Eurasia, creating a "hunter's paradise" of plentiful large game.
        (1) The Upper Paleolithic people became very successful, and this period saw the highest human population densities up to that time in Europe and perhaps Africa.
      ii) Cultural innovations in Eurasia such as warmer, better-fitting sewn clothing allowed Upper Paleolithic peoples to occupy eastern Europe and northern Asia for the first time.
        (1) The warming trend ended about 20 kya as the last, most intense period of glaciation began.
      iii) The Upper Paleolithic is distinguished by the appearance of new tool types as well as the increased use of materials such as bone, antler, and ivory.
        (1) The spear thrower, or atlatl, as well as barbed harpoons appear during the Magdalenian.
        (2) The punch blade technique provided abundant standardized blades that were fashioned into a variety of tools such as burins and borers.
          (a) C. Loring Brace suggests that the reduction of tooth size and the decreased protrusion of the face reflect an increase in the use of technology for food production.
      iv) The Upper Paleolithic of western Europe is also famous for the appearance of various forms of art, including the cave art of France and Spain, sculptures, engravings, and "portable art" (engravings on tools and tool handles).
        (1) Female figurines known as "Venuses" appear in western, central, and eastern Europe, and Siberia.
        (2) The function of the famous cave art of Lascaux of southern France and Altimira in Spain is not fully understood. It could have been religious or magical, a form of visual communication, or simply art for the sake of art.
        (3) The Grotte Chauvet dates to the Aurignacian period (about 30 kya) and includes never before documented images of a panther, a hyena, and an owl.
          (a) Also present at Grotte Chauvet, and seen in later Magdalenian caves and rock shelters, are the outlines of human hands and bas-relief sculptures of animals.
        (4) Among the lingering questions about cave art are: whether religious ritual and magic were associated with the images; whether dots-and-lines motifs are a form of writing or a type of calendar; why certain areas of caves were used for painting; and why certain animals are represented.
          (a) The fluorescence of cave art seems to coincide with the last glacial period (20 kya to 18 kya), and these caves could have been used as meeting places to share valuable information crucial to surviving the rigorous climate.

b) Southern **Africa** has rock art that is about as old as that found in Europe (28 kya to 19 kya), and personal adornment in the form of ostrich shell beads date to about 38 kya.
   i) The most important sites are the Apollo 11 rock shelter, Blombos Cave, and Katanda.
   ii) Katanda, in the Democratic Republic of the Congo, has three sites that have yielded finely crafted bone tools (similar to European Upper Paleolithic harpoons) made from either the ribs or splinters of long bones of large mammals.
      (1) The bone tools have not been precisely dated, but based on TL, and ESR they are believed to be as early as 80 kya.
      (2) The antiquity of the bone tools has not been universally accepted.

VI. Summary of Upper Paleolithic Culture
   a) The Upper Paleolithic is the culmination of 2 million years of cultural evolution.
   b) Late Pleistocene humans had a faster pace of cultural innovation than any previous group of humans.
      i) In Europe and central Africa, cultural innovations included big game hunting and new deadly weapons such as the atlatl, the harpoon, and possibly the bow and arrow. Upper Paleolithic humans had body ornaments, needles, tailored clothing, and more elaborate burials.
   c) After 10 kya, the climate slowly warmed and the glaciers retreated. Grinding hard seeds and roots became increasingly important, and eventually the domestication of plants and animals ensued.

Learning Objectives

After reading Chapter 14, the student should be able to:
1. Discuss the hypotheses regarding the appearance of anatomically modern *Homo sapiens*.
2. Provide details of the geographic distribution of *H. sapiens* for the period between 120 kya and 10 kya.
3. Discuss the issues surrounding the interpretation of the Flores skeletal material.
4. Characterize the climatic, technological, and subsistence changes evident in the Upper Paleolithic.
5. Compare the cultural innovations in Europe with those in Africa.
6. Discuss the appearance and significance of "art" in Eurasia and Africa, especially with regard to cave paintings and their possible cultural significance.

Key Terms and Concepts

Aurignacian	p. 366
Burins	p. 370
Cro-Magnon	p. 366
Magdalenian	p. 370

Lecture Suggestions and Enrichment Topics

1. Remind students that the various models for the origins of modern humans are hypotheses that must be tested in the archaeological and fossil records, and that no matter which one is finally accepted, it is certain that the population-level interactions throughout the Old World must have been complex.
2. Students often ask whether the modern humans, or Cro-Magnons, killed off the Neandertals through warfare. We have no evidence pointing to this scenario. Remind them that population densities throughout the Old World near the beginning of the Upper Paleolithic must have been very low, and it is therefore possible that modern *H. sapiens* and Neandertals were rarely at odds with each other for resources.

3. You should take a few minutes to mention the populating of the New World, since it occurred during the late Upper Paleolithic. Since you are on the subject, you could discuss the controversy over the Kennewick skeleton. Information about Kennewick can be found at http://www.archaeology.org/online/news/kennewick.html and http://www.kennewick-man.com/. Also, be sure to check for late breaking news on the controversy. For example, as of 2004, the Kennewick remains were released to scientists for intensive analysis.

Student Media Exercises

1. From J. Kappelman's *Virtual Laboratories for Physical Anthropology* CD: Students should complete Lab 12: *The Origin and Evolution of Modern Humans.*
2. In *InfoTrac* do a keyword search on "Lake Mungo" and read some of the abstracts and articles that are retrieved. What is the newest date for the Lake Mungo remains?
3. In *InfoTrac* search for the article The caveman convention: did Neanderthals and Cro-Magnons mingle? (Sharon Begley, *Newsweek*, May 27, 1996 v127 n22 p61). Answer the following questions: How did scientists determine that the remains at the Arcy-sur-Cure are from Neandertals? What is actually known about the interactions between Neandertals and modern humans (Cro-Magnons) in Europe?
4. Go online to the French Ministry of Culture's website on Lascaux Cave (http://www.culture.gouv.fr/culture/arcnat/lascaux/en/index.html /) for a virtual tour of the site.
5. Go online to the Bradshaw Foundation (http://www.bradshawfoundation.com/) for an interactive world map of rock art locations.

Multiple Choice Questions

1. According to the most recent evidence, the first modern *Homo sapiens* evolved in Africa around _____ years ago.
    A. 150,000
    B. 1,500,000
    C. 50,000
    D. 500,000
    E. 5,000,000

    ANS: A
    PG: 353

2. According to the *Compete Replacement Model*, the transition from pre-modern to modern *Homo sapiens*
    A. occurred in several regions of the Old World simultaneously.
    B. occurred first in Europe.
    C. only occurred once; in Africa.
    D. began about 10,000 years ago in Indonesia.
    E. began about 100,000 years ago in Asia.

    ANS: C
    PG: 354

3. According to the *Complete Replacement Model*, anatomically modern *Homo sapiens* first appeared in Africa
    A. and dispersed to Europe where they interbred with local pre-modern *H. sapiens* populations.
    B. and migrated to other areas completely displacing all pre-modern *H. sapiens* populations without interbreeding with them.
    C. remained there while pre-modern populations elsewhere evolved more slowly.
    D. around 500,000 years ago.
    E. B and D only

    ANS: B
    PG: 354

4. Which of the following has NOT been proposed as a model to explain the origin of modern *Homo sapiens*?
    A. An origin in Africa followed by migration to other areas where indigenous pre-modern populations were replaced.
    B. An origin in Africa followed by migration to other areas where both interbreeding and replacement occurred.
    C. Several origins in different areas where modern forms evolved from local populations.
    D. Separate origins in Africa and Australia with migrations from both these areas to displace all other populations.
    E. A and C only

    ANS: D
    PG: 354-357

5. According to Partial Replacement Models, modern humans first appeared in Africa
    A. and interbred with pre-modern populations of Eurasia, thus partially displacing them.
    B. and remained there until modern humans from Asia displaced them.
    C. about 500,000 years ago.
    D. but were later displaced by European Neandertals.
    E. A and B only

    ANS: A
    PG: 356

6. Several different Partial Replacement Models have been proposed. They differ from each other with respect to
    A. the geographic origin of modern humans.
    B. the timing of the origin of modern humans.
    C. whether a speciation event occurred at the origin of modern humans.
    D. the degree of interbreeding between pre-modern and modern human populations.
    E. all of these

    ANS: D
    PG: 356

7. The *Regional Continuity Model* of modern *Homo sapiens* origins proposes that
   A. modern humans did not appear solely in Africa.
   B. pre-modern populations in Europe, Asia and Africa all evolved into modern *Homo sapiens*.
   C. there was gene flow between pre-modern populations from different regions of the Old World.
   D. all of these
   E. A and B only

   ANS: D
   PG: 356-357

8. According to the *Regional Continuity Model*, _____ prevented local populations of pre-modern *Homo sapiens* from becoming separate species.
   A. founder's effect
   B. gene flow
   C. displacement by African *Homo sapiens*
   D. mitochondrial DNA
   E. genetic drift

   ANS: B
   PG: 356-357

9. Although there is not complete agreement, current evidence indicates that the earliest anatomically modern *Homo sapiens* fossils are from
   A. China.
   B. India.
   C. Germany.
   D. France.
   E. Africa.

   ANS: E
   PG: 354-357

10. Early anatomically modern *Homo sapiens* remains, dated from 90,000 to perhaps over 155,000 years ago, have been found in
    A. Australia.
    B. South America.
    C. North America.
    D. none of these
    E. A and B only

    ANS: D
    PG: 357-359

11. The earliest anatomically modern *Homo sapiens* fossils from Africa have been dated to about _____ years ago.
    A. 100,000-70,000
    B. 200,000-150,000
    C. 160,000-80,000
    D. 35,000
    E. 65,000

    ANS: C
    PG: 357-359

12. The Herto remains are
    A. from South Africa.
    B. from the Bouri formation.
    C. considered to be modern *Homo sapiens*.
    D. considered to be *Ardipithecus*.
    E. B and C only

    ANS: E
    PG: 359

13. The analysis of the Herto remains indicate they are
    A. most similar to *Australopithecus*.
    B. indistinguishable from modern *Homo sapiens*.
    C. most similar to late *Homo erectus* from China.
    D. not specifically similar to any one group of modern *Homo sapiens*.
    E. none of these

    ANS: D
    PG: 359

14. Early modern *Homo sapiens* remains have been found at _____ in Israel.
    A. Kow Swamp
    B. Skhūl
    C. Qafzeh
    D. all of these
    E. B and C only

    ANS: E
    PG: 360

15. The Skhūl site in Israel is dated to approximately _____ years ago.
    A. 150,000
    B. 75,000
    C. 200,000
    D. 115,000
    E. 40,000

    ANS: D
    PG: 360

16. Of the sites listed below, the most important one for determining the morphology of the earliest *Homo sapiens sapiens* in Central Europe is
   A. Cro-Magnon.
   B. Tabun.
   C. Katanda.
   D. Mladeč.
   E. none of these

   ANS: D
   PG: 363-366

17. Among the sites in central Europe that may offer evidence for genetic continuity between Neandertals and modern humans are
   A. Mladeč and Vindija.
   B. Tabun and Qafzeh.
   C. Qafzeh and Skhūl.
   D. Border Cave and Vindija.
   E. none of these

   ANS: A
   PG: 363-365

18. _____ is a site in France dated to 30,000 years ago. Fossil material from this site became the archetype for Upper Paleolithic Europeans.
   A. Skhūl
   B. La Chapelle-aux-Saints
   C. Cro-Magnon
   D. Qafzeh
   E. Zhoukoudian

   ANS: C
   PG: 365-366

19. Some Chinese paleoanthropologists suggest that the modern *Homo sapiens* material from China indicates that
   A. all pre-modern *H. sapiens* populations in China were replaced by modern *H. sapiens* from Europe.
   B. all pre-modern *H. sapiens* populations in China were replaced by modern *H. sapiens* from Africa.
   C. modern *H. sapiens* in China are the direct descendants of Chinese pre-modern *H. sapiens*.
   D. modern *H. sapiens* in China are the direct descendants of Neandertals.
   E. none of these

   ANS: C
   PG: 361-363

20. The skeletal remains from _____ are from Inner Mongolia and date to about 50,000 years ago.
    A. Upper Cave
    B. Zhoukoudian
    C. Lake Mungo
    D. Border Cave
    E. Ordos

    ANS: E
    PG: 361-363

21. The question of whether continuous local evolution produced anatomically modern groups directly from some regions of Eurasia
    A. was settled about ten years ago.
    B. was never an issue among paleoanthropologists.
    C. is far from settled.
    D. was called into question with the discoveries at Zhoukoudian.
    E. A and B only

    ANS: C
    PG: 361-363

22. The Lagar Velho specimen
    A. is from Portugal.
    B. is dated to about 24,500 years ago.
    C. may be an example of admixture between Neandertals and early modern humans.
    D. A and C only
    E. all of these

    ANS: E
    PG: 365-366

23. The mtDNA extracted from the Lake Mungo specimen
    A. MAY indeed be ancient.
    B. MAY be contaminated.
    C. is DEFINITELY ancient.
    D. A and B only
    E. B and C only

    ANS: D
    PG: 363

24. Archaeological sites in Australia have been dated to _____ years ago.
    A. 25,000
    B. 30,000
    C. 75,000
    D. 55,000
    E. 100,000

    ANS: D
    PG: 363

25. A newly published controversial date for the Lake Mungo remains indicates they may be as old as
_____ years.
    A. 60,000
    B. 400,000
    C. 10,000
    D. 600,000
    E. none of these

    ANS: A
    PG: 363

26. The Kow Swamp remains
    A. are more robust than the Lake Mungo remains.
    B. are less robust than the Lake Mungo remains.
    C. are from Australia.
    D. A and C only
    E. B and C only

    ANS: D
    PG: 363

27. The Upper Paleolithic
    A. began at the onset of the Pleistocene.
    B. is a cultural period attributed primarily to Neandertals.
    C. is characterized by the invention of iron tools.
    D. began about 150,000 years ago.
    E. none of these

    ANS: E
    PG: 369

28. The Upper Paleolithic culture period is divided into categories based on stone tool technologies.
These include
    A. Solutrean.
    B. Magdalenian.
    C. Aurignacian.
    D. all of these
    E. none of these

    ANS: D
    PG: 369

29. The Upper Paleolithic culture period began in Western Europe about _____ years ago.
    A. 40,000
    B. 10,000
    C. 5,000
    D. 70,000
    E. 100,000

    ANS: A
    PG: 369-371

30. During the last glaciation in Eurasia
    A. human habitation was impossible.
    B. the entire area was permanently covered with ice-sheets.
    C. a warming trend at about 30,000 y.a. partially melted the glacial ice.
    D. hunting was impossible because there were no animals in the region.
    E. none of these

    ANS: C
    PG: 369-373

31. During the Upper Paleolithic, humans in Eurasia relied heavily on
    A. deep sea fishing.
    B. hunting.
    C. small-scale farming.
    D. large-scale agriculture.
    E. domesticated animals.

    ANS: B
    PG: 369-373

32. The atlatl
    A. is a type of projectile point.
    B. is used for starting fires.
    C. is used to increase the distance of a spear throw.
    D. is a drill.
    E. is used for fishing.

    ANS: C
    PG: 370

33. Technological changes typical of the Upper Paleolithic include
    A. the use of the barbed harpoon.
    B. the increased use of bone and antler.
    C. the use of metal.
    D. all of these
    E. A and B only

    ANS: E
    PG: 369-371

34. Upper Paleolithic peoples made symbolic depictions on
    A. cave walls.
    B. rock faces (carved).
    C. fired clay.
    D. bone and antler.
    E. all of these

    ANS: E
    PG: 372-373

35. Types of Upper Paleolithic art include
    A. engravings.
    B. cave paintings.
    C. sculptured figurines.
    D. all of these
    E. A and B only

    ANS: D
    PG: 372-373

36. Lascaux and Altamira
    A. are well known Neandertal sites.
    B. are 20,000 year-old campsites.
    C. contain evidence of butchered mammoths.
    D. are famous for their numerous cave bear skulls.
    E. are famous for their elaborate cave paintings.

    ANS: E
    PG: 373-375

37. The cave paintings in the Grotte Chauvet
    A. are relatively crude and primitive.
    B. mostly depict landscapes.
    C. mostly depict female humans.
    D. date to about 10,000 y.a.
    E. none of these

    ANS: E
    PG: 372-375

38. Upper Paleolithic cave paintings
    A. are found in France and Spain.
    B. may have served as "encoded information" passed from generation to generation.
    C. were painted mostly during the last glacial maximum.
    D. all of these
    E. A and C only

    ANS: D
    PG: 372-375

39. Early rock art from Africa may be as old as _____ years.
    A. 10,000
    B. 68,000
    C. 100,000
    D. 28,000
    E. 40,000

    ANS: D
    PG: 373

40. If the early dates for bone tools found at Katanda are correct, then
    A. this technology dates to about 1.5 million years ago.
    B. African cultural innovations must have lagged behind those of Europe.
    C. this technology dates to about 100,000 years ago.
    D. Africa may be the source for many European Upper Paleolithic innovations.
    E. C and D only

    ANS: E
    PG: 373

41. The Upper Paleolithic
    A. was an age during which there was little innovation in technology and art.
    B. led the way for later more complex cultural accomplishments.
    C. was restricted to Europe.
    D. was an age during which there was extraordinary innovation in technology and art.
    E. B and D only

    ANS: E
    PG: 373-375

42. The rate of cultural and technological change
    A. increased dramatically during the Upper Paleolithic.
    B. slowed dramatically during the Upper Paleolithic.
    C. increased during the European Upper Paleolithic, but slowed during the same time period everywhere else in the Old World.
    D. remained stable until after the Upper Paleolithic.
    E. none of these

    ANS: A
    PG: 373-375

True/False Questions

1. The transition between pre-modern and anatomically modern forms of humans may have occurred as early as 500,000 years ago in Africa.

    ANS: False
    PG: 353

2. Specimens that we refer to as *Homo sapiens sapiens* are considered to be a side branch of human evolution, and therefore not closely related to contemporary humans.

    ANS: False
    PG: 353

3. As a group, the specimens from Skhūl all have modern human features and none show any hints of pre-modern features.

    ANS: False
    PG: 360

4. Current evidence suggests the earliest modern *Homo sapiens* fossils come from Africa, but not everyone agrees on their dates.

    ANS: True
    PG: 354

5. The fossils from Mladeč, in the Czech republic, have been cited as evidence for local genetic continuity with Neandertals.

    ANS: True
    PG: 363-364

6. The morphology of the child's skeleton from Lagar Velho in Portugal has been cited as support for the *Complete Replacement Model*.

    ANS: False
    PG: 365-366

7. Cultural innovations of the Upper Paleolithic allowed humans to occupy easternmost Europe for the first time.

    ANS: True
    PG: 369

8. The Upper Paleolithic was a period during which there were rapid shifts in climatic conditions.

    ANS: True
    PG: 369

Short Answer Questions

1. Summarize the main points of the *Complete Replacement Model*.
    (pp. 354-357)

2. Summarize the main points of *Partial Replacement Models*.
    (p. 356)

3. Summarize the main points of the *Regional Continuity Model*.
    (pp. 356-357)

4. Summarize the importance of the discovery of the child's skeleton from the Abrigo do Lagar Velho relative to the debate on modern human origins.
    (pp. 365-366)

5. Review the evidence relative to the timing of the habitation of Australia.
    (pp. 363)

6. What do the Upper Paleolithic cave paintings depict? Where are most of these caves found, and why do anthropologists think the paintings may have been produced?
    (pp. 369-373)

7. Define the term "portable art." When and where do we find it?
    (pp. 370-372)

Essay Questions

1. Review the evidence for the earliest appearance of modern human morphology throughout the Old World.

2. Using your knowledge of the fossil record and the genetic evidence, which model of modern human origins is best supported by the current data?

3. What were the environmental and climatic conditions from 40,000 y.a. to 10,000 y.a. in Eurasia? How did these factors influence the technological and cultural innovations of Upper Paleolithic humans?

CHAPTER 15: MODERN HUMAN BIOLOGY: PATTERNS OF VARIATION

Chapter Outline

I. **Introduction**
   a) This chapter deals with past and current views concerning human phenotypic variation.
      i) The traditional view of human variation focused on attempts to classify humans into races. Now, we tend to focus on the genetics and adaptive significance of human variation.

II. **Historical Views of Human Variation**
   a) Because differences in skin color were apparent when different human groups came into contact, skin color became one of the most common traits of racial classification.
   b) Johann Friedrich Blumenbach (1752-1840) classified humans into four races.
      i) He used skin color (white, yellow, brown, and black) as well as other traits, but emphasized that humans do not fall neatly into these categories.
   c) Believing that head shape was a stable "racial trait," Anders Retzius developed the cephalic index in 1842 to describe the shape of the head.
      i) A head with a width that measures less than 75% of its length is termed dolichocephalic, one with a width that measures between 75 to 80% of its length is termed mesocephalic, and one with a width that is more than 80% of its length is termed brachycephalic.
         (1) The cephalic index ceased to be used as a racial trait when it was discovered that allegedly superior dolichocephalic northern Europeans shared a similar head shape with some so-called "inferior" African populations.
   d) After 1850 biological determinism, the belief in a biologically inherited association between physical characteristics and behavioral attributes, became a dominant theme in the European and American schools of racial classification.
      i) Charles Darwin's cousin, Francis Galton, wrote and lectured on eugenics, the theme of race improvement through selective breeding. The Eugenics movement became very popular in America throughout the 1930s, and the Eugenics movement in Germany formed the basis of Nazi ideas of racial purity.
      ii) The 1930s synthesis of natural selection with Mendelian genetics caused many physical anthropologists to apply evolutionary principals to the study of human variation.

III. **The Concept of Race**
   a) Humans are all members of the same polytypic species, Homo sapiens.
      i) Geographically localized peoples possessing particular combinations of skin color, face form, and nose form, etc. have been lumped together in racial categories.
         (1) The term "race" is not well defined. Since the 1960s, race has referred to culturally as well as biologically defined groups of people.
            (a) References to national origin in the guise of ethnicity have become increasingly popular lately, and this term is incorrectly equated with the more emotionally charged term of race.
            (b) In biological usage, race refers to geographically patterned phenotypic variation within a species. The modern emphasis is on using the tools of population genetics to discovering the adaptive significance of human phenotypic and genotypic variation.
   b) Broadly defined racial categories have little biological reality because the genetic variation within groups is vastly greater than the genetic variation between groups.
      i) Forensic anthropologists concentrate on phenotypic variables because they are called on by law enforcement agencies to identify sex, age, stature, and ancestry (racial background) from skeletal remains.
         (1) They are able to establish broad population affinities with about 80% accuracy.

ii) Other physical anthropologists argue that race is a meaningless, cultural construct that has no basis in biology.

c) It is clear that traditional racial traits have a continuous range of phenotypic variation and it is impossible to construct discrete phenotypic or genotypic boundaries around populations.

i) It is the job of the anthropologist to inform the general public of new information regarding the causes of human variation.

IV. Racism

a) Racism stems from a belief in biological determinism and rests on the false assumption that one's own group is superior to other groups.

i) These beliefs often lead to violence, warfare, and genocide.

b) In fact, the biological variation that we presently see, such as differences in face shape, and eye and skin color, are products of our evolutionary past. These traits preserve the evolutionary record of human populations that have adapted to various environmental conditions.

V. Intelligence

a) There is no evidence to suggest that there are any genetically-based between-group differences in behavioral traits.

i) Certainly both genetic and environmental factors contribute to intelligence, but intelligence is almost impossible to measure accurately.

(1) IQ scores and intelligence are not the same things, and claims that between-group differences in IQ are indicative of between-group differences in intelligence are false.

(2) Individual differences in cognitive abilities result from complex interactions between genetics and the environment, but these innate variations are apparent only at the level of the individual and not at the level of the population.

VI. Contemporary Interpretations of Human Variation

a) **Human polymorphisms**

i) Contemporary studies of human variation focus on polymorphisms, characteristics that have different phenotypic expressions (the genetic locus governing the trait has two or more alleles).

(1) Populations often differ with respect to their allele frequencies for polymorphic traits and this requires evolutionary explanations.

(2) A popular alternative to the racial approach is the study of the clinal distributions of polymorphic traits.

(a) Clinal distributions are thought to reflect the microevolutionary processes of gene flow and/or natural selection.

ii) The ABO system is of anthropological interest because its three alleles vary among human populations and their frequencies follow a clinal distribution.

(1) The A or B allele rarely reach frequencies of 50% in human populations.

(2) South American Indian populations have frequencies of O that approach 100%.

(a) High frequencies of O are also found in northern Australians.

(b) These unusually high frequencies may be the product of genetic drift.

b) **Patterns of polymorphic variation**

i) Analyzing single traits can lead to confusions regarding population relationships, so multivariate approaches have become more commonplace.

(1) Lewontin's study of the allele frequencies for 17 polymorphic traits in seven geographic human populations indicates only 6.3% of the total genetic variation is explained by differences among major populations.

(2) Nevertheless, there are interesting geographic patterns in human genetic diversity. Compared to all other areas, African populations have much more genetic diversity due to their long occupation of that continent.

c) **Polymorphisms at the DNA Level**
   i) Analyses of human mitochondrial DNA (mtDNA) indicate that humans have less within-species variability than chimpanzees. This indicates a recent origin for Homo sapiens.
   ii) Studies of nuclear DNA include the analysis of RFLPs, Alus, microsatellites, SNPs, and the Y chromosome. The hope is that these new techniques will shed further light on the origins and dispersal of modern humans, as well as the microevolution of various human groups.

VII. **Population Genetics**
   a) A population is a group of interbreeding individuals who share a common gene pool.
      i) Mate choice is conditioned by geographical, ecological, and social factors.
         (1) Breeding isolates are populations who tend to mate with individuals in their immediate vicinity.
         (2) Populations have relative amounts of endogamy and exogamy, and social, ethnic, and religious boundaries may further subdivide populations into smaller breeding units.
   b) The Hardy-Weinberg equilibrium is a hypothetical state and describes a population that is not evolving.
      i) If the observed allele frequencies differ significantly from the predicted frequencies under Hardy-Weinberg, evolution must be occurring at the locus in question.

VIII. **Evolution in Action: Modern Human populations**
   a) Mutation, gene flow, genetic drift, and natural selection cause changes in allele frequencies. Nonrandom mating acts to redistribute alleles throughout the population.
   b) **Nonrandom mating** includes assortative mating, and inbreeding.
      i) When individuals of similar phenotypes mate, it is called positive assortative mating, and when individuals of dissimilar phenotypes mate, it is called negative assortative mating.
   c) Inbreeding occurs when relatives mate more often than expected, and this tends to increase homozygosity.
      i) Incest avoidance is a feature of all living human societies.
      ii) Selective pressures may also play a part since inbreeding reduces offspring viability.
      iii) When related individuals mate, there is an increased chance of inheriting two copies of a harmful recessive allele from a relative that they share in common.

IX. **Human Biocultural Evolution**
   a) Because humans live in a cultural environment, human evolution is only understandable within this context.
   b) For example, before humans developed agriculture, they rarely lived near mosquito breeding areas.
      i) With the advent of slash-and-burn agriculture some 2,000 y.a., prime mosquito breeding areas were created near human living areas.
         (1) RFLP studies indicate the origin of the HbS mutation in Senegal to be between 1,250 to 2,100 ya.
         (2) Following WWII, DDT spraying was initiated to control mosquito populations. Both mosquito populations and the frequency of the HbS allele declined initially, but natural selection eventually resulted in DDT-resistant strains of mosquitoes. This also caused a rise in the frequency of the HbS allele.
         (3) The HbS allele is an example of a balanced polymorphism.
   c) Lactose intolerance (the reduced production of the enzyme lactase) follows a simple Mendelian pattern of inheritance.
      i) Most adult humans are lactose intolerant. However, European groups who share partial descent from Middle Eastern populations and some African groups such as the Tutsi and Fulani, have high rates of lactose tolerance.
         (1) These groups have a recent history of pastoralism. It is likely that their cultural dependence on milk products has increased the frequency of lactose tolerant individuals through natural selection.

Learning Objectives

After reading Chapter 15, the student should be able to:
1. Trace the historical views of human variation.
2. Discuss modern race concepts and distinguish them from racist beliefs.
3. Critically discuss the issues surrounding the concept of I.Q.
4. Draw on their knowledge of natural selection and other evolutionary forces to discuss the adaptive aspects of human genotypic and phenotypic variation.
5. Understand the application of population genetics to the study of human diversity.
6. Calculate allele frequencies using the Hardy-Weinberg equilibrium formula.
7. Discuss examples of evolution in modern human populations.
8. Define and discuss human biocultural evolution.

Key Terms And Concepts

Balanced polymorphism	p. 396	Hardy-Weinberg theory of genetic equilibrium	p. 391
Biological determinism	p. 380	Inbreeding	p. 395
Breeding isolates	p. 390	Lactose intolerance	p. 397
Cline	p. 385	Nonrandom mating	p. 395
Endogamy	p. 390	Polymorphisms	p. 385
Eugenics	p. 380	Polytypic	p. 381
Exogamy	p. 390	Population genetics	p. 388
Gene pool	p. 390	Slash-and-burn agriculture	p. 396

Lecture Suggestions and Enrichment Topics

1. Expand on the historical views and attitudes regarding human phenotypic variation. Trace the rise of the Eugenics movement in America and Europe and put it in the context of misapplied Darwinism. It becomes easier to understand that the Nazi emphasis on "racial hygiene" developed in part from late nineteenth century views that were popular in Europe and the United States. Also, stress that the "Aryan race" concept is a myth!
2. Show your students the video *Human Evolution and Human Equality*, a tape of a lecture by Stephen J. Gould that is based on his book *The Mismeasure of Man*. This is an excellent and provocative introduction to the history of scientific racism.

Student Media Exercises

1. In *InfoTrac* do a keyword search on "Human Population Genetics". How many citations are returned? What are some of the research questions being addressed with this type of research?
2. In *InfoTrac* search for the article <u>Mapping human history: Perspectives: human genetics</u> (Mary-Claire King and Arno G. Motulsky, *Science*, Dec 20, 2002 v298 i5602 p2342). Read the article and answer the following questions: What genetic markers have been used in this type of research. What results have been reported with regard to the degree of within and between group genetic variations?
3. Go online to the American Association of Physical Anthropology website (http://www.physanth.org) and choose the "Position statements" link. Briefly outline the main points of their position on the biological aspects of race.
4. Go online and search for "clinal variation". How many examples of the clinal distribution of genotypes and/or phenotypes can you find?

Multiple Choice Questions

1. Categorizing people on the basis of skin color
   A. is mostly a twentieth century phenomenon.
   B. has been practiced only by Western Europeans.
   C. is a valid approach to racial taxonomy.
   D. has a long history and has been practiced by many peoples.
   E. began with Christopher Columbus.

   ANS: D
   PG: 379

2. The first scientific attempt to classify humans based on biological variation was by
   A. Christopher Columbus.
   B. the ancient Egyptians.
   C. J. F. Blumenbach.
   D. C. Linnaeus
   E. none of these

   ANS: D
   PG: 380

3. Deterministic (or racist) views concerning human variation were held by
   A. Benjamin Franklin.
   B. Thomas Jefferson.
   C. Oliver Wendell Holmes.
   D. none of these
   E. all of these

   ANS: E
   PG: 380

4. The false belief that there is a relationship between physical traits and certain behavioral traits such as intelligence and morals is called
   A. eugenics.
   B. monogenism.
   C. polygenism.
   D. biological determinism.
   E. homeostasis.

   ANS: D
   PG: 380

5. The philosophy of "race improvement" through the forced sterilization of some groups and the encouraged reproduction of others is termed
   A. eugenics.
   B. genetics.
   C. monogenism.
   D. polygenism.
   E. none of these

   ANS: A
   PG: 380

6. The person responsible for popularizing eugenics among 19th century Europeans was
    A. Charles Darwin.
    B. Georges Cuvier.
    C. Charles Lyell.
    D. Francis Galton.
    E. Thomas Jefferson.

    ANS: D
    PG: 380

7. The Eugenics movement
    A. formed the basis for notions of racial purity in Nazi Germany.
    B. was popular throughout the 1930's.
    C. is a now discredited view of racial purity.
    D. all of these
    E. A and C only

    ANS: D
    PG: 380-381

8. A polytypic species
    A. is one that has no phenotypic variability.
    B. has never been observed in nature.
    C. is one composed of local populations that differ from one another with regard to the expression of NO MORE THAN three traits.
    D. is one composed of local populations that differ from one another with regard to the expression of ONE OR MORE traits.
    E. A and B

    ANS: D
    PG: 381

9. The application of evolutionary principles to the study of human variation
    A. reinforced traditional views of races as fixed biological entities that do not change.
    B. allowed scientists to ignore the adaptive significance of most traits.
    C. allowed scientists to divide the human species precisely into well-defined races.
    D. helped replace earlier views based solely on observed phenotypes..
    E. has been of little value for understanding human variation.

    ANS: D
    PG: 381

10. The modern biological usage of the term race
    A. has precise definitions agreed upon all anthropologists.
    B. refers to the geographically patterned phenotypic variation within a species.
    C. refers only to skin color.
    D. refers only to I. Q.
    E. refers to a person's nationality.

    ANS: B
    PG: 381-382

11. It is scientifically valid to assign people to particular "racial" groups solely on the basis of
    A. skin color.
    B. hair color.
    C. ABO blood type.
    D. all of these
    E. none of these

    ANS: E
    PG: 381

12. The characteristics that have traditionally been used to define races
    A. are the product of Mendelian inheritance.
    B. are affected by environmental/genetic interactions.
    C. do not vary within groups.
    D. are polygenic.
    E. B and D only

    ANS: E
    PG: 381-382

13. Intelligence
    A. is determined solely by genetic factors.
    B. is determined solely by environmental factors.
    C. can be accurately measured by IQ tests.
    D. is a Mendelian trait.
    E. is the result of both genetic and environmental factors.

    ANS: E
    PG: 384

14. IQ
    A. and intelligence are the same thing.
    B. is inherited in a Mendelian fashion (low IQ is a recessive trait).
    C. is useful for making racial distinctions.
    D. varies between groups only.
    E. none of these

    ANS: E
    PG: 384

15. The existence of clines
    A. illustrates that allele frequencies do NOT vary with geography.
    B. illustrates that some allele frequencies DO vary with geography.
    C. demonstrates that natural selection does not alter allele frequencies.
    D. has never been convincingly demonstrated for any allele.
    E. A and D only

    ANS: B
    PG: 386

16. Which of the following is a polymorphic trait in most human populations?
    A. ABO blood type
    B. DNA microsatellites
    C. SNP's
    D. B and C only
    E. all of these

    ANS: E
    PG: 386-389

17. The frequency of the O allele is almost 100 percent in _____.
    A. Northern Europeans
    B. Chinese
    C. Eurasians
    D. African blacks
    E. South American Indians

    ANS: E
    PG: 386

18. The frequencies of the A, B and O alleles
    A. are the same in all populations.
    B. vary between populations.
    C. are definitely NOT affected by natural selection.
    D. have never been measured for different populations.
    E. are definitely NOT affected by genetic drift.

    ANS: B
    PG: 386

19. The existence of clines
    A. illustrates that allele frequencies do NOT vary with geography.
    B. illustrates that some allele frequencies DO vary with geography.
    C. demonstrates that natural selection does not alter allele frequencies.
    D. has never been convincingly demonstrated for any allele.
    E. A and D only

    ANS: B
    PG: 385

20. Which of the ABO alleles has the highest frequency worldwide?
    A. A
    B. B
    C. O
    D. They are all equally frequent.

    ANS: C
    PG: 385

21. Which is NOT a red blood cell antigen system?
   A. MN
   B. HLA
   C. Rh
   D. ABO
   E. none of these

   ANS: B
   PG: 385-386

22. The _____ system is involved in the immune response.
   A. Xg
   B. Rh
   C. MN
   D. ABO
   E. HLA

   ANS: E
   PG: 386-387

23. Current evidence suggests that certain HLA antigens appear to function to
   A. resist malaria.
   B. cause sickle-cell anemia.
   C. cause malaria.
   D. cause HIV.
   E. none of these

   ANS: A
   PG: 387

24. According to the population geneticist, R.D. Lewontin,
   A. human races have specific genetic markers.
   B. about 94 percent of human genetic variation is found WITHIN major population groups.
   C. geographical and local races account for about 85 percent of human variation.
   D. geographical and local races account for about 15 percent of human variation.
   E. A and B only

   ANS: D
   PG: 387-388

25. The areas in the DNA that contain repeated segments are
   A. termed microsatellites.
   B. termed SNP's.
   C. the basis for DNA fingerprinting.
   D. A and C only
   E. none of these

   ANS: D
   PG: 388

26. Factors that influence mate choice are
    A. geographical.
    B. ecological.
    C. social.
    D. A and C only
    E. all of these

    ANS: E
    PG: 390

27. The gene pool concept
    A. refers to the total complement of genes shared by non-reproductive members of a population.
    B. is no longer used by modern anthropologists.
    C. refers to the total complement of genes shared by reproductive members of a population.
    D. refers to the total complement of mutations shared by reproductive members of a population.
    E. refers to any type of genetic mutation.

    ANS: C
    PG: 390

28. Endogamy refers to
    A. mating outside of a group.
    B. marrying, but not mating inside of a group.
    C. advantageous traits that evolve in a population over time.
    D. **dis**advantageous traits that evolve in a population over time.
    E. none of these

    ANS: E
    PG: 390

29. A group of interbreeding individuals that shares a common gene pool is a
    A. group of species.
    B. population.
    C. polytypic species
    D. race.
    E. clinal distribution.

    ANS: B
    PG: 390

30. Population geneticists use the Hardy-Weinberg equilibrium equation to determine
    A. whether evolution is occurring at all loci throughout the genome simultaneously.
    B. whether evolution is occurring at a given locus.
    C. the mode of inheritance of Mendelian traits.
    D. whether a particular trait is polygenic.
    E. B and C only

    ANS: B
    PG: 391

31. The Hardy-Weinberg genetic equilibrium formula assumes that
    A. the population under study is infinitely large.
    B. there is constant mutation of alleles in the population under study.
    C. the population under study is very small.
    D. B and C only
    E. A and B only

    ANS: A
    PG: 391

32. If the observed allele frequencies in a population differ significantly from those predicted by the Hardy-Weinberg equilibrium theory, then
    A. the population is in genetic equilibrium.
    B. evolution is not occurring.
    C. mutations have stopped occurring.
    D. the population is a breeding isolate.
    E. evolution is occurring.

    ANS: E
    PG: 391

33. Which of the following statements explains why a population must be infinitely large in order to be in genetic equilibrium?
    A. There are no mutations in large populations.
    B. Small populations have higher rates of mutation than do large populations.
    C. Natural selection cannot act on large populations.
    D. Mating must be random in large populations.
    E. Large populations are less likely to have chance changes in allele frequencies.

    ANS: E
    PG: 391

34. If mating is random, then
    A. mate choice is based on social factors such as religion or level of education.
    B. mate choice is biased.
    C. mating is promiscuous.
    D. any female has an equal chance of mating with any male.
    E. mating must be monogamous.

    ANS: D
    PG: 391

35. Under idealized Hardy-Weinberg conditions, which of the following statements is FALSE?
    A. No new alleles will be added to a population's gene pool.
    B. No alleles will be removed from a population's gene pool.
    C. There will be no change in allele frequencies in a population over time.
    D. There are no molecular changes in the gametes.
    E. Mutation rates will increase with each generation.

    ANS: E
    PG: 391

36. The ratio of one allele to all the other alleles at a given locus in a population is the definition of
    A. the allele frequency.
    B. a polymorphism.
    C. genetic drift.
    D. the mutation rate.
    E. none of these

    ANS: A
    PG: 391-392

37. In the Hardy-Weinberg genetic equilibrium formula, p is the
    A. frequency of the recessive allele.
    B. mutation rate.
    C. frequency of heterozygotes.
    D. frequency of the dominant allele.
    E. none of these

    ANS: D
    PG: 392

38. Using the Hardy-Weinberg equilibrium formula, if $p = .25$, then q must equal _____.
    A. 0.50
    B. 0.25
    C. 0.35
    D. 0.60
    E. 0.75

    ANS: E
    PG: 391-393

39. According to the Hardy-Weinberg genetic equilibrium formula, if the frequency of q is .4, then the frequency of heterozygotes in the population should be
    A. 1.0
    B. 0.36
    C. 0.16
    D. 0.48
    E. none of these

    ANS: D
    PG: 393-394

40. According to the Hardy-Weinberg genetic equilibrium formula, if the frequency of q is .4, then the frequency of homozygous recessives in the population should be _____.
    A. 16
    B. 0.24
    C. 0.48
    D. 1.6
    E. none of these

    ANS: E
    PG: 393-394

41. According to the Hardy-Weinberg genetic equilibrium formula, if the frequency of q is .4, then the frequency of homozygous dominants in the population should be _____ .
    A. 0.16
    B. 0.24
    C. 0.36
    D. 1.6
    E. none of these

    ANS: C
    PG: 393-394

42. What can cause allele frequencies to change in populations?
    A. Genetic drift
    B. Gene flow
    C. Natural selection
    D. all of these
    E. A and B only

    ANS: D
    PG: 394

43. A balanced polymorphism discussed in the text is
    A. lactose intolerance.
    B. the A, B, and O alleles.
    C. the HbS allele.
    D. malaria.
    E. C and D only

    ANS: C
    PG: 395

44. Lactose intolerance
    A. results from the lack of lactase.
    B. has a genetic basis.
    C. is a good example of biocultural evolution.
    D. can be influenced by the environment.
    E. all of these.

    ANS: E
    PG: 397

45. _____ is an/are example/examples of biocultural evolution.
    A. The relationship between malaria, agricultural practices, and the sickle-cell allele
    B. The relationship between lactase deficiency and cultural practices
    C. Variations in head shape
    D. The worldwide distribution of ABO allele frequencies
    E. A and B only

    ANS: E
    PG: 396-397

True/False Questions

1. Anders Retzius was the first European scientist to classify humans into races.

   ANS: False
   PG: 379-380

2. Francis Galton, Darwin's cousin, originated the eugenics approach to "race improvement".

   ANS: True
   PG: 380

3. The term race currently has only biological connotations and is without any social significance.

   ANS: False
   PG: 381

4. The term ethnicity was originally proposed in order to avoid the emotional baggage associated with the term race.

   ANS: True
   PG: 381

5. Forensic anthropologists must deal with the race concept because they are asked by law enforcement agencies to identify an individual's race from skeletal remains.

   ANS: True
   PG: 382

6. Breeding isolates are groups that are clearly separated geographically and/or socially from other breeding groups.

   ANS: True
   PG: 390

7. If the expected frequencies of genotypes calculated from the Hardy-Weinberg equilibrium formula do NOT differ significantly from those measured in the population being studied, then evolution is clearly occurring.

   ANS: False
   PG: 392-393

8. Inbreeding is a form of random mating.

   ANS: False
   PG: 394

9. The risk of genetic defects among the offspring of first-cousin marriages is no higher than that of the general population.

    ANS: False
    PG: 394

10. A genetic trait is considered a polymorphism if the locus governing that trait has two or more alleles.

    ANS: True
    PG: 385-386

Short Answer Questions

1. Define the terms dolichocephalic and brachycephalic.
   (p. 379-380)

2. What does it mean when one states that humans are members of the same polytypic species?
   (pp. 380-381)

3. Contrast the concept of race as it is currently employed with racism.
   (pp. 381-382)

4. What polymorphisms exist at the DNA level?
   (pp. 388-389)

5. How are the concepts of population, gene pool, and breeding isolates related to each other?
   (p. 390)

6. Write the equation for the Hardy-Weinberg theory of genetic equilibrium and list four of the five assumptions that must be met in an idealized population at equilibrium.
   (pp. 390-394)

7. If the frequency of the recessive allele in a population is 0.3, what is the frequency of the dominant allele? Now, use the Hardy-Weinberg formula to calculate the expected genotypic frequencies.
   (pp. 392-394)

8. The frequency of the recessive allele in a population is 0.4 and the observed genotypic frequencies are 0.75 for the homozygous dominants, 0.15 for the heterozygotes, and 0.1 for homozygous recessives. Is this population evolving? Show your work.
   (pp. 392-394)

9. What is the physiological mechanism of lactose intolerance? Why is the ability to digest milk sugars an example of biocultural evolution?
   (pp. 396-397)

Essay Questions

1. Define the term race. How does the modern use of race differ from the 19th Century use of race?

2. Why is the study of clines so important to our understanding of human variation?

3. What have population geneticists discovered about human polymorphisms of the DNA?

4. Use your knowledge of genetics to explain why inbreeding tends to increase homozygosity.

CHAPTER 16: MODERN HUMAN BIOLOGY: PATTERNS OF ADAPTATION

Chapter Outline

I. **Introduction**
    a) Modern human populations live in a variety of climates. They are adapted to varying degrees of UV radiation, different altitudes, different temperature extremes, and different infectious diseases.

II. **The Adaptive Significance of Human Variation**
    a) Adaptation refers to long-term evolutionary (genetic) change that occurs in all individuals in a population.
      i) Examples in humans are physiological responses to heat and heavily pigmented skin in tropical regions.
    b) Acclimatization is a physiological response to a change in environmental conditions.
      i) Examples of acclimatization include tanning in response to exposure to ultraviolet radiation, and increased hemoglobin production on exposure to hypoxia.
      ii) Developmental acclimatization results from exposure to a changing environment during growth.
    c) The relationship between **solar radiation and skin color** is an example of adaptation and natural selection.
      i) Skin color in native populations follows a particular geographic pattern: the darkest skin is found in populations living in the tropics, and lighter skin tones are found in more northern latitudes.
        (1) Skin color is primarily influenced by the pigment melanin, which is produced in the epidermis by melanocytes. Although all humans possess about the same number of melanocytes, human populations differ with respect to the amount and size of the melanin granules produced by the melanocytes.
          (a) Because melanin absorbs ultraviolet (UV) radiation, it provides protection against the damaging effects of ultraviolet radiation such as skin cancer.
          (b) Natural selection has favored dark skin near the equator because of the high levels of UV radiation there.
          (c) An additional benefit of darkly pigmented skin is that it prevents degradation of folate, an important B vitamin, by UV radiation.
      ii) Heavily pigmented skin would have been adaptive to early hominids living in Africa, but as hominids migrated out of Africa the environmental factors changed. Hominids living in northern Eurasia encountered lower levels of UV radiation and the selective pressure for heavily pigmented skin was relaxed.
        (1) The need for vitamin D production in the skin (through the interaction of UV radiation and a cholesterol-like compound in skin cells) to protect individuals from the deleterious effects of rickets was probably the most significant selective force for depigmentation.
        (2) The above is referred to as the *vitamin D hypothesis*.
      iii) **The thermal environment** that *Homo sapiens* populations face ranges from very hot (above 120°F) to very cold (below -60°F).
        (1) **Responses to heat** are more effective than our physiological responses to cold, indicating our tropical ancestry.
          (a) All human populations are effective at dissipating heat through sweating, since all humans have about 1.6 million sweat glands, resulting in the ability to sweat up to 3 liters of water per hour while engaged in heavy work in high heat.
          (b) Vasodilation, the widening of the capillaries near the surface of the skin to permit increased blood flow, is another mechanism for radiating body heat.

(2) Human populations vary in body size and proportions in general accordance with Bergmann's and Allen's rules, both of which describe the relationship between mass-to-surface ratios and heat retention and loss.

    (a) The optimal body shape in hot climates is linear with long arms and legs, whereas the most suitable body type for cold climates is stocky with shorter limbs.

(3) **Responses to cold** include heat retention and heat production.

    (a) Increased metabolic rate, shivering, and vasoconstriction to shunt blood to the body core are all short-term responses to cold.

        (i) Populations exposed to chronic cold maintain higher metabolic rates than populations not exposed to chronic cold.

    (b) Long-term responses to cold include prolonged vasoconstriction when there is no threat of frostbite, and intermittent vasoconstriction and vasodilation when frostbite is a threat.

d) **High altitude** populations (those that live at altitudes of 10,000 feet or more) are subjected to multiple stressors, including hypoxia, more intense solar radiation, cold, low humidity, wind, and a reduced nutritional base.

   i) Responses to hypoxia include increased respiration rate, heart rate, and production of red blood cells.

   ii) High altitude natives exhibit developmental acclimatization in the form of slowed growth and maturation, a larger chest size, a larger heart, and more efficient oxygen diffusion to the tissues of the body.

    (1) There is some evidence that Tibetans and Quechuans have genetically adapted to high altitudes.

III. **Infectious Disease**

   a) Infectious diseases have exerted selective pressure on human populations, influencing the frequency of alleles involved in the functioning of the immune system.

   b) Cultural factors have played an important role in the spread of diseases, because up until 10 to 12 k.y.a., all humans lived in small nomadic hunting and gathering groups. As humans came to live in large settled communities, their living conditions increasingly favored the transmission of diseases.

   i) Malaria with its relationship to the HbS allele, AIDS with its possible relationship to the allele that blocks an important receptor site on T4 and other immune cells, and smallpox with its relationship to higher rates of infection in blood type A and AB individuals, are all examples of the selective role of infectious diseases in human populations.

IV. **The Continuing Impact of Infectious Disease**

   a) Infectious diseaseas a selective force in contemporary human populations cannot be denied.

   i) HIV is the best-documented case of evolution and adaptation of a pathogen.

    (1) HIV-2, a HIV variant found in human populations in West Africa, is similar to the form of SIV found in the sooty mangabey. It is likely that HIV-2 evolved from SIV, and since sooty mangabeys are hunted for meat and kept for pets, it is likely that SIV was transmitted to humans from monkeys.

    (2) Another HIV variant, HIV-1, almost certainly evolved from a strain of SIV found in *Pan troglodytes troglodytes*, although it is not known when the transmission of SIV to humans actually occurred.

   ii) The past few years has seen the reemergence of many bacterial diseases such as influenza, pneumonia, tuberculosis, and cholera. These diseases are resistant to antibiotics because the indiscriminant use of antibiotics has selected for antibiotic-resistant strains of bacterial diseases.

    (1) Other nonbacterial diseases have reemerged due to the evolved resistance to drugs and pesticides intended to kill disease vectors. Additionally, humans are more mobile and some populations are living in more crowded and unsanitary conditions due to population growth.

Learning Objectives

After reading Chapter 16, the student should be able to:

1. Outline the hypotheses concerning the adaptive advantages of skin color relating them to levels of UV radiation and the incidence of rickets.
2. Discuss human responses to heat, cold, and high altitude. Include the application of Bergmann's and Allen's rules to population-level variations in human body size and proportions.
3. Discuss the possible interactions between natural selection and human infectious diseases.

Key Terms and Concepts

Acclimatization	p. 404	Spina bifida	p. 406
Antibodies	p. 414	Stress	p. 403
Endemic	p. 413	Vasoconstriction	p. 411
Evaporative cooling	p. 409	Vasodilation	p. 411
Homeostasis	p. 403	Vectors	p. 413
Neural tube	p. 406	Zoonotic	p. 413
Pathogens	p. 414		

Lecture Suggestions and Enrichment Topics

1. Further explore the role of infectious disease in human evolution. In addition to hemoglobin polymorphisms (sickle cell, thalassemia, and G6PD deficiency), it has been suggested that malaria was a selective agent on the MHC locus. In this context, it is also useful to discuss the relationship between the ABO blood types and certain infectious diseases. For example, people with blood type A appear to have increased susceptibility to smallpox, while those with type O may be susceptibility to bubonic plague. These examples illustrate how allele frequencies at the ABO locus can shift through the actions of natural selection.

2. Scientists have considered the possibility that HIV-2, the less virulent form of HIV found in West Africa, evolved from a form of SIV (simian immunodeficiency virus) found in sooty mangabeys (SIVsm). Recently published research demonstrates that HIV-1, the form responsible for most AIDS cases, almost certainly evolved from a type of SIV (SIVcpz) that occurs in West African populations of chimpanzees (Pan troglodytes troglodytes). Researchers postulate that transmission from chimpanzees to humans occurred at least three different times, probably while human hunters butchered carcasses of chimpanzees killed for food. This evidence provides the opportunity to discuss the evolutionary history of the HIV virus. Point to the fact that chimpanzees apparently suffer few, if any, ill effects from SIVcpz infection. This illustrates that it is beneficial for pathogens to be sufficiently benign so as not to kill their hosts immediately, since less lethal pathogens are able to infect more hosts and increase their own reproductive success.

Student Media Exercises

1. Have students go to the Map Exercises sub-section of the Cultural Anthropology section of the Wadsworth Anthropology Resource Center and complete the *Aids Epidemic* map quiz.
2. In *InfoTrac* do a keyword search on "SARS" (Severe Acute Respiratory Syndrome). What are the symptoms for SARS? Where do health experts believe SARS originated? Are there currently any effective treatments for SARS?
3. In *InfoTrac* search for the article Vitamins B6, B12 and folate. Nutrition & Dietetics (The Journal of the Dieticians Association of Australia, March 2003 v60 i1 p51). Take this quiz and learn more about folate.
4. Go online to http://news.nationalgeographic.com/news/2004/02/0224_040225_evolution.html and read about high altitude adaptations.
5. Go online and do a search for "Bergmann's rule". Does this ecogeographic rule apply to nonhuman species of mammals?

Multiple Choice Questions

1. Adaptation
   A. is seen only in nonhuman animals.
   B. is the same as acclimatization.
   C. is always temporary.
   D. is a genetic adjustment to environmental conditions.
   E. B and D only

   ANS: D
   PG: 403

2. Biological systems are balanced systems maintained by the interaction of physiological mechanisms that compensate for both external and internal changes. Such a balanced system is in
   A. hypoxia.
   B. homeostasis.
   C. heterostasis.
   D. acclimatization.
   E. polystasis.

   ANS: B
   PG: 403

3. Acclimatization refers to
   A. long-term adaptations of species to certain environmental conditions.
   B. an individual's short-term physiological responses to the environment.
   C. the appearance of a new species.
   D. slow genetic changes in populations.
   E. none of these

   ANS: B
   PG: 404

4. Which of the following contributes most to skin color?
   A. Hemoglobin
   B. Melanin
   C. Carotene
   D. Vitamin D
   E. none of these

   ANS: B
   PG: 405

5. Which of following absorbs ultraviolet radiation?
   A. Carotene
   B. Hemoglobin
   C. Vitamin D
   D. Melanin
   E. Melanocytes

   ANS: D
   PG: 404-405

6. Melanocytes
    A. are cells that produce carotene.
    B. cause skin cancer.
    C. only occur in dark-skinned individuals.
    D. absorb ultraviolet radiation.
    E. produce melanin.

    ANS: E
    PG: 405

7. Ultraviolet radiation can be an important factor in selection for increased melanin production
   because UV radiation can cause
    A. rickets.
    B. albinism.
    C. skin cancer.
    D. the destruction of folate.
    E. C and D only

    ANS: E
    PG: 406-407

8. A temporary increase in melanin production in response to exposure to ultraviolet radiation is
    A. called tanning.
    B. an acclimatization response.
    C. impossible for albinos.
    D. all of these
    E. A and B only

    ANS: D
    PG: 405

9. Dark skin is advantageous in the tropics because it
    A. protects from frostbite.
    B. protects from overexposure to ultraviolet radiation.
    C. helps prevent rickets.
    D. promotes vitamin D synthesis.
    E. increases the skin's exposure to ultraviolet radiation.

    ANS: B
    PG: 405

10. Rickets is caused by
    A. overexposure to ultraviolet radiation.
    B. too much vitamin D.
    C. an insufficient amount of melanin.
    D. too few melanocytes.
    E. insufficient amount of vitamin D.

    ANS: E
    PG: 406-407

11. Studies have shown that UV radiation rapidly depletes _____, which plays a crucial role in neural tube development of the embryo.
    A. melanin
    B. melanocytes
    C. carotene
    D. folate
    E. A and B only

    ANS: D
    PG: 405-407

12. The folate hypothesis
    A. contradicts the importance of the relationship between UV radiation and skin cancer.
    B. purports to explain why dark skin is advantageous in high UV environments.
    C. CANNOT explain why dark skin is advantageous in high UV environments.
    D. explains why dark-skinned individuals often have rickets.
    E. A and C only

    ANS: B
    PG: 404-407

13. The vitamin D hypothesis
    A. helps explain why dark skinned populations are found near the equator.
    B. has never been challenged.
    C. cannot explain why light skin may be adaptive in low UV environments.
    D. remains the primary hypothesis explaining why skin color lightened as populations moved out of Africa.
    E. A and B only

    ANS: D
    PG: 407

14. Sweating
    A. is a uniquely human ability.
    B. has no detrimental effects.
    C. is NOT an effective means of dissipating heat.
    D. permits cooling through evaporation.
    E. is an ability that varies from one human population to another.

    ANS: D
    PG: 408-409

15. Mechanisms for radiating body heat include
    A. increased production of red blood cells.
    B. vasodilation.
    C. vasoconstriction.
    D. increased activity levels.
    E. increased metabolic rate.

    ANS: B
    PG: 408-409

16. Vasodilation
    A. facilitates heat loss at the skin's surface.
    B. can be caused by exposure to heat and some drugs including alcohol.
    C. is the widening or opening up of capillaries which, in turn, increases blood flow to the skin.
    D. all of these
    E. A and C only

    ANS: D
    PG: 408-411

17. Bergmann's rule
    A. states that a linear body with long arms and legs is optimal for cold climates.
    B. concerns the relationship between climate and shape and size of appendages.
    C. states that bodies with increased mass or volume to surface area are optimal for cold climates.
    D. is based upon the principle that as arms increase in length, there is a corresponding increase in surface area.
    E. is based on the principle that heat is retained at the body surface.

    ANS: C
    PG: 410

18. Physiological methods of either producing or retaining body heat include
    A. shivering.
    B. an increased metabolic rate.
    C. vasoconstriction.
    D. all of these
    E. A and C only

    ANS: D
    PG: 410

19. Hypoxia
    A. is the reduced availability of oxygen.
    B. occurs at higher altitudes because the atmosphere contains less oxygen than at sea level.
    C. exerts no stress on humans.
    D. is a problem for people living at sea level.
    E. none of these

    ANS: A
    PG: 411

20. Stresses imposed by living at high altitude include
    A. reduced availability of oxygen.
    B. increased exposure to cold and wind.
    C. a reduced nutritional base.
    D. all of these
    E. A and B only

    ANS: D
    PG: 411-412

21. Which is true of populations living at high altitudes compared to those living at sea level?
    A. Low birth weights are more frequent at high altitudes.
    B. Low birth weights are more frequent at low altitudes.
    C. People produce fewer red blood cells at high altitudes.
    D. Growth and maturation occur more rapidly at high altitudes.
    E. Chest and lung size are reduced at higher altitudes.

    ANS: A
    PG: 411-412

22. Infectious diseases
    A. affect only children and infants.
    B. are associated with aging.
    C. are always fatal.
    D. have had no evolutionary effects on humans.
    E. are caused by microorganisms such as viruses and bacteria.

    ANS: E
    PG: 413

23. Fleas and mosquitoes sometimes transmit disease pathogens such as bacteria and viruses from one
    individual to another. Such agents (fleas and mosquitoes) are called
    A. pathogens.
    B. vectors.
    C. pandemics.
    D. endemics.
    E. none of these.

    ANS: B
    PG: 413

24. When a disease is continuously present in a population it is said to be
    A. pandemic.
    B. chronic.
    C. epidemic.
    D. lethal.
    E. endemic.

    ANS: E
    PG: 413

25. HIV attacks
    A. all cells in the body.
    B. liver cells.
    C. red blood cells.
    D. T4 cells.
    E. T6 cells.

    ANS: D
    PG: 413-414

26. Which of the following provides the best-documented example of the evolutionary role of infectious disease in humans?
    A. Bubonic plague
    B. Malaria
    C. Tuberculosis
    D. Smallpox
    E. Influenza

    ANS: B
    PG: 414

27. AIDS is caused by
    A. mosquito bites.
    B. a bacterium.
    C. a mutation on a cell's receptor site.
    D. a virus.
    E. all of these

    ANS: D
    PG: 414

28. Recent evidence suggests that
    A. HIV is closely related to SIV.
    B. HIV was initially transmitted to humans from primates with a similar disease.
    C. HIV has two main forms, HIV-1 and HIV-2.
    D. SIV has a long evolutionary history in monkeys.
    E. all of these

    ANS: E
    PG: 413-415

29. The most mutable and genetically variable virus known is
    A. tuberculosis.
    B. cholera.
    C. AIDS.
    D. malaria.
    E. HIV.

    ANS: E
    PG: 415

30. HIV-2 is
    A. the most common form of HIV.
    B. is the form of HIV found in chimpanzees..
    C. found only in the United States.
    D. found only in human populations in West Africa.
    E. A and C only

    ANS: D
    PG: 415

31. The emergence over the past few years of diseases, such as pneumonia, tuberculosis, and cholera is due to the
    A. fact that these diseases are viral in origin.
    B. indiscriminant use of antibiotics.
    C. action of natural selection.
    D. B and C only
    E. all of these

    ANS: D
    PG: 415-417

32. The World Heath Organization lists _____ as the world's leading killer of adults.
    A. car crashes
    B. reality show stunts
    C. tuberculosis
    D. cholera
    E. AIDS

    ANS: C
    PG: 417

33. Recent outbreaks of cholera in South America, India, and elsewhere, have been attributed, in part, to
    A. rising ocean temperatures.
    B. lack of sanitation.
    C. reduced population sizes.
    D. A and B only
    E. all of these

    ANS: D
    PG: 418

34. The increased prevalence and reemergence of some infectious diseases
    A. is due, in part, to the overuse of antibiotics.
    B. is due, in part, to the reduction in human population sizes.
    C. is due, in part, to the disturbance of the environment by humans.
    D. A and C only
    E. all of these

    ANS: D
    PG: 417-418

True/False Questions

1. Adaptations refer to short-term physiological responses to stress.

   ANS: False
   PG: 403

2. Developmental acclimatization occurs in high-altitude natives during growth and development.

   ANS: True
   PG: 404

3. The most interesting fact about human skin color is that there appears to be no adaptive significance whatsoever to population-level variations in skin color.

   ANS: False
   PG: 404-405

4. Of the three types of skin cells found in the epidermis, only melanocytes are susceptible to cancerous changes.

   ANS: False
   PG: 405-406

5. BCCs and SCCs tend to appear in middle age long after underlying genetic damage that occurred during childhood and adolescence.

   ANS: True
   PG: 408-409

6. Bergmann's rule concerns the shape of the body, especially the appendages.

   ANS: False
   PG: 410

7. Hypoxia results from reduced barometric pressure.

   ANS: True
   PG: 411-413

8. In Colorado, infant deaths are about twice as common above 8,200 feet as at lower elevations.

   ANS: True
   PG: 412

9. The oldest evidence of human infection by HIV is an HIV-positive blood sample taken from a West African patient in 1959.

   ANS: True
   PG: 416

10. Thanks to the modern medicine, many infectious diseases such as tuberculosis and cholera are no longer a threat to human populations.

    ANS: False
    PG: 417

Short Answer Questions

1. Define homeostasis.
   (p. 403)

2. What are the three types of acclimatization responses described in your text?
   (p. 404)

3. What are neural tube defects and how might they affect reproductive fitness?
   (p. 405)

4. What is the physiological role of vitamin D? What are the dietary and non-dietary sources of Vitamin D?
   (p. 406)

5. What are the various physiological mechanisms for reducing heat stress?
   (pp. 408-409)

6. Define vasoconstriction and describe its role in the human physiological response to cold.
   (p. 410)

7. Discuss two physiological challenges faced by populations that live at high altitudes.
   (pp. 411-413)

8. What is the nature of the evidence suggesting that HIV was initially transmitted to humans from nonhuman primates?
   (pp. 415-418)

9. What does the term *zoonotic disease* mean?
   (p. 413)

10. Your text indicates that HIV provides the best-documented example of evolution and adaptation of a pathogen. Why is this so?
    (pp. 415-418)

Essay Questions

1. What is the adaptive value of dark skin tones in equatorial regions such as Africa? If all humans are ultimately from Africa, what hypothesis has been offered to explain why skin tones lightened as humans came to occupy more northern latitudes?

2. Outline the general principles of Bergmann's and Allen's rules. Can we use these rules to explain human phenotypic variation at the level of the population? Support your answer with examples.

3. How did the adoption of a settled lifestyle affect patterns of infectious disease in human populations?

4. Discuss three factors that are contributing to the reemergence of infectious diseases that used to be close to extinction.

CHAPTER 17: LEGACIES OF HUMAN EVOLUTIONARY HISTORY

Chapter Outline

I. **Introduction**
   a) Human biology is the result of millions of years of evolution.
      i) Human beings are unique because we are the product of biocultural evolution.
   b) Humans are a generalized species; we can live in a variety of climates, have a varied diet, and respond to the environment both behaviorally and physically.
   c) The legacies of human evolution impact the individual, society, and the planet.

II. **Evolution of Behavior and the Life Course**
   a) Behavioral ecology examines human social behavior in an evolutionary framework.
      i) Humans (like other animals) behave in ways that increase their fitness.
         (1) Reproductive efforts are viewed as a series of trade-offs in time, energy, and resources invested in mating and parenting.
         (2) This paradigm argues that males seek to increase their reproductive success by maximizing the number of mates they have, whereas females maximize their reproductive success by maintaining the health of their offspring. This means that a female attempts to find a mate that will supply resources to her and her children.
   b) Evolutionary psychology is the study of how humans and other primates think. They examine topics such as mate attraction, sexuality, aggression, and violence.
      i) Wrangham and Peterson use the evolutionary psychology paradigm to investigate male aggression and violence by contrasting male-male interactions in chimpanzee society with more peaceful, female-dominated bonobo society.
         (1) Apparently, aggression and interpersonal violence are part of our evolutionary heritage shared with these hominoids, although there are clearly cultural and social variables that affect human behavior.
   c) Optimal foraging strategy (a behavioral ecology approach) is used to predict the hunting strategies of human foraging societies.
      i) The optimal foraging model predicts that hunters should pursue a strategy that maximizes their return by minimizing the time and energy invested in hunting prey.

III. **Biocultural Evolution and the Life Cycle**
   a) Modern human beings are the result of biocultural evolution.
      i) An examination of the human life course (how humans develop from embryos to adults) allows us to explore the interaction of biology and culture.
         (1) Some genetically based traits, such as albinism, will be expressed in the same way regardless of the environmental context.
         (2) Other traits are influenced by environmental/genetic interactions. Some examples include intelligence, body shape, and growth.
   b) Anthropologists use life history theory to answer questions about nonhuman primate and human growth and development.
      i) The premise of life history theory is that an organism has a limited amount of energy for investment in its life course. There is a continual tradeoff in energy investment among life history traits, and natural selection shapes these tradeoffs.
   c) Not all animals have the same number of phases during their lives, nor do all animals have clearly demarcated phases.
      i) Most primates have four distinct phases: gestation, infancy, juvenile, and adult.
      ii) Monkeys, apes, and humans have added the subadult phase, and only humans have a postreproductive phase for females that follows menopause.
         (1) Humans are unique among primates in that our life cycle stages are marked by both biological and culturally determined social changes.

d) **Growth in gestation, infancy and childhood**
   i) Humans have a relatively large brain, a trait shared to some degree by other primates.
      (1) Human babies have an undeveloped brain at birth (it's about 25% of its adult size), making them more helpless than most monkey infants.
         (a) The human pattern of brain growth is unusual; the brain doubles in size by 6 months after birth (making it 50% of adult size), it reaches 75% of adult size by age 2½, and 90% by age 5.

e) **Nutritional effects on growth and development**
   i) The nutrients needed for proper growth and development include proteins, carbohydrates, lipids, vitamins, and minerals.
      (1) The fact that we require certain amino acids in our diet reflects our ancestral diet, which was high in animal proteins.
         (a) The preagricultural diet was high in animal protein, complex carbohydrates, and calcium, and low in fats and salt.
         (b) Modern diets tend to have the opposite composition.
      (2) Our evolved capacity to store fats due to high variance in its abundance has become a detriment in societies where fatty foods are abundant.
         (a) Type II diabetes is clearly linked to dietary and lifestyle behaviors that de-emphasize physical activity and emphasize the consumption of fats and refined carbohydrates.

f) **Onset of reproductive functioning in humans**
   i) Researchers note that there is a trend towards a lowered age of first menstruation (menarche) in many societies.
      (1) This trend may be explained, in part, by environmental variables such as the accumulation of body fat at earlier ages than in previous generations.
         (a) Early sexual maturation should be favored by natural selection, and this biological heritage may account for the fact that many cultures are experiencing high rates of adolescent pregnancies.
   ii) The behavioral ecology approach has been used to help us understand why some parenting behaviors that at first glance seem to decrease reproductive success, continue to occur.
      (1) Mothers may actually abandon their children when economic and social circumstances conspire to decrease the likelihood that the child will survive. Thus, it is better (in an evolutionary sense) to let the child die so that the mother can try again to reproduce.
   iii) Menopause may also be understood when the behavioral ecology approach is applied.
      (1) Throughout most of human evolution, females did not survive past age 50, the approximate onset of menopause. Now, females survive well past menopause to lead healthy lives.
         (a) It has been suggested that human females are biologically "programmed" to live 10 to 15 years past the age when they can have their last child, thus ensuring the child's survival, and the female's last chance at reproductive success.
         (b) The "grandmother hypothesis" asserts that natural selection favors menopause because postmenopausal women can provide high-quality care for their grandchildren.
         (c) Alternately, menopause may be an artificial byproduct of the extension of the human life span.

g) **Human longevity**
   i) Humans have a relatively long lifespan. One explanation for why we age is that genes that enhance reproduction in early years have detrimental effects later in life. Genes with multiple effects are called pleiotropic genes.
      (1) Others have pointed to the effects of free radicals (molecules that damage cells) on senescence.

(2) The telomere hypothesis argues that as cells continually divide, their telomeres (the DNA sequence at the end of each chromosome) become progressively shorter, somehow negatively impacting the longevity of the cell.

(3) The rate at which we age is also affected by lifestyle factors such as smoking, physical activity, diet, and the quality of medical care.

(4) Also, women universally have higher life expectancies than men.

h) **Evolutionary medicine**

    i) An evolutionary view can help us to understand contemporary health challenges.

        (1) We must realize that pathogens can evolve resistance to drugs.

           (a) One evolutionary approach to this problem is to "domesticate" pathogens.

        (2) Evolutionary medicine helps to distinguish traits that may have evolved because they enhance reproductive success.

           (a) Tay-Sachs is one such example, and another is cystic fibrosis.

    ii) The sequencing of the chimpanzee and human genomes confirms how genetically similar we are to each other.

        (1) There are also minute differences which may help to explain why humans, but not chimpanzees, are susceptible to certain diseases such as cholera, malaria, and influenza.

IV. **Human Impact on the Planet and Other Life-Forms**

a) The most urgent challenge facing humanity is the overpopulation of the world.

    i) Currently human population increases at an annual rate of 1.8% worldwide.

        (1) 10 kya, only about 5 million people inhabited the Earth. There were about 500 million by the year 1650.

        (2) Given the past history of population growth, it appears that we add about 1 billion people to the world's population every 11 years.

        (3) Given that about half of all people living in the developing world are less than 15 years old, it is unlikely that populations will cease to grow in the near future.

           (a) It is unlikely that world resources can keep up with the current rate of population expansion.

b) **Impact on Biodiversity**

    i) Humans have the ability to alter global ecology and to destroy us and all other life forms on the planet (with the probable exception of the cockroach [this author's comment]).

           (a) There have been at least 15 mass extinctions in the past 570 my caused by natural events.

           (b) Since the onset of the late Pleistocene or early Holocene, recent and ongoing extinctions are or have been caused by *Homo sapiens*.

               (i) Overhunting by humans has been implicated in the extinctions of many large mammals that occurred near the end of the Pleistocene.

                  1. Humans certainly were responsible for the more recent extinction of the moa, numerous species of lemurs, and many bird and mammal species.

           (c) Humans are responsible for the reduction of the habitats of elephants, pandas, rhinos, tigers, and gorillas.

               (i) Humans destroy about one football field-sized area of rainforest every second, seriously contributing to the loss of biodiversity. Biodiversity is central to the ecology of this planet, and many potentially beneficial compounds may never be discovered if biodiversity continues to decline.

c) **Acceleration of Evolutionary Processes**

    i) Human-invented antibiotics are one example of how humans have accelerated the evolutionary process in other organisms.

        (1) HIV-AIDS, dengue hemorrhagic fever, Legionnaire's disease, Lyme disease, and drug-resistant strains of bacteria are all examples of the impact of human behavior on the evolution of infectious diseases.

           (a) The overuse of DDT has now rendered it virtually useless in fighting mosquito-borne malaria.

V. Is There Any Good News?
- i) The rate of growth of human populations has slowed somewhat.
    - (1) Decreases in family sizes may result in improvements in the environment.
- ii) International efforts to preserve primate populations have increased.
- iii) Developing and developed countries are beginning to discuss new ways of reducing global poverty.

VI. Are We Still Evolving?
- a) Yes, but we cannot answer the question of whether we will become a different species in the future; since extinction is the ultimate fate of almost every other species on the Earth, it is likely we will go extinct at some point in the future.
    - i) Culture has enabled us to transcend most of our biological limitations.
        - (1) Yet, since humans are constantly exposed to new environments and new diseases, and children continue to die due to limited medical care and malnutrition, gene frequencies continue to change.

Learning Objectives

After reading Chapter 17, the student should be able to:
1. Discuss the insights of behavioral ecology into human behavior patterns and the evolution of human life cycle stages.
2. Discuss the nutritional effects on growth and development.
3. Describe the life cycle stages of humans, with special attention to the postreproductive phase. Also discuss the hypotheses concerning human senescence.
4. Discuss the field of evolutionary medicine.
5. Discuss the future of the Earth and the human species in light of the threat of overpopulation.
6. Answer the question "Are we still evolving?"

Key Terms and Concepts

Holocene	p. 439
Menarche	p. 427
Menopause	p. 427
Pleiotropic genes	p. 436
Senescence	p. 434

Lecture Suggestions and Enrichment Topics

1. Have the students keep a 3-day food intake diary and see how their diets compare with the pre-agricultural diet and with the typical contemporary diet. There are several computer programs available for analyzing nutrient intake. Searching the Internet for "diet analysis software" will return several websites from which this software can be obtained.
2. Recent research suggests that women who postpone reproduction until their 30s or 40s run a significant risk of having children with physical or mental disabilities, or of not being able to have children at all, due to the degeneration of the female's eggs. Discuss how social evolution in industrialized societies has favored women joining the work force and delaying pregnancy.
3. The number of children born to families in industrialized societies is decreasing, while the number of children born to families in developing nations continues to increase. If this trend continues, a small aging population will control the vast majority of the world's resources. Discuss how this will contribute to problems in developing nations.

Student Media Exercises

1. Have students go to the Map Exercises sub-section of the Cultural Anthropology section of the Wadsworth Anthropology Resource Center and complete the *Global Population and Life Expectancy* map quiz.
2. Have students go to the Map Exercises sub-section of the Cultural Anthropology section of the Wadsworth Anthropology Resource Center and complete the *Global Water Supply* map quiz.
3. Have students go to the Map Exercises sub-section of the Cultural Anthropology section of the Wadsworth Anthropology Resource Center and complete the *Global Environment* map quiz.
4. In *InfoTrac* do keyword search on "global warming" and read through the titles of the articles. What are some of the likely economic and environmental crises that global warming could cause?
5. In *InfoTrac* search for the article <u>Famine: is there a lesson in Africa?</u> (Janet Raloff, *Science News*, Feb 23, 1985 v127 p118). Contrast the responses by Africa and China to the problems related to population growth.
6. Go online to the U.S. Environmental Protection Agency website for an overview of the global warming problem (http://epa.gov/climatechange/index.html).

Multiple Choice Questions

1. The behavioral ecology approach
    A. stresses that humans behave in ways that increase their fitness.
    B. argues that reproductive efforts do NOT require trade-offs in time, energy, and resources.
    C. stresses that evolutionary processes do NOT have an impact on human behavior.
    D. B and C only
    E. none of these

    ANS: A
    PG: 423-424

2. Human forager groups are examined in the context of optimal foraging strategy in order to
    A. determine the optimal number of offspring they should have.
    B. determine the optimal number of wives men should have.
    C. analyze their hunting practices.
    D. determine the causes of interpersonal violence.
    E. A and B only

    ANS: C
    PG: 425

3. Life history theory
    A. seeks to answer why humans have long periods of infancy and childhood.
    B. does NOT have an evolutionary perspective.
    C. seeks to understand the impact of natural selection on life cycles.
    D. all of these
    E. A and C only

    ANS: E
    PG: 427

4. Which of the following life cycle stages may be unique for humans?
    F. Gestation
    G. Adolescence or juvenile
    H. Childhood
    I. Post-reproductive
    J. Infancy

    ANS: D
    PG: 427

4. The subadult life cycle phase is present in
    A. all mammals.
    B. all primates.
    C. humans only.
    D. monkeys, apes, and humans.
    E. none of these

    ANS: D
    PG: 427

5. For humans, approximately what percent of adult brain size is completed by the time of birth?
    A. 10%
    B. 25%
    C. 50%
    D. 75%
    E. 100%

    ANS: B
    PG: 428

6. The language centers of the human brain
    A. are fully developed at birth.
    B. develop during the first 3 years of life.
    C. develop throughout the individual's life.
    D. finish their development at puberty.
    E. develop after the 5th year of life.

    ANS: B
    PG: 428-429

7. Chimpanzees, gorillas, and women in foraging societies nurse their infants for approximately how many years?
    A. ½
    B. 1
    C. 2
    D. 4
    E. 6

    ANS: D
    PG: 429

8. The human preagricultural diet was
   A. high in fats and low in carbohydrates.
   B. high in fats and animal proteins.
   C. low in fats and high in animal proteins.
   D. low in complex carbohydrates and calcium.
   E. A and D only

   ANS: C
   PG: 429-430

9. The disorder that is clearly linked to dietary and lifestyle behaviors, such as decreased activity levels and increased consumption of fats and refined carbohydrates is
   A. HIV.
   B. SIV.
   C. malaria.
   D. small pox.
   E. diabetes.

   ANS: E
   PG: 430-431

10. A female's first menstruation is known as
    A. menopause.
    B. menarche.
    C. andropause.
    D. andrenarche.
    E. cyclopause.

    ANS: B
    PG: 427

11. The age of onset of menarche is determined by
    A. genetic patterns.
    B. nutrition.
    C. stress.
    D. disease.
    E. all of these

    ANS: E
    PG: 433

12. Paleodemographic studies indicate a mortality rate of at least _____ in subadults in preindustrial populations.
    A. 0%
    B. 10%
    C. 50%
    D. 75%
    E. 100%

    ANS: C
    PG: 433

13. Primates such as monkeys, apes, and humans typically give birth to _____ infant at a time.
    A. 1
    B. 2
    C. 3
    D. 4
    E. none of these

    ANS: A
    PG: 434

14. The birth interval in humans can be reduced by
    A. increased nutrition of the infant.
    B. reduced calorie intake of the mother.
    C. not nursing the infant.
    D. early weaning.
    E. C and D only

    ANS: E
    PG: 434

15. If the number of offspring reaching reproductive maturity is lower in individuals and families with 2-year birth intervals than those with 4-year birth intervals, then natural selection will favor individuals with
    A. 1-year birth intervals.
    B. 2-year birth intervals.
    C. no children.
    D. 4-year birth intervals.
    E. 5-year birth intervals.

    ANS: D
    PG: 434

16. Instances in which mothers abandon their newborn infant
    A. cannot be explained with an evolutionary perspective.
    B. have not been well-documented in any mammals.
    C. are thought to occur when the mother will increase her reproductive success by abandoning the infant.
    D. only occur when the infant is sick.
    E. A and D only

    ANS: C
    PG: 434

17. The period following the last menstrual cycle in human women is known as
    A. menarche.
    B. menopause.
    C. adrenarche.
    D. egg-pause.
    E. cyclopause.

    ANS: B
    PG: 435

18. Evidence suggests that the average life span for preagricultural humans was about _____ years.
    A. 12
    B. 15
    C. 35
    D. 45
    E. 65

    ANS: E
    PG: 435

19. A long period of female postreproductive time is found in
    A. chimpanzees.
    B. gorillas.
    C. all monkeys.
    D. A and B only
    E. none of these

    ANS: E
    PG: 435

20. The "grandmother hypothesis" proposes to explain
    A. the age of onset of menopause.
    B. the age of puberty for males.
    C. the age of onset of menarche.
    D. the existence of menopause.
    E. A and D only

    ANS: D
    PG: 435

21. _____ genes have multiple effects at different times in the life span or under different conditions.
    A. Ontogenetic
    B. Telomere
    C. Pleiotropic
    D. Hidden
    E. Dominant

    ANS: C
    PG: 436

22. One hypothesis that proposes to explain senescence notes that cells that divide throughout the life course have shortened DNA sequences at the end of the chromosomes. This is referred to as the _____ hypothesis.
    A. hadromere
    B. carsonomere
    C. telomere
    D. intron
    E. none of these

    ANS: C
    PG: 435

23. The gene for telemerase
    A. codes for an enzyme that can lengthen telomeres.
    B. can make cells young again.
    C. has been called the "immortalizing gene."
    D. A and B only
    E. all of these

    ANS: E
    PG: 436

24. Before the AIDS epidemic in Africa, Zimbabweans had a life expectancy of 65 years. Now it is about _____ years.
    A. 15
    B. 39
    C. 60
    D. 75
    E. 85

    ANS: B
    PG: 436-437

25. The one single challenge facing humanity, to which all other problems can be tied, is
    A. overpopulation.
    B. the lowered age of menarche.
    C. loss of biodiversity.
    D. the decrease in the maximum life span of humans.
    E. double-cheeseburgers.

    ANS: A
    PG: 438

26. Scientists estimate that around 10,000 years ago the Earth's population was about _____ people.
    A. 2
    B. 200,000
    C. 5 million
    D. 5 billion
    E. 25 million

    ANS: C
    PG: 438

27. Humans have profound effects on the Earth's ecology, including the
    A. extinction of numerous mammalian species.
    B. extinction of the dinosaurs.
    C. loss of biodiversity.
    D. A and C only
    E. all of these

    ANS: D
    PG: 439

28. Habitat reduction on the Earth is the direct result of
    A. the need for building materials.
    B. the need for agricultural land.
    C. the increase in human populations.
    D. all of these
    E. none of these

    ANS: D
    PG: 439-440

29. Reasons for maintaining the Earth's biodiversity include
    A. the need for research into potentially useful rainforest products.
    B. the maintenance of all species that fill various econiches.
    C. the ethical dilemma of destroying species that are the product of millions of years of evolution.
    D. A and B only
    E. all of these

    ANS: E
    PG: 440

30. One impact of human activities has been
    A. the acceleration of the evolutionary process for several life forms.
    B. the deceleration of the evolutionary process for several life-forms.
    C. to increase the biodiversity on the Earth.
    D. to increase of available habitat for numerous species such as the mountain gorilla.
    E. none of these

    ANS: A
    PG: 440

31. Human technology and lifestyle are responsible for the deadly nature of some diseases, such as
    A. HIV-AIDS.
    B. Lyme disease.
    C. Legionnaire's disease.
    D. resistant strains of tuberculosis.
    E. all of these

    ANS: E
    PG: 440-441

32. The overuse of DDT, after it was first developed, resulted in DDT resistant strains of
    A. bald-eagles.
    B. *Staphylococcus.*
    C. mosquitoes.
    D. tuberculosis.
    E. *E. coli.*

    ANS: C
    PG: 441

33. Whether we will become a different species in the future
   A. is not a question we can easily answer.
   B. is not a question that anthropologists have considered.
   C. is certain; we will all have big heads, big eyes, and four fingers on each hand.
   D. depends on the future course of evolution.
   E. A and D only

   ANS: E
   PG: 443

True/False Questions

1. In the United States, the primary determinant of health and nutrition is economic status.

   ANS: True
   PG: 426-427

2. The prenatal life cycle phase begins with conception and ends at weaning.

   ANS: False
   PG: 427-428

3. Only humans have a large brain relative to their body size.

   ANS: False
   PG: 428

4. Nutrition has an effect ONLY on the prenatal period of the human life cycle.

   ANS: False
   PG: 429

5. The contemporary diet typical of industrialized societies is basically unchanged from preagricultural diets.

   ANS: False
   PG: 429-431

6. Our ability to store fat was adaptive in the past but is maladaptive in industrialized societies.

   ANS: True
   PG: 430

7. Both nutritional deficiencies and excesses can cause health problems and interfere with childhood growth.

   ANS: True
   PG: 431

8. Lifestyle factors, such as smoking, physical activity, and diet are far more important than the effects of genes on the aging process.

   ANS: True
   PG: 436

9. Throughout the world, men have higher life expectancies than women.

    ANS: False
    PG: 436

10. Recently, there have been several international agreements designed to preserve endangered species and their habitats.

    ANS: True
    PG: 442

Short Answer/Essay Questions

1. What are the effects of biocultural evolution on the individual?
    (pp. 426-427)

2. List and briefly define the life cycle stages of humans and monkeys and apes.
    (pp. 427-428)

3. What is the importance of delayed brain growth in humans?
    (pp. 428-429)

4. What percentage of human adult brain growth is accomplished by birth, 6 months of age, 2½ years of age, 5 years of age, and 10 years of age?
    (p. 428)

5. Compare the hypothesized preagricultural diet with that consumed by most Americans today.
    (pp. 429-432)

6. Why do all humans have the capacity to efficiently store fat? What effects does this have on human health in light of high fat and refined carbohydrate diets and low activity lifestyles?
    (pp. 429-432)

7. Define senescence and discuss the hypotheses that attempt to explain it.
    (pp. 429-432)

Essay Questions

1. What is the behavioral ecology approach? How can this approach help us to understand why mothers may behave in ways that run counter to claims that there is a natural "instinct" for motherly love?

2. Why do human females have such a long period of time during which they can no longer reproduce?

3. Discuss the nature of the dangers posed from human overpopulation of the planet.

4. Are humans still evolving? Defend your answer.

Appendix A

Video, Film, and Slide Resources

APPENDIX: VIDEO, FILM, AND SLIDE RESOURCES

The following list of distributors of audiovisual materials is not complete. Unfortunately, there is no single clearinghouse for film/video information. Pennsylvania State University and the University of California-Berkeley are probably the best sources for locating audiovisual materials. Most of the suppliers listed below offer free catalogs on request.

You may contact the supplier included in the video descriptions only to learn they no longer carry that item. Distribution rights can change quickly. If this occurs, you should contact Penn State University, as they will probably know who currently offers the title you need.

Inquiries regarding the Nature series should be directed to WNET (see below). Inquiries regarding NOVA should go to WGBH-Boston for Films for the Humanities & Sciences (see below).

Be sure to give yourself plenty of time if you decide you want to rent one of the films.

Films for Anthropological Teaching, 8th Edition, 1995, AAA Special Publication No. 29, is available from the American Anthropological Association, 4305 North Fairfax Drive, Suite 640, Arlington, VA 22203-1620 ($19.95 for AAA members, $24.95 for others; shipping included). It lists over 3000 film and video entries in all fields of anthropology and provides brief descriptions or review comments for most.

I. Distributors

Ambrose Video Publishing
145 West 45th Street, Suite 1115
New York, NY 10036
      Tel: (800) 526-4663
      Fax: (212) 768-9282
      e-mail: ambrosevid@aol.com
      www.ambrosevideo.com/

Annenberg/CPB Collection
409 9th St., NW
Washington, DC 20004
      Tel: (800) LEA-RNER
      Fax: (802) 864-9846
      e-mail: info@learner.org
      www.learner.org

Carolina Biological Supply Co.
2700 York Rd.
Burlington, NC 27215
      Tel: (800) 334-5551 or
               (910) 584-0381
      Fax: (910) 584-3399
      e-mail: carolina@carolina.com
      http://carolina.com

Britannica Films
310 S. Michigan Ave.
Chicago, IL 60604
      Tel: (800) 554-9862 or
               (312) 347-7900
      Fax: (312) 347-7966

Bullfrog Films, Inc.
P.O. Box 149
Oley, PA 19547
      Tel: (800) 543-3764 or
               (610) 779-8226
      Fax: (610) 370-1978
      e-mail: bullfrog@igc.org
      http://bullfrogfilms.com

Documentary Educational Resources
101 Morse St.
Watertown, MA 02472
      Tel: (800) 569-6621 or
               (617) 926-0491
      Fax: (617) 926-9519
      e-mail: docued@der.org
      http://der.org

Center for Humanities, Inc.
Box 1000
Mount Kisco, NY 10549
        Tel: (800) 431-1242 or
                 (914) 666-4100
        Fax: (914) 666-5319
        e-mail: gavideoi@aol.com

Chip Taylor Communications
15 Spollet Dr.
Derry, NH 03038
        Tel: (800) 876-2447 or
                 (603) 434-9262
        Fax: (603) 432-2723
        e-mail:
chip.taylor@chiptaylor.com
        www.chiptaylor.com

Columbia TriStar Home Video
SONY Pictures Plaza
10202 W. Washington Blvd.
Culver City, CA 90232
        Tel: (310) 280-5418
        Fax: (310) 280-2485
        www.spe.sony.com

Coronet/MTI Film and Videos
(Phoenix Learning Group)
2349 Chaffee Dr.
St. Louis, MO 63146
        Tel: (800) 221-1274
        www.phoenixlearninggroup.com

Insight Media
2162 Broadway
New York, NY 10024-0621
        Tel: (800) 233-9910 or
                 (212) 721-6316
        Fax: (212) 799-5309
        E-mail: cs@insight-media.com
        www.insight-media.com

Educational Video Network
1336 19th St.
Huntsville, TX 77340
        Tel: (800) 762-0060 or
                 (409) 295-5767
        Fax: (409) 294-0233
        www.edvidnet.net/users/comments.php
        www.edvidnet.net

Films for the Humanities & Sciences
P.O. Box 2053
Princeton, NJ 08543-2053
        Tel: (800) 257-5126 or
                 (609) 275-1400
        Fax: (609) 275-3767
        e-mail: custserv@films.com

        www.films.com

Handel Film Corporation
8730 Sunset Blvd.
Los Angeles, CA 90069
        Tel: (800) 395-8990 or
                 (310) 652-3887
        Fax: (310) 657-2746

Home Vision Cinema
4423 N. Ravenswood Ave.
Chicago, IL 60640-1199
        Tel: (800) 826-3456 or
                 (773) 878-2600
        Fax: (773) 878-8406
        www.homevision.com

Knowledge Unlimited, Inc.
Box 52
Madison, WI 53701-0052
        Tel: (800) 356-2303 or
                 (608) 836-6660
        Fax: (608) 831-1570
        e-mail: csis@newscurrents.com
        www.thekustore.com/

Instructional Technology Center
Iowa State University
1200 Communications Bldg.
Ames, IA 50011
      Tel: (800) 447-0060
      (online catalog & online ordering –
      please confirm online order by
      calling their toll-free number)

Instructional Video
2219 C. St.
Lincoln, NE 68502
      Tel: (800) 228-0164 or
             (402) 475-6570
      Fax: (402) 475-6500
      e-mail:
      www.insvideo.com/contactus.asp
      www.insvideo.com

ISS Media Resources
Indiana University
Franklin Hall 0009
601 E. Kirkwood
Bloomington, IN 47405-1223
      Tel: (800) 552-8620 or
             (812) 855-8765
      Fax: (812) 855-8404
      e-mail: issmedia@indiana.edu
      www.indiana.edu/~mediares/rental.
      html

Journal Films, Inc.
1560 Sherman Ave., Suite 100
Evanston, IL 60201
      Tel: (800) 323-9084
      Fax: (708) 328-6706

New Dimensions Media, Inc.
611 E. State
Jacksonville, IL 62650
      Tel: (800) 288-4456
      Fax: (800) 242-2288
      e-mail: info@ndmquestar.com
      www.ndmccc.com/index.jsp

Lucerne Media
37 Ground Pine Rd.
Morris Plains, NJ 07950
      Tel: (800) 341-2293 or
             (973) 538-1401
      Fax: (973) 538-0855
      e-mail: lm@lucernemedia.com
      www.lucernemedia.com

MTI Film and Video
14216 SW 136th St.
Miami, FL 33186
      Tel: (305) 255-8684
      Fax: (305) 233-6943
      e-mail: mti@mtivideo.com
      www.mtivideo.com

National Gallery of Art
Department of Education Resources
4th and Constitution Ave., NW
Washington, DC 20565
Tel: (202) 842-6273
e-mail: mail@nga.gov
www.nga.gov/education/education.htm

National Geographic Society
c/o Educational Services
P.O. Box 98019
Washington, DC 20090
      Tel: (800) 627-5162 or
             (202) 857-7378
      Fax: (202) 857-7300
      e-mail: info@nationalgeographic.com
      www.nationalgeographic.com/foundation

University of California Extension
Center for Media and Independent Learning
2000 Center St., 4th Fl.
Berkeley, CA 94704
      Tel: (510) 642-1340
      Fax: (510) 643-9271
      e-mail: cmil@uclink.berkeley.edu
      http://ucmedia1.ucxonline.berkeley.edu

PBS Home Video
Catalog Fulfillment Center
P.O. Box 751089
Charlotte, NC 28275-1089
        Tel: (800) 531-4727 or
                (800) 645-4PBS
        e-mail: info@pbs.org
        www.pbs.org

PBS Videofinders/KCET Videofinders
425 E. Colorado Street, Suite B10
Glendale, CA 91205
        Tel: (800) 343-4727
                (818) 637-5291

The Pennsylvania State University
Media Tech Support Services
Special Services Bldg.
1127 Fox Hill Rd.
State College, PA 16803-1824
        Tel: (800) 826-0132
        www.libraries.PSU.edu/mtss/

Primate Info Net
Wisconsin Reg. Primate Research Center
1220 Capitol Court
Madison, WI 53715-1299
        Tel: (608) 263-3512
        Fax: (608) 263-4031
        Audiovisual Archive
        www.primate.wisc.edu/pin/av.html
        general:
http://primate.wisc.edu/pin/

Time-Life Video and Television
1450 E. Parham Rd.
Richmond, VA 23280
        Tel: (800) 621-7026 or
                (804) 266-6330
        www.timelife.com

Wards Natural Science Establishment, Inc.
P.O. Box 92912
5100 W. Henrietta Rd.
Rochester, NY 14692
        Tel: (800) 962-2660
        www.wardsci.com

WGBH Boston Video
P.O. Box 2284
S. Burlington, VT 05407
        Tel: (888) 255-9231
        www.wgbh.org/shop/

WNET
P.O. Box 2284
S. Burlington, VT 05407
        Tel: (800) 336-1917
        Fax: (802) 864-9846
        www.wnet.org
        (they have several *Nature* episodes)

Teacher's Video Company
P.O. Box 4455
Scottsdale, AZ 85261
Tel:(800) 262-8837
www.teachersvideo.com

The Discovery Channel
Tel:(800) 889-9950
http://shopping.discovery.com

II. Audiovisuals by Topic

GENETICS

- *Cracking the Code of Life* A NOVA series featuring the Human Genome Project. *Teacher's Video Company* (2001) 120 min.

- *Chromosomes and Genes* A non-threatening look at the transmission of Mendelian traits for those who have difficulty conceptualizing the subject. *Teacher's Video Company* (2000) 43 min.

- *Decoding the Book of Life* This BBC/WGBH production for NOVA portrays the goals of the Human Genome Project. *Films for the Humanities & Sciences* (Item No. 3999) (1989) 58 min.

- *Dissected World of Biology* An award-winning educational video that introduces the cell and its organelles. It includes information on chromosomes. *Teacher's Video Company* (1996) 135 min.

- *DNA* A History Channel production about DNA structure and function. *Teacher's Video Company* (1996) 50 min.

- *Genetics* Examines various aspects of the Human Genome Project including ethical issues. *Films for the Humanities & Sciences* (Item No. 3046) (1993) 30 min.

- *The Human Genome* Covers advances in genetics since the 1950s and explores some of the ethical dilemmas surrounding identification of individuals who carry deleterious genes. *Films for the Humanities & Sciences* (1990) 26 min.

- *Mendelian Genetics* This introductory video demonstrates concepts of classical genetics, focusing on dominance, segregation, and independent assortment. It shows how Mendel studied the principles of inheritance and illustrates how Punnett squares are used to predict both the genotype and phenotype of the offspring of a genetic cross. *Insight Media* (1991) 28 min.

- *Twin Stories* A lighthearted look at human twins. *Teacher's Video Company* (1997) 46 min.

- *Understanding Genetics: The Molecular Basis of Inheritance* This video chronicles Mendel's experiments and then details the relationships among DNA, genes, and chromosomes. *Insight Media* (1995) 35 min.

- *Who Are You?* Part of the *Secret of Life* series written and narrated by David Suzuki and produced by WGBH Boston and the BBC. This episode focuses on the role of genetic and environmental factors in behavior. *Films for the Humanities & Sciences* (to purchase) (1993) 58 min.

EVOLUTION

- *The Blind Watchmaker: The Evolutionary Ideas of Richard Dawkins* A BBC production that features Richard Dawkins and creationists debating each other. The evolutionists win. *Films for the Humanities & Sciences* (1987) 49 min.

- *Evolution* A Discovery Channel production of the scientific basis of Darwinian evolution. This is a 7-part series on 7 videotapes. *The Discovery Channel* (2001) 8 hrs.

- *Evolution I: Natural Selection* Concepts of population, gene pool, and fitness are introduced. The role of natural selection in altering allele frequencies is examined. *Carolina Biological Supply* 31 min.

- *Evolution II: Sources of Variety* Recombination and mutation are presented as sources of genetic variation in populations. *Carolina Biological Supply* 32 min.

- *Evolution III: Speciation* Presents the concept of species and the process of speciation. Examines isolating mechanisms and adaptive radiation and looks at racial variation in humans. *Carolina Biological Supply* 46 min.

- *Evolution: What About God?* The publisher's description: Of all the species on earth, only humans try to explain who they are and how they came to be, through the prisms of both science and religion. Today, the theory of evolution is dogged by this tension. What About God? explores the controversy by drawing on real human stories of people struggling to find a balance between religion and science. Through their perceptions, the film underscores the point that these realms are compatible, although they play very different roles in assigning order to the universe and a purpose to life. *WGBH* (2001) 60 min.

- *Gene Frequencies, Natural Selection, and Speciation* This video explores how genetic drift, gene flow, mutation, and random mating alter the gene pool. It visits the Burgess Shale and features paleontologist Desmond Collins' discussion of natural selection and speciation. *Insight Media* (1997) 29 min.

- *The Hardy-Weinberg Principle* The underlying concepts of population genetics are presented in this video. *Insight Media* (1997) 29 min.

- *I+I: A Natural History of Sexuality* An examination of the evolution of sexual reproduction. *Films for the Humanities & Sciences* (2000) 53 min.

- *Sociobiology: The Human Animal* Produced for *NOVA*, this documentary considers the pros and cons of sociobiological theory. Discussion by E. O. Wilson and Richard Lewontin. *Penn State* (rental) (1977) 54 min.

MODERN HUMANS: DIVERSITY AND ADAPTATION

- *The Aging Process* Discusses the physical process of aging and examines various physiological systems as they age. *Films for the Humanities & Sciences* (Item No. 3142) (1986) 26 min.

- *Antibiotics* A History Channel production that traces the history of antibiotic use and warns of the dangers of the overuse of antibiotics. *Teacher's Video Company* (1996) 50 min.

- *Ebola* A NOVA episode that details the 1995 Ebola outbreak in Zaire. *Teacher's Video Company* (1996) 60 min.

- *Evolution and Human Equality* Dr. Stephen Jay Gould uses evidence from paleontology, genetics, evolutionary biology, social history, and the history of science to discuss human differences and human equality. A historical perspective of variation is presented. Gould explains that misconceptions about human diversity have been used by scientists and others to justify prejudice, exploitation, and persecution. *Indiana University* (rental only) (1987) 43 min; also available for purchase from *Insight Media*.

- *Hot and Cold* (part of *The Living Body* series) Demonstrates the physiological mechanisms that the body uses to maintain a constant internal body temperature while being exposed to heat and cold. *Films for the Humanities & Sciences* (Item No. 837) (1986) 26 min.

- *Human Nutrition* An educational video about human nutrition and health issues. *Teacher's Video Company* (1998) 120 min.

- *The Miracle of Life* An Emmy Award winning NOVA episode tracing the development of the human fetus. *Teacher's Video Company* (1986) 60 min.

- *Outbreaks: New Plagues* This A&E video traces scientists as they travel to plague "hot spots". *Teacher's Video Company* (1996) 50 min.

- *Understanding Race* A Discovery Channel production that examines the history of the race concept and current ideas about human variation. *Films for the Humanities & Sciences* 52 min.

PRIMATES

- *Among the Wild Chimpanzees* Depicts chimpanzee behavior as explored by Jane Goodall at Gombe National Park, Tanzania. Contains some footage from the earlier 1966 *National Geographic* film *Miss Goodall and the Wild Chimpanzees*. It also discusses the violent conflicts that occurred in the early 1970s and the infanticidal female, Passion. A very good film with excellent photography. *National Geographic* (1984) 60 min. (Note: Specify catalog number 51297)

- *The Ape: So Human* This video includes sequences of the Gardners and Sue Savage Rumbaugh working with apes. The parallels of ape and human behavior and cognition are examined. *Films for the Humanities & Sciences* (1998) 41 min.

- *Baboon Tales* This documentary-style video focuses on Shirley Strum's research work on a troop of olive baboons. *Insight Media* (1998) 52 min.

- *Behavior of the Macaques of Japan: Macaca fuscata of the Takasakiyama and Koshima Colonies* Includes communication, mother-infant relationships, territorial behavior, and potato washing. *Penn State* (1969) (Rental) 28 min.

- *Can Chimps Talk?* A recent *NOVA* episode. Very good, up-to-date treatment of the great ape language studies. Much of the focus is on the recent work with bonobos by Sue Savage-Rumbaugh and Duane Rumbaugh, but early footage of the Washoe study is included. The ongoing work with Washoe by Roger and Debbi Fouts is also shown. *WGBH* (1993) 55 min.

- *Chimpanzees Today* This video addresses the decline of chimpanzee populations and reviews Jane Goodall's research at Gombe. Insight Media (2001) 36 min.

- *First Signs of Washoe* Produced by *WGBH* for *NOVA*, this review of language studies involving nonhuman primates includes the early work of Allen and Beatrice Gardner, Duane Rumbaugh and Roger Fouts. *Penn State* (rental only). (1974) 54 min.

- *Five Species* This video compares three monkey species (the vervet, the blue monkey, and the black and white colobus) and two ape species (the common chimpanzee and the eastern lowland gorilla) living in their natural habitats in Africa. Filmed by a primatologist, the footage reveals behavior and social interactions. *Insight Media* (1997) 53 min.

- *Gelada* Shows social behavior and organization in free-ranging geladas in the Ethiopian highlands. *Penn State* (1974) (Rental and purchase) 18 min.

- *Gorillas* Excellent footage of mountain gorillas filmed in the Parc des Volcans of Rwanda. Discussion includes endangered status of the mountain gorilla. Part of the *Nature* series. *WNET* (c. 1987) 60 min.

- *Gorilla* Depicts the work of Dian Fossey with mountain gorillas, the large captive group of lowland gorillas at England's Howlett Park Zoo, and the work of Penny Patterson with the signing gorilla, Koko. *National Geographic* (1981) 58 min.

- *Gorilla-King of the Congo* Actually there is not much footage of lowland gorillas in this recent *Nature* episode, but what there is apparently represents the first time this subspecies has been filmed in the wild. Also shows a sequence of black and white colobus foraging on the ground. Filmed in the remote Ndoki Forest of Northern Congo. Direct inquiries to *WGBH-Boston*. (1993) 58 min.

- *Jane Goodall, My Life with the Chimpanzees* An overview of 30 years of living with and studying wild chimpanzees. *National Geographic* (1990) 60 min.

- *Keeli and Ivy: Chimps Like Us* A Discovery Channel production that examines the research of Sally Boyson as she attempts to teach two chimps at the Primate Research Center at Ohio State University to read and write. *The Discovery Channel* (2002) 50 min.

- *Life in the Trees* Episode 12 of the *Life on Earth* series. This is probably still the best introductory film to the non-human primates. Free-ranging prosimians, monkeys, and apes are all depicted and vocalizations are included. There are a few inaccuracies in David Attenborough's narration. *Time-Life* (1978) 60 min.

- *Monkey Island* Excellent footage of 7 groups of free-ranging rhesus macaques on Cayo Santiago Island. Various behaviors are shown, including aggression, submission, courtship, and mating. Discussion focuses partly on matrilineal social organization. Part of the *Nature* series. *Time-Life; WNET* (1990) 57 min.

- *Monkeys on the Edge* This excellent film depicts endangered New World monkeys and includes outstanding footage of muriquis, emphasizing locomotor patterns. Direct inquiries to *WGBH-Boston* (617) 492-2777 ext. 5300. Part of the *Nature* series. (1991) 57 min.

- *Mother Love* This classic black and white film depicts the research of Harry Harlow demonstrating how isolation reared infant macaques react to surrogate mothers. *Penn State* (1960) 26 min.

- *Mozu, the Snow Monkey* Students like this sentimental but worthwhile depiction of a provisioned group of Japanese macaques. It focuses on one female, Mozu, born with severely malformed hands. Part of the *Nature* series. *Time-Life* (1987) 57 min.

- *The Nut-Cracking Chimpanzees of Tai Forest* Depicts wild chimpanzees in the Ivory Coast's Tai Forest using stones to crack nuts. It compares the nut-cracking behavior of males and females and explores other aspects of social behavior. Filmed by Christophe Boesch and Hedwige Boesch-Achermann. *Penn State* (rental or purchase) (1991) 25 min.

- *People of the Forest* Footage shot at Gombe National Park by Baron Hugo van Lawick during the early years of Jane Goodall's research. Although the narrative contains inaccuracies and the scoring is overdone, the footage is excellent. Especially interesting are the scenes depicting the young male, Flint, after the death of his mother, Flo. *KCET Videofinders* (1992) (ca. 1.5 hours).

- *Search for the Great Apes* Depicts the early work of Dian Fossey and Birute Galdikas. *National Geographic* (1975) 59 min.

- *Spirits of the Forest* Excellent footage and descriptions of various lemur species. All animals are free-ranging. Part of the *Nature* series. *WNET* 60 min.

- *The Uncommon Chimpanzee* An examination of Bonobo society and their evolutionary relationship to humans. *Insight Media* (1993) 32 min.

- *Urban Gorilla* This video focuses on captive gorillas with an emphasis on intelligence. *National Geographic* (1992) 60 min.

PALEOANTHROPOLOGY

- *Dr. Leakey and the Dawn of Man* This film depicts the earlier discoveries of Louis and Mary Leakey at Olduvai Gorge. *National Geographic* (1966) 60 min.

- *The Fate of the Neanderthals* Harvard archaeologist Ofer Bar-Yosef discusses new hypotheses concerning the fate of Neanderthals. *Insight Media* (1997) 50 min.

- *Frozen in Time: Life in the Upper Paleolithic Age* Anthropologist Richard Rudgley discusses the Upper Paleolithic of Europe. *Films for the Humanities & Sciences* (1999) 51 min.

- *History of the Anthropoid* Friedmann Schrenk and Meave Leakey discuss early hominid evolution. *Films for the Humanities & Sciences* (no date) 46 min.

- *Homo sapiens: A look into a Distant Mirror* Modern human origins are discussed by a number of scientists from different disciplines, including Bernard Saladin D'Anglure (ethnologist), Polly Wiessner (ethnoarcheologist), and Bernard Vandermeersch (anthropologist). *Films for the Humanities & Sciences* (1999) 53 min.

- *The Human Story: Traces of Humankind's Oldest Relatives* Anthropologist Richard Rudgley discusses the origins of modern humans. Included is a discussion of the Lagar Velho skeleton. *Films for the Humanities & Sciences* (1999) 51 min.

- *The Ice World* The publisher's description: Join a tribe of primitive Europeans as they teeter on the brink of annihilation, struggling to cope with the most extreme living conditions anyone has ever faced – ever-encroaching sheets of ice that swallowed every bit of fertile land and a climate that was on average 70 degrees colder than it is today. *The Discovery Channel* 100 min.

- *In Search of Human Origins* This three part series was coproduced by *WGBH-Boston* and the *Institute of Human Origins.* Narrated by Don Johanson, the first two episodes concern the discovery of the first *Australopithecus afarensis* material and theories about early australopithecine lifestyle. The third episode concerns later hominids and the development of culture. The third episode is the most useful for college-level audiences. Episodes are available separately or as a set. *WGBH* (1993) 60 min.

- *Lucy and the First Family* An episode of the *Odyssey* series that depicts the discovery of the two famous *A. afarensis* sites, "Lucy" (AL 288-1) and the "first family" (AL 333) in Ethiopia. Discussion of the analysis and interpretation is also presented. *Iowa State* (1980) 60 min.

- *Lucy in Disguise* Documentary about the discovery of the "Lucy" skeleton (*A. afarensis*) in 1974. It presents conflicting theories (as of the late 1970s) pertaining to early hominid evolution. Much of the latter part of the film shows discussion between various scholars. *Penn State* (1981) 58 min.

- *The Making of Mankind* Very well done seven part series based on Richard Leakey's book by the same title. The series presents human evolution beginning with the Laetoli footprints up to the present. Features several scholars and differing views. Available as a set or sold separately. *Ambrose Video* (1982) each episode 55 min.

- *Mysteries of Mankind* This is a good paleoanthropology film for an introductory class. One good feature is footage of earlier research and scientists, including Raymond Dart with the Taung specimen. *National Geographic* (1988) 59 min.

- *Neanderthal's World* A (bit overdone) Discovery Channel production of the possible interactions of Neanderthals and modern humans based on the research of Chris Stringer and Paul Pettitt. Good for stimulating class discussions. *The Discovery Channel* (2000) 97 min.

- *Origins of Homo sapiens: East African Roots*   A discussion of Australopithecines and *H. rudolfensis*. *Films for the Humanities & Sciences* (no date) 47 min.

- *Out of Asia: New Theories on Evolution*   A BBC production examining the implications of very early dates for hominid fossils from Java. *Films for the Humanities & Sciences* (1997) 50 min.

- *The Real Eve* Another overdone, but nevertheless interesting, Discovery Channel production. This time, modern human origins are chronicled based on mtDNA and fossil evidence. It relies entirely on the "Out of Africa" model of modern human origins. It is good for stimulating class discussions. The downfall is that there is no discussion of the evolutionary history of premodern humans and Neandertals appear in Europe seemingly without a history of their own. *The Discovery Channel* (2002) 100 min.

- *Search for the Ultimate Survivor*   The publisher's description: More has been learned in the last 10 years about how we became human than in the previous 50 years. Through elaborate recreations and computer animation along with expedition footage, National Geographic explores fascinating new discoveries including a hobbit-size human and an ancient super hominid that help shed new light on the mysteries of our origins. *National Geographic Films* (2005) 90 min.

- *The Shanidar Neandertals*   A set of 20 slides of the Shanidar fossil material. *Pictures of Record.*

- *Walking With Cavemen* The publisher's description: Take a stroll with the most personal and captivating entry in the *Walking with...* series yet – a kaleidoscope of 3.5 million years of human evolution, presented by Golden Globe nominee Alec Baldwin. *The Discovery Channel* 100 min.

GENERAL INTEREST

- *Archaeological Dating: Retracing Time* Uses sites in the Southwestern United States to demonstrate applications of relative dating and absolute dating techniques. A good introduction and survey. *Britannica Films* (1976) 18 min.

- *Blades and Pressure Flaking* French Paleolithic archaeologist Dr. François Bordes and Don Crabtree demonstrate the fine points of creating delicate flint blades and other tools by using punches for pressure flaking. A companion to *Early Stone Tools* (see below). *University of California Extension* (1969) 21 min.

- *Bones of Contention: Native American Archaeology* This *BBC* production deals with the ongoing controversy over the thousands of Native American skeletal remains held in U.S. museum collections. Physical anthropologists, archaeologists, museum curators, and Native peoples express their viewpoints on the significance of the bones. *Films for the Humanities & Sciences* (1995) 49 min.

- *Digging Up the Past* This video includes dating techniques such as C-14 and dendrochronology, plus fossil pollen analysis. *Films for the Humanities & Sciences* (no date) 23 min.

- *Early Stone Tools* This vintage film (a companion to *Blades and Pressure Flaking*, above) remains a classic, in which Dr. François Bordes, the eminent Paleolithic archaeologist, demonstrates flint-knapping techniques to produce tools such as handaxes and Mousterian flakes. *University of California Extension* (1967) 20 min.

- *Haunted Vision* This video demonstrates the use of ground penetrating radar and facial reconstruction in body recovery and identification. *Films for the Humanities & Sciences* (1999) 26 min.

- *The Iceman* A video about the discovery and analysis of the 5,300 year-old mummy discovered in the Alps. *Films for the Humanities & Sciences* (1998) 97 min.

- *The Talking Skull: Forensic Anthropology* Dr. Michael Charney and others analyze the skeletal remains of a murder victim. *Films for the Humanities & Sciences* (1998) 26 min.

- *This Is Archaeology!* Introduces the basic techniques of modern archaeology, using a Near Eastern site as the case study. Emphasizes careful stratigraphic excavation and recordkeeping and illustrates the concept of cultural analogies from prehistoric, classical, and contemporary cultures. *Insight Media* (1995) 25 min.

III. Internet Features

Primate InfoNet
http://www.primate.wisc.edu/pin/

> This excellent site, developed and maintained by the Wisconsin Regional Primate Research Center, University of Wisconsin – Madison, provides a wide range of information and resources related to nonhuman primates. These resources include, among others, a primate meetings calendar, primate taxonomies, primate ethograms, information on endangered species, bibliographic searches, and links to other primate-related sites. There is also an extensive listing of primate films.

On Line Mendelian Inheritance in Man (OMIM)
http://www.ncbi.nlm.nih.gov/entrez/query.fcgi?db=OMIM

> Very up to date online version of the McKusick catalog of Mendelian traits in humans. Word searches provide full text information, current bibliographies and some journal abstracts. See the main menu for citation procedures. Developed by the National Center of Biotechnology Information and maintained by Johns Hopkins University.

Bio-Journals
http://www.bio.net

> Numerous biological journals and tables of contents for current and past issues.

Fossil Hominids and Evolution
http://www.talkorigins.org

> It provides overviews of fossil hominid species, usually with extensive bibliographies. It also has discussions of evolution/creationism controversies.

IV. Equipment and Supplies

Candent
1602 Matheson Blvd. E., Unit 21
Mississauga, Ontario L4W 5A8
Canada
Tel: (905) 629-7688

> Candent offers anatomical supplies and charts as well as modern human skeletal casts. You may request a catalog.

Carolina Biological Supply
2700 York Rd.
Burlington, NC 27215
Tel: (800) 334-5551
www.carolina.com

> One of the largest suppliers of biological materials, their inventory includes a wide variety of laboratory equipment including microscopes, calipers, and blood typing equipment. They also offer a few fossil hominid and modern human cranial casts.

Edmund Scientific
101 E. Gloucester Pike
Barrington, NJ 08007-1380
Tel: (800) 728-6999 (orders)
www.edsci.com

Offers a wide assortment of scientific equipment with an emphasis on optical equipment including microscopes and various magnifiers. They also have a wide variety of other kinds of supplies including dissecting kits and numeric and digital read out calipers. Catalogs available.

Forestry Suppliers, Inc.
P.O. Box 8397
Jackson, MS 39284-8397
Tel: (800) 752-8460 or
     (601) 354-3565
Fax: (800) 543-4203
e-mail: fsi@forestry-suppliers.com
www.forestry-suppliers.com

Provides an extensive inventory of forestry, educational, environmental and engineering supplies. They offer inexpensive plastic sliding calipers suitable for undergraduate student use in a laboratory setting. They also have electronic calipers with computer interface for direct data entry. Numerous geological tools, useful for archeological excavation, including Marshalltown trowels. 500 page catalog available.

France Casting
1713 Willox Ct., Unit A
Ft. Collins, CO 80524
Tel: (970) 221-4044
http://www.francecasts.com/

High quality casts of various types of osteological specimens including the Suchey-Brooks and Suchey-Sutherland age and sex determination models and a wide assortment of pathological lesions of both traumatic and disease origin. You may request a catalog.

Lithic Casting Lab
577 Troy-O'Fallon Rd.
Troy IL 62294
Tel: (618) 667-2447
e-mail: lcl@ezl.com
http://lithiccastinglab.com

High-quality replicas and plastic casts of a variety of New and Old World stone artifacts are available for classroom or display purposes, as well as slide sets and posters featuring outstanding Paleo-Indian, Hopewell, and Mississippian specimens.

National Museums of Kenya
Casting Department
P.O. Box 40658
Nairobi
Kenya
www.museums.or.ke/casting.html

Excellent quality fossil hominid casts, including WT 1700, ER 1813, ER 1470, various specimens of *A. afarensis* from Laetoli, *A. boisei*, *H. havilis*, *H. erectus*, and *H.sapiens*. Also, Miocene hominoids and Plio-pleistocene cercopithecoids. There are also casts of choppers, flakes and bifaces from Koobi Fora and Olorgesailie. There is a catalog available.

Paleo-Tech Concepts
e-mail: sales@paleo-tech.com
http://www.paleotech.com/index.cfm

Paleo-Tech Concepts manufactures and distributes instruments used in osteology, physical anthropology, bioanthropology, bioarchaeology, forensic anthropology, and the forensic sciences. These include, coordinate calipers, simometers, radiometers, osteometric boards, spreading calipers, and a variety of commercially available traditional calipers. Paleo-Tech Concepts will also design and manufacture custom osteometric instruments.

Pictures of Record
119 Kettle Creek Rd.
Weston, CT 06883
Tel: (203) 277-3387
Fax: (203) 222-9673
www.picturesofrecord.com

Sets of high-quality, annotated slides that deal with archaeological techniques, ethnoarchaeology, and many individual New and Old World archaeological sites are available. Request catalog or view it online.

Piltdown Productions
2 Fredonia Ave.
Lynchburg, VA 24503
Tel:(804) 528-3444
www.errettcallahan.com/piltdown.htm

Replicas and plastic casts of a variety of New and Old World stone artifacts for classroom or display purposes are available, as are raw materials for lithic tool experiments and flint-knapping demonstrations.

University of Pennsylvania
Casting Program
University Museum
33rd and Spruce St.
Philadelphia, PA 19140
Attn: Alan Mann or Janet Monge
Tel: (215) 898-6986
Fax: (215) 898-7462
www.sas.upenn.edu/~jmonge/

The University of Pennsylvania Casting Program provides a wide array of fossil hominid casts. They have a reputation for producing high quality materials.

Ward's Natural Sciences Establishment, Inc.
P.O. Box 92912
5100 W. Henrietta Rd.
Rochester, NY 14692
Tel: (800) 962-2660 or
   (800) 872-7289

Ward's offers an extensive inventory of biological and geological materials including osteometric and anthropometric supplies. They also offer a limited choice of fossil hominid cast material including *A. boisei*, Neanderthal, and modern *H. sapiens*. They offer two catalogs (biology and geology).

Appendix B

Wadworth's Case Study Catalog: Case Studies in Anthropology, 2007

table of contents

pages 4–5 **pages 6–17** **pages 18–20**

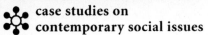

case studies on
contemporary social issues

edited by John A. Young

This series explores how anthropology is used today in understanding and addressing problems faced by human societies around the world. Each case study in this new and acclaimed series examines an issue of socially recognized importance in the historical, geographical, and cultural context of a particular region of the world, and includes comparative analysis that highlights not only the local effects of globalization, but also the global dimensions of the issue. Each author in this series writes with a highly readable narrative style as they explain, sometimes illustrating from personal experience, how their work has implications for advocacy, community action, and policy formation.

case studies in
cultural anthropology

edited by George Spindler &
Janice E. Stockard

Since its inception in 1960, the Spindler series has influenced the teaching of countless undergraduate and graduate students of anthropology. Now, Thomson Wadsworth offers you a selection of over 60 classic and contemporary ethnographies in this series, representing geographic and topical diversity. Newer case studies focus on culture change and culture continuity, reflecting the globalization of the world and treating students to first-hand accounts of the interface between formerly separate ethnic groups and their strategies for survival. Students come to more fully grasp the enormity of the changes they see in the world around them.

case studies in
archaeology

edited by Jeffrey Quilter

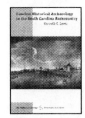

Enrich your students' study of archaeology with the many contemporary case studies in this acclaimed series! Students will read how archaeologists study human behavior through analysis of material remains. They will learn about new interpretations and developments within the field—and the importance of the archaeological perspective in understanding how the past informs our experience of the present. These engaging accounts of cutting-edge archaeological techniques, issues, and solutions—as well as studies discussing the collection of material remains—range from site-specific excavations to types of archaeology practiced.

build your own coursepack or reader using TextChoice

PROGRAM DESCRIPTION

The Anthropology and Archaeology Case Study library allows you to select content from over 75 case studies from the following best selling series:

 ### Case Studies on Contemporary Social Issues
John A. Young, Series Editor

 ### Case Studies in Cultural Anthropology
George Spindler & Janice E. Stockard, Series Editors

 ### Case Studies in Archaeology
Jeffrey Quilter, Series Editor

FEATURES

- You can combine full case studies or select chapters from case studies in any order you wish. You can also combine this content with your textbook or your own materials to create a customized book.
- You can personalize these case studies to an even greater extent; you may insert your own class notes, syllabi, and course materials.
- Upon completion your coursepack or reader is delivered in a polished format that students can reference as they continue their studies in Anthropology.

GETTING STARTED

- Go to **www.TextChoice.com** and click on "Register Now" to begin the process.
- In the "Featured Programs" dialog box a list of case studies will appear. In this section you can view entire titles and mark which selections or chapters you wish to include. As you continue to add chapters to your project you will receive a running total of selections, page count and pricing. Other features include moving your selections around and adding your own materials.
- Create a cover will allow you to create a title and imprint for the project. If you want a custom cover that is also an option for an additional cost.
- Finish the Project by submitting your order clicking on the "Save and Submit for Quote."

HOW TO ORDER

- Go to **www.TextChoice.com** to start the process
- Call Customer Service at **1-800-355-9983** with questions or contact you local Thomson sales representative.

Once you have submitted the list of selections, a Thomson Custom Representative will contact you to confirm the specifications and price of your book. Within five business days an ISBN will be forwarded to you. Please use this ISBN to place an order with your bookstore at least six weeks prior to the start of your classes to ensure on-time delivery.

PRICING INFORMATION

Pricing is as follows:
- ▶ $5.50 base price
- ▶ .08 cents per page for customization

One complete case study can be bundled for free with a Thomson core text. (this is also true for non-TextChoice versions).

All prices are subject to change. Please confirm pricing when you place your order.

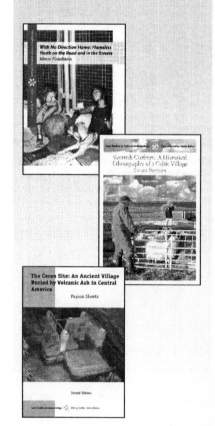

special topics also available

Globalization and Change in Fifteen Cultures: Born in One World, Living in Another

George Spindler—Stanford University
Janice E. Stockard—Mills College

304 pages | Paperbound | 6-3/8 x 9-1/4 | 1-color | ©2006 | **0-534-63648-9**

The original articles presented in this anthology reflect a world changed by globalization, and an anthropology committed to documenting the effects of the vast cultural flows of people, information, goods, and technology, now in motion the world over. Spindler and Stockard write an introduction to the topic of cultural change, and each of the fifteen anthropologists in the anthology take students on a return visit to their original field sites, asking questions for a new era and writing of peoples to some extent familiar, but at the same time changed, transformed by global forces.

SEE PAGE 16 FOR MORE INFORMATION.

Violence and Culture: A Cross-Cultural and Interdisciplinary Approach

Jack David Eller—Community College of Denver

272 pages | Paperbound | 6-3/8 x 9-1/4 | 1-color | ©2006 | **0-534-52279-3**

Violence and Culture: A Cross-Cultural and Interdisciplinary Approach brings together in a single readable volume the widest possible range of material on violence as a modern and international cultural problem. It uniquely combines comprehensive theoretical discussion with rich empirical description and analysis in a global approach. Violence, if not more prevalent, is definitely attracting more attention than ever before in academic arenas as well as the public arena. It has become a central feature of the 21st century and students and the American public are hungry to know and understand the roots of violence.

case studies on contemporary social issues

EDITED BY JOHN A. YOUNG

A Precious Liquid: Drinking Water and Culture in the Valley of Mexico

Michael Ennis-McMillan, Skidmore College

192 pages | Paperbound | 6-3/8 x 9-1/4 |
1-color | ©2006 | 0-534-61285-7

The text provides an ethnographic analysis of the social and cultural aspects of installing and managing a piped drinking water system in La Purificacion Tepetitla, a community located in the densely populated and semiarid region of the Valley of Mexico. The account shows how politics and culture shape community initiatives to develop adequate and equitable drinking water supplies in the Valley of Mexico's changing ecology. The research is based on 22 months of ethnographic fieldwork, carried out from 1993 to 2000. The book applies the culture concept to drinking water issues and furthers students' understanding of human diversity in terms of economics, ecological adaptation, politics, kinship, gender, ethnicity, health beliefs and practices, and religion and ritual.

KEY FEATURES

- This case study responds to the need to offer students ethnographic case studies that link small-scale cultures with global processes of social and culture change.
- Drinking water, which is the main focus of the text, is a subject students can identify with and many can understand why water scarcity is becoming a major global issue.
- The case study is presented as a personal account of how an anthropologist goes about studying health and environmental issues in the context of culture.
- Commonly used Spanish terms will be introduced in the text and included in the glossary.

TABLE OF CONTENTS

Junkie Business: The Evolution and Operation of a Heroin Dealing Network

Lee D. Hoffer, Washington University School of Medicine

192 pages | Paperbound | 6-3/8 x 9-1/4 |
1-color | ©2006 | 0-534-64495-3

Junkie Business is the result of an intensive three-year ethnographic study of the formation and eventual demise of a heroin dealing network in Denver. While earlier books have dealt with marijuana dealers and cocaine dealers, this will be the first study ever to provide an "insider's perspective" on the business of dealing heroin.

KEY FEATURES

- This text provides a unique look at addiction and the "business" of heroin dealing: it is the first study ever to provide an 'insider's perspective' on the business of dealing heroin.
- The ethnographic account represents the everyday reality of being addicted to heroin and having to sell the drug to support a lifestyle, and documents how the business of dealing heroin progressed from a loose knit street-based partnership to a private business with a clear and well organized division of labor.
- Basic concepts of anthropology are illustrated, and the book also demonstrates how ethnographic research can be applied.

TABLE OF CONTENTS

With No Direction Home: Homeless Youth on the Road and in the Streets

Marni Finkelstein, Albert Einstein College of Medicine/Montefiore Medical Center

192 pages · Paperbound · ©2005 · **0-534-62649-1**

This book gives voice to the homeless youth and is rich with material on their everyday lives, including living conditions and street experiences. The case study's strength lies in its ethnographic methodology, which combines direct observations and qualitative interviews. Finkelstein discusses her own experiences with the street kids, including how she was able to develop a rapport within the "street scene."

A Crisis of Births: Population Politics and Family-Making in Italy

Elizabeth L. Krause, University of Massachusetts, Amherst

192 pages · Paperbound · ©2005 · **0-534-63693-4**

This book tells the story of one society's remarkable experience when Italians in the late 1990s attained the lowest birthrate per women of any nation in the world. This case study draws on two years of ethnographic fieldwork over a five year period, to examine the conflicts as well as the possibility that this trend in family-making has created for an otherwise family-centered culture.

Bravo for the Marshallese: Regaining Control in a Post-Nuclear, Post-Colonial World

Holly M. Barker, Senior Advisor to the Ambassador, Embassy of the Republic of the Marshall Islands (RMI)

192 pages · Paperbound · ©2004 · **0-534-61326-8**

This case study describes the role an applied anthropologist takes to help Marshallese communities understand the impact of radiation exposure on the environment and themselves, and addresses problems stemming from the U.S. nuclear weapons testing program conducted in the Marshall Islands from 1946-1958.

Conservation and Globalization: A Study of National Parks and Indigenous Communities from East Africa to South Dakota

Jim Igoe, University of Colorado, Denver

200 pages · Paperbound · ©2004 · **0-534-61317-9**

Conservation and Globalization opens with a discussion of these two broad issues as they relate to the author's fieldwork with Maasai herding communities on the margins of Tarangire National Park in Tanzania. It explores different theoretical perspectives (Neo-Marxist and Foucauldian) on globalization and why both are relevant to the case studies presented.

New Capitalists: Law, Politics, and Identity Surrounding Casino Gaming on Native American Land

Eve Darian-Smith, University of California, Santa Barbara

144 pages · Paperbound · ©2004 · **0-534-61308-X**

This case study examines the impact of casino gaming on Native American reservations, and also explores why the idea of "rich Indians" and their participation in corporate America disrupts dominant assumptions and attitudes about indigenous peoples, their cultural authenticity, and their place in mainstream urban society.

Slaughterhouse Blues: The Meat and Poultry Industry in North America

Donald D. Stull, The University of Kansas, and
Michael J. Broadway, Northern Michigan University, Foreword by Eric Schlosser

208 pages · Paperbound · ©2004 · **0-534-61303-9**

Slaughterhouse Blues: The Meat and Poultry Industry in North America draws on more than 15 years of research by the authors, a cultural anthropologist and a social geographer, to present a detailed look at the meat and poultry industry in the United States and Canada and how the industrialization of agriculture affects communities economically, environmentally, and socially.

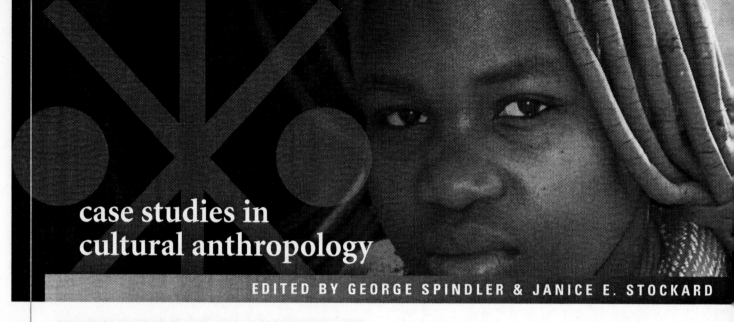

case studies in cultural anthropology

EDITED BY GEORGE SPINDLER & JANICE E. STOCKARD

AFRICA

The Dobe Ju/'hoansi, 3e

Richard B. Lee, University of Toronto

220 pages | Paperbound | ©2002 | **0-15-506333-2**

This classic, best-selling study of the !Kung San, foragers of the Dobe area of the Kalahari Desert describes relatively recent changes to the !Kung rituals, beliefs, social control, marriage and kinship. It documents their determination to take hold of their own destiny—despite exploitation of their habitat and relentless development—to assert their political rights and revitalize their communities.

Watch and Pray: A Portrait of Fante Village Life in Transition

Nancy Lundgren, University of Cape Coast, Ghana

178 pages | Paperbound | ©2002 | **0-15-505933-5**

This case study provides an intimate look at the Fante, who now reside in towns and villages, are predominantly Christian and earn their living primarily as traders, farmers and fishing people, but are found in all walks of life including: government officials, teachers, University professors, lawyers and doctors.

A Bagful of Locusts and the Baboon Woman: Constructions of Gender, Change, and Continuity in Botswana

David N. Suggs, Kenyon College

160 pages | Paperbound | ©2002 | **0-15-507038-X**

Set in the Saharan Africa in a contemporary context, this ethnography represents over 12 years of field research that focuses on the popular twin themes of culture change and gender roles amongst the BaKgatla of BaTswana.

The Rashaayda Bedouin: Arab Pastoralists of Eastern Sudan

William C. Young, Georgia Southern University

224 pages | Paperbound | ©1996 | **0-15-501513-3** | **TextChoice**

This is the only available book-length study of an Arab Bedouin society that supplements customary observations with data about gender and race. This case study integrates cultural meanings with the pastoral economy in clear, non-technical language.

The Lugbara of Uganda, 2e

John Middleton, Yale University

128 pages | Paperbound | ©1992 | **0-534-96895-3** | **TextChoice**

Middleton's sensitive account dramatizes how this complex sociopolitical society, once reliant on feud or warfare to control competition, became refugees of harassment and victims of famine.

The Sebei: A Study in Adaptation

Walter Goldschmidt, University of California, Los Angeles

182 pages | Paperbound | ©1987 | **0-534-97147-4**

The Sebei live on the north slope of a giant extinct volcano, Mount Elgon, in Uganda, in the heart of Africa. This case study is about their adaptation to their environment over time.

The Swazi: A South African Kingdom, 2e

Hilda Kuper, University of California, Los Angeles

187 pages ⁞ Paperbound ⁞ ©1986 ⁞ **0-03-070239-9** ⁞ **TextChoice**

Based upon information collected during half a century of field research in Swaziland, this case study presents rare insight into the dynamics of the country's independence, problems facing traditional leaders, and conflicts of interest and personalities.

The Mbuti Pygmies: Change and Adaptation

Colin M. Turnbull, American Museum of Natural History

161 pages ⁞ Paperbound ⁞ ©1983 ⁞ **0-03-061537-2** ⁞ **TextChoice**

This case focuses on the Mbuti pygmy hunter/gatherers of Zaire and their adaptation to change both before and after independence.

The Igbo of Southeast Nigeria

Victor C. Uchendu, Northwestern University

111 pages ⁞ Paperbound ⁞ ©1965 ⁞ **0-03-052475-X** ⁞ **TextChoice**

This book examines the Igbo social system and view of the world, covers their contact with European culture, and the warfare that raged within the Igbo borders.

Bunyoro: An African Kingdom

John Beattie, Oxford University

96 pages ⁞ Paperbound ⁞ ©1960 ⁞ **0-534-97128-8** ⁞ **TextChoice**

This study examines the conflicts that arise when a feudal and bureaucratic administration struggles against the influences of European and traditional standards of behavior.

ASIA

Challenging Gender Norms: Five Genders Among Bugis in Indonesia

Sharyn Graham—Auckland University of Technology–Auckland, New Zealand

192 pages ⁞ Paperbound ⁞ 6-3/8 x 9-1/4 ⁞ 1-color ⁞ ©2007 ⁞ **0-495-09280-0**

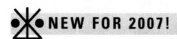

✳ NEW FOR 2007!

As part of the Case Studies in Cultural Anthropology series, edited by George Spindler and Janice Stockard, Sharyn Graham brings us *Challenging Gender Norms: Five Genders Among Bugis in Indonesia*. This case study explores the Bugis ethnic group, native to the Indonisian island of Sulawesi, that recognizes five gender categories rather than the two acknowledged in most societies. The Bugis acknowledge three sexes (female, male, hermaphrodite), four genders (women, men, calabai, and calalai), and a fifth meta-gender group, the bissu.

This ethnography presents individuals' stories, opinions and deliberations, grounding discussions of how gendered identities are constructed in a rapidly changing cultural milieu. The rich ethnographic material contained in this book challenges two types of Western theory—queer theory, which tends to focus on sexuality, and feminist theory, which tends to focus on social gender enactment. Neither theory is well-equipped for articulating the complexities of multiple gender identities and a multifarious gender system. By unraveling social negotiations and examining both individual embodiment and the impact of global forces on localized identities, the book proposes a new theory of gender which incorporates appreciation of variously gendered subjectivities.

TABLE OF CONTENTS

ASIA

A Sinhalese Village in Sri Lanka: Coping with Uncertainty

Victoria J. Baker, Eckerd College, Comparative Cultures Collegium

192 pages ⋮ Paperbound ⋮ ©1998 ⋮ **0-15-505176-8**

The most detailed case study of South Asia available, this book documents the ways in which the members of a remote agricultural village cope with the dangers that plague them by employing a complex system of ritual practices and beliefs in supernatural forces.

Himalayan Herders

Naomi H. Bishop, California State University, Northridge

212 pages ⋮ Paperbound ⋮ ©1998 ⋮ **0-534-44060-6** **TextChoice**

This first general case study about the Sherpa people in the Yolmo region of Nepal helps to place the more familiar Sherpa of the Solu-Khumbu region of Mt. Everest in comparative context.

Ethnic Identity in China: The Making of a Muslim Minority Nationality

Dru C. Gladney, University of Hawaii, Manoa; East-West Center

176 pages ⋮ Paperbound ⋮ ©1998 ⋮ **0-15-501970-8** **TextChoice**

This case study introduces students to the problems of ethnic diversity in China, a modern nation-state that is normally thought of and taught as culturally monolithic.

The Balinese

Stephen H. Lansing, University of Southern California

148 pages ⋮ Paperbound ⋮ ©1995 ⋮ **0-15-500240-6**

This study of the complex Balinese culture examines Balinese concepts of personhood and society; the integration of art into every aspect of Balinese life; the effects of the Guen Revolution on Balinese agriculture; the ecological role of their water temples in an age-old system of inigrate rice terraces; and the ethnohistory of Bali, including both colonial and Balinese views.

China's Urban Villagers: Changing Life in A Beijing Suburb, 2e

Norman A. Chance, University of Connecticut

230 pages ⋮ Paperbound ⋮ ©1991 ⋮ **0-534-97156-3** **TextChoice**

This book describes life in a small village within the borders of a large state farm on the outskirts of Beijing.

Friend by Day, Enemy by Night: Organized Vengeance in a Kohistani Community

Lincoln Keiser, Wesleyan College

131 pages ⋮ Paperbound ⋮ ©1991 ⋮ **0-03-053332-5** **TextChoice**

This exploration of the blood feuding and its ramifications in Thull, a Kohistani tribal community in the Hindu-Kush Mountains of Pakistan shows how 'mar dushmani' (literally "death enmity") has come to interpenetrate the mountaineer's lives.

Gopalpur: A South Indian Village, Fieldwork Edition

Alan R. Beals, University of California, Riverside

140 pages ⋮ Paperbound ⋮ ©1980 ⋮ **0-03-045371-2** **TextChoice**

From a Western point of view, the problem-solving techniques (including wrestling matches) of the people of Gopalpur seem strange, but this study provides an inside view of Gopalpur's rich and fulfilling life.

A Mountain Village in Nepal

John Thayer Hitchcock

156 pages ⋮ Paperbound ⋮ ©1980 ⋮ **0-534-97173-3** **TextChoice**

This village is in Gurkha country, home of the famed fighters that have served everywhere the British have been. Hitchcock describes their way of life focusing on the land and it uses, family, marriage and farmstead, kin, and recent change.

CENTRAL & SOUTH AMERICA/MEXICO

Aztecs of Central Mexico: An Imperial Society, 2e

Frances Berdan, California State University, San Bernardino

192 pages ┊ Paperbound ┊ ©2005 ┊ **0-534-62728-5**

Berdan's book covers the compelling story of a complex, imperial society in Central Mexico during the 15th and 16th centuries. It uses pre- and post-Spanish conquest documents and illustrations, as well as archaeological discoveries, to reconstruct the variety and "feel" of Aztec daily life at various status levels.

The Canela: Kinship, Ritual and Sex in an Amazonian Tribe, 2e

William H. Crocker, National Museum of Natural History, Smithsonian Institution, and **Jean G. Crocker**

174 pages ┊ Paperbound ┊ ©2004 ┊ **0-534-17491-4**

This text is a case study of one people, the Canela, which traces changes through time, a group uniquely held together by social and sexual bonds, and reveals the ethnographer's fieldwork practices. A companion website provides students with a study guide for the BBC films available through Films for the Humanities.

Katun: A Twenty-Year Journey with the Maya

Cindy L. Hull, Grand Valley State University

208 pages ┊ Paperbound ┊ ©2004 ┊ **0-534-61290-3**

The focus of this case study is the changing social and economic structure of the henequen zone in northwest Yucatan, Mexico, with special attention paid to women's economic participation.

From the Bush: The Front Line of Health Care in a Caribbean Village

Marsha B. Quinlan, Ball State University

168 pages ┊ Paperbound ┊ ©2004 ┊ **0-15-508567-0**

This case study is the first to deal with a topic in medical anthropology. It explores the world of folk medicine in the Caribbean (Dominica)—local beliefs and practices concerning how the body functions and malfunctions and the home remedies Dominicans use to cure common illnesses.

The Yanomamö, 5e

Napoleon A. Chagnon, University of California, Santa Barbara

165 pages ┊ Paperbound ┊ ©1997 ┊ **0-15-505327-2**

Based on the author's extensive fieldwork, this classic ethnography, now in its fifth edition, focuses on the Yanomamö. These truly remarkable South American people are one of the few primitive sovereign tribal societies left on earth.

Yanomamö Interactive: The Ax Fight on CD-ROM

Peter Biella, San Francisco State University, **Napolean A. Chagnon**, University of California, Santa Barbara, and **Gary Seaman**, University of Southern California

©1997 ┊ **0-15-505428-7**

Yanomamö Interactive: The Ax Fight sets a standard in the teaching of cultural anthropology, using the power of multimedia to enhance and extend the experience of viewing Chagnon and Asch's classics ethnographic film.

The Isthmus Zapotecs: A Matrifocal Culture of Mexico

Beverly N. Chinas, California State University, Chico

133 pages ┊ Paperbound ┊ ©1992 ┊ **0-03-055057-2**

This case study has long been valued for its unique gender role model and focus on the only matrifocal indigenous culture in Latin America.

Life Under the Tropical Canopy: Tradition and Change Among the Yucatec Maya

Ellen R. Kintz, State University of New York, Geneseo

170 pages ┊ Paperbound ┊ ©1990 ┊ **0-03-032592-7** **TextChoice**

This case study describes how the Maya have lived and benefited from their environment for 13 centuries.

The Zinacantecos of Mexico: A Modern Maya Way of Life, 2e

Evon Z. Vogt, Harvard University

157 pages ┊ Paperbound ┊ ©1990 ┊ **0-03-033344-X** **TextChoice**

This case study explores the Zinacanteco belief system as represented in ceremonies, rituals, and daily life, and discusses how that belief system also serves as a philosophy, cosmology, theology, code of values, and science.

Yuqui: Forest Nomads in a Changing World

Allyn Maclean Stearman, University of Central Florida

164 pages ┊ Paperbound ┊ ©1989 ┊ **0-534-97074-5** **TextChoice**

This book examines the effects of 20th century social and cultural changes on the Yuqui, a group of fewer than 100 nomadic foragers who've survived without houses or the ability to produce fire.

EUROPE

Scottish Crofters: A Historical Ethnography of a Celtic Village, 2e

Susan Parman, California State University, Fullerton

192 pages | Paperbound | ©2005 | 0-534-63324-2

This case study focuses on Geall, a community in the Scottish Outer Hebrides. With an understanding gained from an intimate, long-term relationship with Scotland, things Scottish, and the people of Geall. The author describes a human community and places it in the wider cultural, historical, economic, and sociopolitical contexts of maintaining relationships to Scotland, England and Europe.

Nazare: Women and Men in a Prebureaucratic Portuguese Fishing Village

Jan Brogger

148 pages | Paperbound | ©1992 | 0-03-043382-7 | **TextChoice**

This case study discusses the various gender roles, as well as equalities and inequalities, that exist among a society of people in Portugal.

Town and Country in Locorotondo

Anthony H. Galt, University of Wisconsin, Green Bay

124 pages | Paperbound | ©1992 | 0-03-073327-8 | **TextChoice**

This look at peasant and elite cultures of the southern Italian town of Locorotondo focuses on its connection and similarities with Italian society and the ways in which both cultures have changed in the past decades.

Vasilika: A Village in Modern Greece

Ernestine Friedl

Paperbound | ©1962 | 0-534-97165-2 | **TextChoice**

This case study focuses on Friedl's extensive study of family economics, consumption habits, dowry and inheritance, and the village as a community.

NORTH AMERICA

Skin and Bones: The Management of People and Natural Resources in Shellcracker Haven, Florida

Jane Gibson, University of Kansas

192 pages | Paperbound | ©2004 | 0-15-508476-3

Skin and Bones relates the history of Shellcracker Haven, a community pseudonym, to the development of fresh water fish and wildlife management in the state of Florida.

Strangers in a Not-So-Strange-Land: Indian Americans in the Global Age

Arthur W. Helweg, Western Michigan University

176 pages | Paperbound | ©2004 | 0-534-61312-8

This text is a case study about Asian Indians in the United States. The case study takes a transnational perspective and discusses the role of globalization and the current world system to form a more comprehensive study than those studies that have dominated migration studies and anthropology to date.

Life in Riverfront: A Middle Western Town Seen Through Japanese Eyes

Mariko Fujita Sano, Hiroshima University and **Toshiyuki Sano**, Nara's Women's University

192 pages | Paperbound | ©2001 | 0-15-506421-5

Life in Riverfront is a unique case study that offers a fresh approach to ethnography because it looks at American culture as seen through the eyes of Japanese anthropologists.

Shadowed Lives: Undocumented Immigrants in American Society, 2e

Leo R. Chavez, University of California, Irvine

224 pages | Paperbound | ©1998 | 0-15-508089-X

The hardships of Hispanic migration are conveyed in the immigrants' own voices while the author's voice raises questions about power, stereotypes, settlement, and incorporation into American society.

Personas Mexicanas: Chicano Highschoolers in a Changing Los Angeles

James Diego Vigil, The Center for the Study of Urban Poverty, University of California, Los Angeles

208 pages | Paperbound | ©1997 | 0-15-503838-9 | **TextChoice**

Vigil's impressive case study explores the real-life situations of both suburban and urban Mexican American high school students in 1974 and 1988.

The Hutterites in North America, 4e

John A. Hostetler, Emeritus, Temple University and **Gertrude Enders Huntington**, University of Michigan, Ann Arbor

178 pages | Paperbound | ©1996 | 0-534-44033-9 | **TextChoice**

This case study in cultural anthropology focuses on the day-to-day living patterns of the Hutterites, a German-dialect-speaking Christian sect whose members live communally in the Great Plains of the United States and Canada.

The Mi'kmaq: Resistance, Accommodation, and Cultural Survival

Harald E.L. Prins, Kansas State University,

250 pages | Paperbound | ©1996 | 0-03-053427-5 | **TextChoice**

Chronicled here are 500 years of the complex dynamics of Mi'kmaq culture. This text explores the group as a tribal nation—their ordeals in the face of colonialism and their current struggle for self-determination and cultural revitalization.

The Ojibwa of Berens River, Manitoba: Ethnography into History

A. Irving Hallowell and **Jennifer S. H. Brown**, University of Winnipeg

148 pages | Paperbound | ©1992 | 0-03-055122-6 | **TextChoice**

This case study conveys the essential qualities and patterns of Ojibwa culture.

Amish Children: Education in the Family, School, and Community, 2e

John A. Hostetler and **Gertrude E. Huntington**

127 pages | Paperbound | ©1992 | 0-03-031592-1 | **TextChoice**

This case study describes a way of life where families are still stable, people live with a high sense of communal obligation, men and women work with their hands, one hears the clop of horse's hooves rather than the whine of tires, and the school and community are joined.

The Inupiat and Arctic Alaska: An Ethnography of Development

Norman A. Chance, University of Connecticut

241 pages | Paperbound | ©1990 | 0-534-44159-9 | **TextChoice**

This exciting case study traces accurately the history of the Inupiat Eskimo of Alaska from pre-contact times to the present.

The Huron: Farmers of the North, 2e

Bruce G. Trigger, McGill University, Montreal

164 pages | Paperbound | ©1990 | 0-03-031689-8

This remarkable reconstruction of the sedentary, agricultural, but warlike life of the Huron underscores the importance of studying Huron life, since the Huron were wiped out by other Iroquoians in the 17th Century.

Chinatown: Economic Adaptation and Ethnic Identity of the Chinese

Bernard P. Wong

160 pages | Paperbound | ©1982 | 0-534-97137-7 | **TextChoice**

This case study analyzes the structural adaptations that Chinese American communities in general, and the New York Chinatown in particular, have made to survive in American society.

Lakota of the Rosebud: A Contemporary Adaptation

Elizabeth Grobsmith, University of Nebraska, Lincoln

160 pages | Paperbound | ©1981 | 0-03-057438-2 | **TextChoice**

This study of the Rosebud Sioux tribe of South Dakota explores the way they meet the challenges of living in the 20th century.

Aleuts: Survivors of the Bering Land Bridge

William S. Laughlin, University of Connecticut

151 pages | Paperbound | ©1981 | 0-534-97119-9 | **TextChoice**

This unusual case study integrates vital data and interpretations to give a complete historical picture of the Aleuts, who have lived for 9,000 years in a remote and inhospitable part of the earth, and whose ancestors are connected with the original human inhabitants of the New World.

The Vice Lords: Warriors of the Streets, Fieldwork Edition

Lincoln Keiser, Weleyan University

116 pages ¦ Paperbound ¦ ©1979 ¦ 0-534-96931-3 ¦ **TextChoice**

This study of a Chicago street gang provides an insightful picture of gangs of similar age and composition operating in depressed areas and ghettos of large American cities.

The Cheyennes: Indians of the Great Plains, 2e

E. Adamson Hoebel, Emeritus, University of Minnesota

137 pages ¦ Paperbound ¦ ©1978 ¦ 0-03-022686-4

This case study traces the Cheyenne Indians from their first contact with the French explorer LaSalle in 1680.

The Urban Poor of Puerto Rico: A Study in Development and Inequality

Helen Icken Safa

116 pages ¦ Paperbound ¦ ©1974 ¦ 0-534-97191-1 ¦ **TextChoice**

A study in the shantytown of the San Juan metropolitan area in Puerto Rico that was built by landless agricultural laborers out of the materials at hand.

Hano: The Tewa Indian Community in Arizona

Edward P. Dozier, University of Arizona

114 pages ¦ Paperbound ¦ ©1966 ¦ 0-03-075653-7 ¦ **TextChoice**

This case study provides a look at Pueblo life as well as the historical forces which shaped the Pueblo communities of today. The author analyzes the relationships of White, Tewa Indians, and Hopi Indians.

PACIFIC OCEANA

✳ NEW FOR 2007!

As part of the Spindler/Stockard Case Studies in Cultural Anthropology Series, *Hawaiian Fisherman* is the first case study that presents the cultural aspects of fishing in Hawaii. Author, Ed Glazier, describes an important socio-cultural domain enacted in a complex cultural context which has received little attention in the anthropological literature. The book articulates local-level issues with macro-scale social and political economic processes with relevant social theory.

KEY FEATURES

- This study comes at a time of renewed national interest in the health of the world's oceans and its resources.
- Students discover what small boat fishing in Hawaii is, how it affects the lives of the participants, other island residents, and the marine environment itself, and how such understanding might influence the future of fishing in Hawaii and maritime settings elsewhere in this rapidly changing world.

Hawaiian Fishermen

Ed Glazier—Research Director and Principal Investigator at Impact Assessment, Inc

192 pages ¦ Paperbound ¦ 6-3/8 x 9-1/4 ¦ 1-color ¦ ©2007 ¦ 0-495-00785-4

TABLE OF CONTENTS

1. Introduction. 2. Small Boat Fishing in Hawai'i. 3. Holoholo. 4. Hardcore Commerical Trolling. 5. Fishing for Food. 6. Some Deeper Analysis of the Fishing Lifestyle in Hawai'i. 7. Conclusions.

The Sambia: Ritual, Sexuality, and Change in Papua New Guinea, 2e

Gilbert Herdt, San Francisco State University

192 pages | Paperbound | 6-3/8 x 9-1/4 | 1-color | ©2006 | **0-534-64383-3**

This cultural and psychological study of gender identity and sexual development in a New Guinea Highlands society includes rich material on initiation rites and socialization studies, and contrasts the Sambia with other societies, including the United States. For example, Sambia boys experience ritualized homosexuality before puberty and continue this practice until marriage, after which homosexual activity is prohibited. The implications are developed cross-culturally and contextualized in gender literature. This new edition contains updated information about the Sambian ritualization and socialization of gender practices and will include a new chapter on sexuality, gender and social change among the Sambia.

KEY FEATURES

- The author has included updated information about the Sambian ritualization and socialization of gender practices.
- This edition adds a new chapter on sexuality, gender and social change among the Sambia.
- Profiles of individuals are updated, as many have experienced significant life changes (death, marriage, children, etc.), and new Sambia women are included.
- Chapter 6, "Ritualized Gender Development: Continuities and Discontinuities," includes coverage of sexual discontinuity, women's real power and how women transform their social inequality into sources of power.
- Chapter 7, "Sexuality and Social Change," includes discussion of globalization and social change.
- By discussing cultural change and cultural continuity, this case study considers the question of sexual identity in the context of culture.

TABLE OF CONTENTS

Introduction. 1. The Behavioral Environment. 2. Warfare and Social Organization. 3. Ordinary People. 4. Gender and Socialization. 5. The Men's Secret Society. 6. Ritualized Gender Development—Continuities and Discontinuities. 7. Sexuality and Social Change. Afterword. Glossary.

Through the Eye of the Needle: A Māori Elder Remembers

Mary Katharine Duffié, University of California, Los Angeles/American Indian Studies Program

224 pages | Paperbound | ©2001 | **0-15-506982-9**

This is a unique ethnography that follows in the tradition of the highly successful book by Marjorie Shostak (*Nisa: The Life and Words of a !Kung Woman.*)

Collaborations and Conflicts: A Leader Through Time

Andrew J. Strathern and **Pamela J. Stewart**, both of University of Pittsburgh

176 pages | Paperbound | ©2000 | **0-15-502147-8**

This is a uniquely dramatic account of life in the Papua New Guinea Highlands as told by a well-known leader of the Kawelka people of Mount Hagen.

Grand Valley Dani: Peaceful Warriors, 3e

Karl G. Heider, University of South Carolina, Columbia

193 pages | Paperbound | ©1997 | **0-15-505173-3**

This case study examines an isolated tribe in Indonesia, West New Guinea, when tribe members were still using stone axes, bows, arrows, and spears, up to more present times spanning 34 years (1961-1995).

Lives on the Line: Women and Ecology on a Pacific Atoll

Alexandra Brewis, University of Auckland

85 pages | Paperbound | ©1996 | **0-15-501969-4**

Lives on the Line examines women's issues in Butaritari, an equatorial Pacific atoll 15 kilometers long and a few hundred meters wide.

From Longhouse to Village: Samo Social Change

R. Daniel Shaw, Fuller Theological Seminary

160 pages | Paperbound | ©1996 | **0-15-502561-9** **TextChoice**

The depth of familiarity with Samo life over 300 years of change is what gives this case study its special character.

The White Man Will Eat You: An Anthropologist Among the Imbonggu of New Guinea

William E. Wormsley, Emory University and Georgia State University

135 pages ┊ Paperbound ┊ ©1993 ┊ **0-534-44015-0** ┊ **TextChoice**

In this fascinating narrative, readers learn about the Imbonggu's social structure, political process, leadership, social and economic exchange and obligations, bridewealth, religion and magic—as well as what it is like to be an anthropologist.

Samoan Village: Then and Now, 2e

Lowell D. Holmes and **Ellen Rhoads Holmes**, both Wichita State University

176 pages ┊ Paperbound ┊ ©1992 ┊ **0-534-97120-2** ┊ **TextChoice**

This case study focuses on the way the acceptance of Christianity brought about major changes within the culture. It also gives readers a working knowledge of the basic elements of traditional Samoan culture including subsistence, principles of rank, ceremonies, and the life cycle.

Simbu Law: Conflict Management in the New Guinea Highlands

Aaron Podolefsky

166 pages ┊ Paperbound ┊ ©1992 ┊ **0-534-97138-5** ┊ **TextChoice**

This case study focuses on the various ways conflicts and disputes are managed and ultimately resolved in the Chimbu province of Papua New Guinea.

The Mardu Aborigines: Living the Dream in Australia's Desert, 2e

Robert Tonkinson, University of Western Australia

204 pages ┊ Paperbound ┊ ©1991 ┊ **0-534-44087-8**

Characterized by a simple technology and a complex socioreligious system, the Mardudjara have survived with much of their traditional culture intact. This edition describes changes as the Mardu adapt to social, economic, and political realities.

Samoan Planters: Tradition and Economic Development in Polynesia

Tim O'Meara, University of North Carolina, Wilmington

266 pages ┊ Paperbound ┊ ©1990 ┊ **0-534-97111-3** ┊ **TextChoice**

Vignettes of villagers enliven this exploration into how traditional customs and values influence economic development among Samoan planters.

The Tiwi of North Australia, 3e

C.W. M. Hart, late of Wayne State University, **Arnold R. Pilling**, Wayne State University, and **Jane C. Goodale**, Bryn Mawr College

179 pages ┊ Paperbound ┊ ©1988 ┊ **0-03-012019-5** ┊ **TextChoice**

This examination of the colorful Tiwi culture from the late 1920s to the 1980s provides a broad picture of cultural change and modernization in a hunting and food gathering tribe.

The Trobrianders of Papua New Guinea

Annette B. Weiner, New York University

184 pages ┊ Paperbound ┊ ©1988 ┊ **0-03-011919-7**

This re-examination of the Trobrianders of Papua New Guinea, the people described in Malinowski's classic ethnographic work of the early 20th century, provides a balanced view of the society from a male and female perspective, including coverage of new discoveries about the importance of woman's work and wealth in the society.

'Elota's Story: The Life and Times of a Solomon Islands Big Man

Roger M. Keesing, The Australian National University

150 pages ┊ Paperbound ┊ ©1983 ┊ **0-534-97146-6** ┊ **TextChoice**

Keesing supplies a sketch of Kwaio culture, set in the time of 'Elota's life span, and has placed 'Elota's life in this cultural and temporal framework.

The Kapauku Papuans of West New Guinea, 2e

Leopold Pospisil, Yale University

142 pages ┊ Paperbound ┊ ©1978 ┊ **0-534-97155-5** ┊ **TextChoice**

This society, first studied by Pospisil when outside influences were just beginning in 1954-55, is characterized by a form of primitve capitalism, with well-developed trade, money, and legal systems.

ETHNOGRAPHIES

The Ghosts of Iceland

Robert Anderson, Mills College

320 pages ┆ Paperbound ┆ ©2005 ┆ **0-534-61052-8**

This ethnography, uniquely set in contemporary Iceland, takes an in-depth look at the way supernatural beliefs and practices (long an important subject of anthropology) thrive as an "unnamed, unpretentious, and quiet, nearly silent, spiritual movement that impacts most of the population either directly or indirectly in deeply personal ways." The author lived and worked in Reykjavik, where friends, acquaintances, students, colleagues and spirit mediums talked with him about their experiences of being in contact with spirits of the dead, including deceased loved ones and spirit doctors. Anderson's book is a primary example of signature anthropology methodology, i.e., ethnographic fieldwork or participant observation. He spent time with spirit mediums, joined in group séances, observed and recorded conversations between the living and the dead, arranged for spirit doctors to treat sick friends, and attended lectures at spiritist schools, and coffee klatches of the 'spirit society.'

Ethnographic Essays in Cultural Anthropology: A Problem-Based Approach

R. Bruce Morrison, Athabasca University; and **C. Roderick Wilson**, University of Alberta

278 pages ┆ Paperbound ┆ ©2001 ┆ **0-87581-445-X**

This collection of ten mini-ethnographies takes a problem-based learning approach, focusing on contextual and cumulative learning to enhance student understanding of the fundamental concepts of cultural anthropology.

Neither Man Nor Woman: The Hijras of India, 2e

Serena Nanda, John Jay College of Criminal Justice

208 pages ┆ Paperbound ┆ ©1999 ┆ **0-534-50903-7**

This ethnography is a cultural study of the Hijras of India, a religious community of men who dress and act like women. It focuses on how Hijras can be used in the study of gender categories and human sexual variation.

READERS

[editors] George Spindler Janice E. Stockard

Globalization and Change in Fifteen Cultures: Born in One World, Living in Another

George Spindler—Stanford University

Janice E. Stockard—Mills College

304 pages ¦ Paperbound ¦ 6-3/8 x 9-1/4 ¦ 1-color ¦ ©2007 ¦ **0-534-63648-9**

NEW FOR 2007!

The original articles presented in this anthology reflect a world changed by globalization, and an anthropology committed to documenting the effects of the vast cultural flows of people, information, goods, and technology, now in motion the world over. Spindler and Stockard write an introduction to the topic of cultural change, and each of the fifteen anthropologists in the anthology take students on a return visit to their original field sites, asking questions for a new era and writing of peoples to some extent familiar, but at the same time changed, transformed by global forces.

KEY FEATURES

■ Emphasizes the effects of globalization and cultural change on flows--people, information, goods and technology.

■ The authors identify four general dimensions of culture change and group chapters accordingly: challenges to identity and power, changing gender hierarchies, new patterns of migration and mobility, and the effects of economic change and modernization.

■ Each chapter begins with a fieldwork biography that makes anthropologists and their field experiences come alive for students.

■ Examples of global coverage include the Bedouin in Sudan, Mardu in Australia, Sambia in New Guinea, Canela in Brazil, Yolmo in Nepal, Ju/'Hoansi in Namibia, Minangkabau in Sumatra, Scottish crofters, Greek villagers, Chinese minorities, the Aztecs and Yucatecans in Mexico, and Mexican immigrants, African-American gang members, and Wisconsin town residents in the U.S.A.

■ Can be used as a core text for courses such as culture change, globalization, and modernization as well as a supplement for any introductory course.

TABLE OF CONTENTS

Current Perspectives: Readings from InfoTrac® College Edition: Cultural Anthropology and Globalization

Thomson Wadsworth

96 pages | Paperbound |©2006 | 0-495-00810-9

This new reader includes hand-selected articles related to the topic of globalization. The articles are drawn from InfoTrac College Edition's vast database of full-length, peer reviewed articles from more than 5,000 top academic journals, newsletters, and periodicals. Ideal to supplement your cultural anthropology textbook, this reader will elicit lively classroom discussions about the real-world challenges and opportunities of globalization.

Classic Readings in Cultural Anthropology

Gary Ferraro, University of North Carolina, Charlotte

136 pages | Paperbound | ©2004 | 0-534-61272-5

Brief, accessible, and inexpensive, this new reader has been carefully edited by text author Gary Ferraro to include those articles and excerpts from works that have been pivotal to the field of anthropology and that have endured over the decades. These eminently relevant selections allow students to further explore anthropological perspectives on key cultural topics such as culture, language and communication, ecology and economics, marriage and family, politics and social control, supernatural belief systems, and issues of culture change.

Distant Mirrors: America as a Foreign Culture, 3e

Philip R. Devita, State University of New York, Plattsburgh, and **James D. Armstrong**, State University of New York

208 pages | Paperbound | ©2002 | 0-534-55648-5

Anthropology has a long history of the "other," yet we can look right here at home for the strangeness we seek. We often neglect to ask the questions that reveal our own culture's underlying value and beliefs. In this volume, we bring the American culture into focus. For students to understand the full impact of ethnography, to experience cultural relativity and to gain a foundation to build informed comparisons, students need a firm grasp of their own culture—and need to use this volume. The Third Edition consists of 19 essays written by anthropologists and other scholars using an ethnographic perspective. The essays enable students to understand themselves better by focusing on their own culture and seeing it from a new perspective. This collection gives anthropology a comparative perspective that provides a reflective lens, a mirror, for understanding ourselves and the world in which we live.

Ethnographic Essays in Cultural Anthropology: A Problem-Based Approach

R. Bruce Morrison, Athabasca University; and **C. Roderick Wilson**, University of Alberta

278 pages | Paperbound | ©2001 | 0-87581-445-X

This collection of ten mini-ethnographies takes a problem-based learning approach, focusing on contextual and cumulative learning to enhance student understanding of the fundamental concepts of cultural anthropology.

Applying Cultural Anthropology: Readings

Gary Ferraro, University of North Carolina, Charlotte

250 pages | Paperbound | ©1988 | 0-534-53324-8

This reader offers a selection of 39 articles written in the words of those cultural anthropologists who are making their discipline useful. The readings are organized into five major sections reflecting those areas that are benefiting from the practice and application of cul-tural anthropology. The intent of the reader is two-fold: first, to provide anthropology students with a wide range of examples as to how the discipline is making meaningful contributions to the mitigation of human problems; and second, to convey through the words of the practicing anthropologists themselves, some of the challenges and rewards involved in making cultural anthropology useful.

case studies in archaeology

Camden: Historical Archaeology in the South Carolina Backcountry

Kenneth E. Lewis, Michigan State University

192 pages ¦ Paperbound ¦ 6-3/8 x 9-1/4 ¦
1-color ¦ ©2006 ¦ **0-534-51323-9**

Camden: Historical Archaeology In The South Carolina Backcountry represents a unique longitudinal study of 25 years of a single site from the colonial era. It uses the distinctive methodology of historical archaeology to investigate behavior associated with a temporal process of change, thereby illuminating the adaptive behavior of colonists. It is also an important study methodologically because it employs a systematic approach to the investigation of large, complex sites using a combination of documentary and material evidence.

KEY FEATURES

- Lewis has a well-developed and well-tested approach to archaeological research; he has a clear, step-by-step method of analysis.
- "The Evolution of a Frontier Community" represents a unique longitudinal study of 25 years of a single site from the colonial era.
- The book uses the distinctive methodology of historical archaeology to investigate behavior associated with a temporal process of change, thereby illuminating the adaptive behavior of colonists.
- It is an important study methodologically because it employs a systematic approach to the investigation of large, complex sites using a combination of documentary and material evidence.

TABLE OF CONTENTS

the Results of the Sampling Excavations: Exploring the Hypotheses for Identity, Function, and Change. 5. Enlarging the Scale of Observation: Households on an Evolving Frontier. 6. Defining Camden's Households in Space. 7. Placing Camden's Households in Time. 8. Exploring Function on a Household Scale. 9. Camden in a Changing Economic and Social Milieu. 10. Camden: An Unfinished Work.

The Ceren Site: An Ancient Village Buried by Volcanic Ash in Central America, 2e

Payson D. Sheets, University of Colorado, Boulder

192 pages ¦ Paperbound ¦ 6-3/8 x 9-1/4 ¦
1-color ¦ ©2006 ¦ **0-495-00606-8**

Discovered in 1976 by Sheets, and under continuous excavation and study since, the spectacular Ceren site provides us with an unusually clear window into the ancient past with which to view family activities on the frontier of the Mayan civilization. Since volcanic ash did not allow people to selectively remove artifacts, the site is well-preserved and it also largely stopped natural processes of decomposition offering this rare opportunity to study the Mayan past through household archaeology.

KEY FEATURES

- Virtually rewritten with new research and personal experiences in the field.
- A new Chapter entitled "The Religious Complex;" Presenting Structures 10 and 12 as a combination to describe where different religious practices occurred. New figures have also been added as well.
- The Ceren household section, previously in Chapter 7, has been expanded and moved to Chapter 8.
- Chapter 2 has been updated with new theory and references sections,

- Chapter 3 is completely updated of as a result of new research in geophysics, volcanology, and biology.
- Chapter 5 includes new clarified descriptions of architecture and artifacts ; updated agriculture section.

TABLE OF CONTENTS

Etlatongo: Social Complexity, Interaction and Village Life in the Mixteca Alta of Oaxaca, Mexico

Jeffrey P. Blomster, Brandeis University

216 pages | Paperbound | ©2004 | **0-534-61281-4**

This case study examines the rise of social complexity and the impact of interregional interaction at the village of Etlatongo, in the Mixteca Alta of Oaxaca.

Tropical Forest Archaeology in Western Pichincha, Ecuador

Ronald D. Lippi, University of Wisconsin, Marathon County

168 pages | Paperbound | ©2004 | **0-534-61294-6**

This case study uniquely covers a tropical forest area in Ecuador. It combines a discussion of the travails of conducting archaeology in the tropical forest and the results of extensive research. Of particular interest are the strategies employed for site survey.

Plants and People in Ancient Ecuador: The Ethnobotany of the Jama River Valley

Deborah M. Pearsall, University of Missouri

200 pages | Paperbound | ©2004 | **0-534-61321-7**

This case study illustrates the contemporary archaeological field of ethnobotany, and explores the interrelationships between the prehistoric residents of a small valley in coastal Ecuador and the dry tropical forest habitat in which they lived.

Copán: The Rise and Fall of an Ancient Maya Kingdom

David L. Webster, Pennsylvania State University; **Ann Corinne Freter**, Ohio University; **Nancy Gonlin**, Bellevue Community College

256 pages | Paperbound | ©2000 | 0-15-505808-8

Webster's case study reconstructs and evaluates the sociopolitical system and culture history of a world-famous Classic Maya Center in the highlands of Western Honduras, whose great temples, palaces, and carved monuments have been investigated since the 1830s.

The Pithouses of Keatley Creek

Brian Hayden, Simon Fraser University and **Jeffrey Quilter**, Series Editor

112 pages | Paperbound | ©1997 | 0-15-503837-0 | **TextChoice**

Brian Hayden's archaeological case study addresses the development of prehistoric and social and economic hierarchies. This archaeology project encompasses a fascinating range of topics making it an ideal case study for all students of archaeology. It also includes a vivid reconstruction of life in one of the largest and most complex Platean communities.

Lambert Farm: Public Archaeology and Canine Burials along Narragansett Bay

Jordan E. Kerber, Colgate University

136 pages | Paperbound | ©1997 | 0-15-505190-3 | **TextChoice**

The discussion of Kerber's trials, tribulations, and ultimate success in investigating the Lambert Farm site captures what real life archaeology in modern day times is like. This particular case study provides a fascinating review of the evidence for dogs in New World archaeology and prehistoric culture.

Purisimeno Chumash Prehistory: Maritime Adaptations Along the Southern California Coast

Michael A. Glassow, University of California, Santa Barbara

180 pages | Paperbound | ©1996 | 0-15-503084-1

This is the only case study available that focuses on the practice of archaeology in California, prehistory coastal adaptations, and cultural resource management. Unique coverage of the Vandenburg region and Santa Barbara Channel not only introduces students to regional archaeology but also allows them to observe the impact of environmental variations on cultural development.

Awatimarka: The Ethnoarchaelology of an Andean Herding Community

Lawrence A. Kuznar, Indiana University

141 pages | Paperbound | ©1995 | 0-15-501528-1

This study discusses the use of analogy in archaeology. It examines the practices of modern goat herders in the southern Andes as a means of understanding ancient human and animal behavior at the prehistoric site of Asana.

Toward a Social History of Archaeology in the United States

Thomas C. Patterson

191 pages | Paperbound | ©1995 | 0-15-500824-2 | **TextChoice**

This case study focuses on the forces influencing archaeological intellectual history and the relationship of history to anthropology and scholarship in general within the United States.

Khok Phanom Di: Prehistoric Adaptation to the World's Richest Habitat

Charles Higham, University of Otago, Dunedin New Zealand, and **Rachanie Thosarat**, Thai Fine Arts Departmetn, Bangkok, Thailand

169 ages | Paperbound | ©1994 | 0-15-500951-6 | **TextChoice**

For the purposes of providing students with an example of how archaeology is done and to what ends, no better example can be found than this account of work conducted in Thailand.

case studies by topic

Author / Title / ISBN	Culture Change/Continuity	Gender/Sexuality	Religion/Spirituality	Environmental/Ecological Issues	Native Americans	Social Organizations/Social Systems	Social Issues/Drugs	Subsistence/Economic Development	Immigrants/Immigration	Health/Medical Anthropology	Linguistics	Politics/Policy/Law	Exclusively from TextChoice
Anderson: **The Ghosts of Iceland**, 0-534-61052-8			■							■			
Baker: **A Sinhalese Village in Sri Lanka: Coping with Uncertainty**, 0-15-505176-8			■				■			■			
Barker: **Bravo for the Marshallese: Regaining Control in a Post-Nuclear, Post-Colonial World**, 0-534-61326-8				■			■				■		
Beals: **Gopalpur: A South Indian Village**, 0-03-045371-2	■					■							■
Beattie: **Bunyoro: An African Kingdom**, 0-534-97128-8			■			■							
Berdan: **The Aztecs of Central Mexico: An Imperial Society, 2e**, 0-534-62728-5			■					■					
Bishop: **Himalayan Herders**, 0-534-44060-6	■			■				■					■
Brewis: **Lives on the Line: Women and Ecology on a Pacific Atoll**, 0-15-501969-4		■		■									
Brogger: **Nazare: Women and Men in a Prebureaucratic Portuguese Fishing Village**, 0-03-043382-7		■											■
Chagnon: **The Yanomamö, 5e**, 0-15-505327-2								■				■	
Chance: **China's Urban Villagers: Changing Life in a Beijing Suburb, 2e**, 0-534-97156-3	■					■		■				■	■
Chance: **The Inupiat and Arctic Alaska: An Ethnography of Development**, 0-534-44159-9	■					■		■				■	■
Chavez: **Shadowed Lives: Undocumented Immigrants in American Society, 2e**, 0-15-508089-X	■								■				
Chinas: **The Isthmus Zapotecs: A Matrifocal Culture of Mexico**, 0-03-055057-2	■	■				■							■
Crocker/Crocker: **The Canela: Kinship, Ritual, and Sex in an Amazonian Tribe, 2e**, 0-534-17491-4		■				■							
Darian-Smith: **New Capitalists: Issues of Law, Politics, and Identity Surrounding Casino Gaming on Native American Land**, 0-534-61308-X					■	■						■	
Dozier: **Hano: The Tewa Indian Community in Arizona**, 0-03-075653-7	■				■								■
Duffié: **Through the Eye of the Needle: A Māori Elder Remembers**, 0-15-506982-9	■	■											
Ennis-McMillan: **A Precious Liquid: Drinking Water and Culture in the Valley of Mexico**, 0-534-61285-7			■	■				■					
Finkelstein: **With No Direction Home: Homeless Youth on the Road and in the Streets**, 0-534-62649-1		■						■					
Friedl: **Vasilika: A Village in Modern Greece**, 0-534-97165-2						■		■					■
Galt: **Town and Country in Locorotondo**, 0-03-073327-8	■					■							■
Gibson: **Skin & Bones: The Management of People and Natural Resources in Shellcracker Haven, FL**, 0-15-508476-3					■			■	■				
Gladney: **Ethnic Identity in China: The Making of a Muslim Minority Nationality**, 0-15-501970-8			■									■	■
Glazier: **Hawaiian Fisherman**, 0-495-00785-4	■			■				■				■	
Goldschmidt: **The Sebei: A Study in Adaptation**, 0-534-97147-4	■		■			■		■					■
Graham: **Challenging Gender Norms: Five Genders Among Bugis in Indonesia**, 0-495-09280-0		■				■							
Grobsmith: **Lakota of the Rosebud: A Contemporary Adaptation**, 0-03-057438-2	■		■		■						■		■
Hallowell/Brown: **The Ojibwa of Berens River, Manitoba: Ethnography into History**, 0-03-055122-6	■		■		■								■
Hart/Pilling/Goodale: **The Tiwi of North Australia, 3e**, 0-03-012019-5	■					■						■	■
Heider: **Grand Valley Dani: Peaceful Warriors, 3e**, 0-15-505173-3	■					■							
Helweg: **Strangers in a Not-So-Strange-Land: Indian Americans in the Global Age**, 0-534-61312-8	■									■			
Herdt: **The Sambia: Ritual and Gender in Papua New Guinea, 2e**, 0-534-64383-3		■						■					
Hitchcock: **A Mountain Village in Nepal**, 0-534-97173-3	■					■							■
Hoebel: **The Cheyennes: Indians of the Great Plains, 2e**, 0-03-022686-4					■		■						

case studies by topic

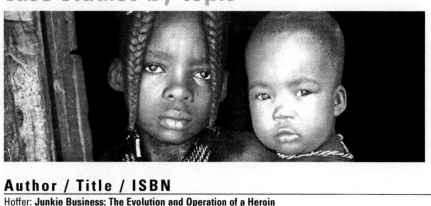

Author / Title / ISBN	Culture Change/Continuity	Gender/Sexuality	Religion/Spirituality	Environmental/Ecological Issues	Native Americans	Social Organizations/Social Systems	Social Issues/Drugs	Subsistence/Economic Development	Immigrants/Immigration	Health/Medical Anthropology	Linguistics	Politics/Policy/Law	Exclusively from TextChoice
Hoffer: **Junkie Business: The Evolution and Operation of a Heroin Dealing Network**, 0-534-64495-3						■	■						
Holmes/Holmes: **Samoan Village: Then and Now, 2e**, 0-534-97120-2	■					■		■					■
Hostetler/Huntington: **Amish Children: Education in the Family, School, and Community, 2e**, 0-03-031592-1	■					■							■
Hostetler/Huntington: **The Hutterites in North America, 4e**, 0-534-44033-9	■					■		■					■
Hull: **Katun: A Twenty Year Journey with the Maya**, 0-534-61290-3	■							■					■
Igoe: **Conservation & Globalization: A Study of National Parks and Indigenous Communities from East Africa to South Dakota**, 0-534-61317-9				■									
Keesing: **'Elota's Story: The Life and Times of a Solomon Islands Big Man**, 0-534-97146-6	■												■
Keiser: **Friend by Day, Enemy by Night: Organized Vengeance in a Kohistani Community**, 0-03-053332-5			■			■	■	■				■	■
Keiser: **The Vice Lords: Warriors of the Street**, 0-534-96931-3						■							■
Kintz: **Life Under the Tropical Canopy: Tradition and Change Among the Yucatec Maya**, 0-03-032592-7	■												■
Krause: **A Crisis of Births: Population Politics and Family-Making in Italy**, 0-534-63693-4		■						■				■	
Kuper: **The Swazi: A South African Kingdom, 2e**, 0-03-070239-9	■					■						■	■
Lansing: **The Balinese**, 0-15-500240-6	■			■									
Laughlin: **Aleuts: Survivors of the Bering Land Bridge**, 0-534-97119-9	■				■	■							■
Lee: **The Dobe Ju/'hoansi, 3e**, 0-15-506333-2						■	■	■					
Lundgren: **Watch and Pray: A Portrait of Fante Village Life in Transition**, 0-15-505933-5	■					■							
Middleton: **The Lugbara of Uganda, 2e**, 0-534-96895-3	■		■			■							
Nanda: **Neither Man Nor Woman: The Hijras of India, 2e**, 0-534-50903-7		■											
O'Meara: **Samoan Planters: Tradition and Economic Development in Polynesia**, 0-534-97111-3						■		■					■
Parman: **Scottish Crofters: A Historical Ethnography of a Celtic Village, 2e**, 0-534-63324-2		■				■		■					■
Podolefsk: **Simbu Law: Conflict Management in the New Guinea Highlands**, 0-534-97138-5						■						■	■
Pospisil: **The Kapauku Papuans of West New Guinea, 2e**, 0-534-97155-5	■					■						■	■
Prins: **The Mi'kmaq: Resistance, Accomodation, and Cultural Survival**, 0-03-053427-5	■					■							■
Quinlan: **From the Bush: The Front Line of Health Care in a Caribbean Village**, 0-15-508567-0		■						■		■			■
Safa: **The Urban Poor of Puerto Rico: A Study in Development and Inequality**, 0-534-97191-1	■							■					■
Sano/Sano: **Life in Riverfront: A Middle Western Town Seen Through Japanese Eyes**, 0-15-506421-5		■				■							■
Shaw: **From Longhouse to Village: Samo Social Change**, 0-15-502561-9	■	■				■		■			■		■
Stearman: **Yuqui: Forest Nomads in a Changing World**, 0-534-97074-5	■					■		■					■
Strathern/Stewart: **Collaborations and Conflict: A Leader Through Time**, 0-15-502147-8	■						■						
Stull/Broadway: **Slaughterhouse Blues: The Meat and Poultry Industry in North America**, 0-534-61303-9				■			■	■					
Suggs: **A Bagful of Locusts and the Baboon Woman: Constructions of Gender, Change, and Continuity in Botswana**, 0-15-507038-X	■	■											
Tonkinson: **The Mardu Aborigines: Living the Dream in Australia's Desert, 2e**, 0-534-44087-8	■		■	■		■							■
Trigger: **The Huron: Farmers of the North, 2e**, 0-03-031689-8					■			■					

case studies by topic

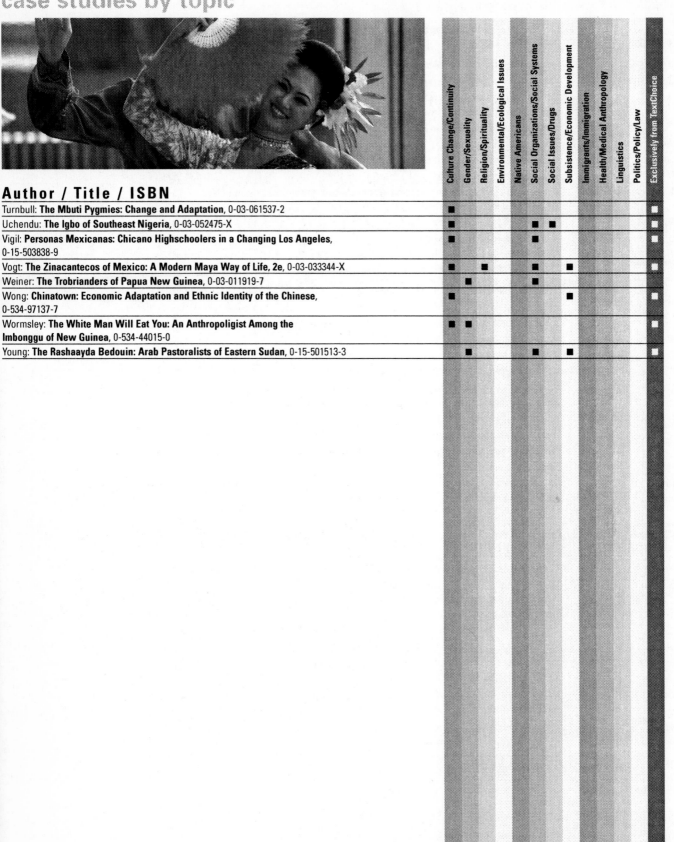

Author / Title / ISBN	Culture Change/Continuity	Gender/Sexuality	Religion/Spirituality	Environmental/Ecological Issues	Native Americans	Social Organizations/Social Systems	Social Issues/Drugs	Subsistence/Economic Development	Immigrants/Immigration	Health/Medical Anthropology	Linguistics	Politics/Policy/Law	Exclusively from TextChoice
Turnbull: **The Mbuti Pygmies: Change and Adaptation**, 0-03-061537-2	■												■
Uchendu: **The Igbo of Southeast Nigeria**, 0-03-052475-X	■					■	■						■
Vigil: **Personas Mexicanas: Chicano Highschoolers in a Changing Los Angeles**, 0-15-503838-9	■					■							■
Vogt: **The Zinacantecos of Mexico: A Modern Maya Way of Life, 2e**, 0-03-033344-X	■	■				■		■					■
Weiner: **The Trobrianders of Papua New Guinea**, 0-03-011919-7		■				■							■
Wong: **Chinatown: Economic Adaptation and Ethnic Identity of the Chinese**, 0-534-97137-7	■							■					■
Wormsley: **The White Man Will Eat You: An Anthropoligist Among the Imbonggu of New Guinea**, 0-534-44015-0	■	■											■
Young: **The Rashaayda Bedouin: Arab Pastoralists of Eastern Sudan**, 0-15-501513-3		■				■		■					■

case studies by geographic region

AFRICA

AUTHOR	TITLE & EDITION	ISBN	SERIES
Beattie	Bunyoro: An African Kingdom	0-534-97128-8	✳ Spindler/▸TC
Goldschmidt	The Sebei: A Study in Adaptation	0-534-97147-4	✳ Spindler/▸TC
Igoe	Conservation & Globalization: A Study of National Parks and Indigenous Communities from East Africa to South Dakota	0-534-61317-9	✳ Young
Kuper	The Swazi: A South African Kingdom, 2e	0-03-070239-9	✳ Spindler/▸TC
Lee	The Dobe Ju/'hoansi, 3e	0-15-506333-2	✳ Spindler
Lundgren	Watch and Pray: A Portrait of Fante Village Life in Transition	0-15-505933-5	✳ Spindler
Middleton	The Lugbara of Uganda, 2e	0-534-96895-3	✳ Spindler/▸TC
Suggs	A Bagful of Locusts and the Baboon Woman: Constructions of Gender, Change, and Continuity in Botswana	0-15-507038-X	✤ Spindler
Turnbull	The Mbuti Pygmies: Change and Adaptation	0-03-061537-2	✳ Spindler/▸TC
Uchendu	The Igbo of Southeast Nigeria	0-03-052475-X	✳ Spindler/▸TC
Young	The Rashaayda Bedouin: Arab Pastoralists of Eastern Sudan	0-15-501513-3	✳ Spindler/▸TC

ASIA

AUTHOR	TITLE & EDITION	ISBN	SERIES
Baker	A Sinhalese Village in Sri Lanka: Coping with Uncertainty	0-15-505176-8	✳ Spindler
Beals	Gopalpur: A South Indian Village	0-03-045371-2	✳ Spindler/▸TC
Bishop	Himalayan Herders	0-534-44060-6	✳ Spindler/▸TC
Chance	China's Urban Villagers: Changing Life in a Beijing Suburb, 2e	0-534-97156-3	✳ Spindler/▸TC
Gladney	Ethnic Identity in China: The Making of a Muslim Minority Nationality	0-15-501970-8	✳ Spindler/▸TC
Graham	Challenging Gender Norms: Five Genders Among Bugis in Indonesia	0-495-09280-0	✳ Spindler
Higham/Thosarat	Khok Phanom Di: Prehistoric Adaptation to the World's Richest Habitat	0-534-44177-7	✤ Quilter/▸TC
Hitchcock	A Mountain Village in Nepal	0-534-97173-3	✳ Spindler/▸TC
Keiser	Friend by Day, Enemy by Night: Organized Vengeance in a Kohistani Community	0-03-053332-5	✳ Spindler/▸TC
Lansing	The Balinese	0-15-500240-6	✳ Spindler
Nanda	Neither Man Nor Woman: The Hijras of India, 2e	0-534-50903-7	Wadsworth

CARIBBEAN, CENTRAL & SOUTH AMERICA/MEXICO

AUTHOR	TITLE & EDITION	ISBN	SERIES
Berdan	The Aztecs of Central Mexico: An Imperial Society, 2e	0-534-62728-5	✳ Spindler
Blomster	Etlatongo: Social Complexity, Interaction, and Village Life in Formative Oaxaca, Mexico	0-534-61281-4	✤ Quilter
Chagnon	The Yanomamö, 5e	0-15-505327-2	✳ Spindler
Chavez	Shadowed Lives: Undocumented Immigrants in American Society, 2e	0-15-508089-X	✳ Spindler
Chinas	The Isthnus Zapotecs: A Matrifocal Culture of Mexico, 2e	0-03-055057-2	✳ Spindler/▸TC
Crocker	The Canela: Kinship, Ritual, and Sex in an Amazonian Tribe, 2e	0-534-17491-4	✳ Spindler
Hull	Katun: A Twenty Year Journey with the Maya	0-534-61290-3	✳ Spindler
Kintz	Life Under the Canopy: Tradition and Change Among the Yucatec Maya	0-03-032593-7	✳ Spindler/▸TC
Kuznar	Awatimarka: The Ethnoarchaeology of an Andean Herding Community	0-15-501528-1	✤ Quilter
Lippi	Tropical Forest Archaeology in Western Pichincha, Ecuador	0-534-61294-6	✤ Quilter
Pearsall	Plants & People in Ancient Ecuador: The Ethnobotany of the Jama River Valley	0-534-61321-7	✤ Quilter
Quinlan	From the Bush: The Front Line of Health Care in a Caribbean Village	0-15-508567-0	✳ Spindler
Sheets	The Ceren Site: An Ancient Village Buried by Volcanic Ash in Central America, 2e	0-495-00606-8	✤ Quilter
Stearman	Yuqui: Forest Nomads in a Changing World	0-534-97074-5	✳ Spindler/▸TC
Vogt	The Zinacantecos of Mexico: A Modern Maya Way of Life, 2e	0-03-033344-X	✳ Spindler/▸TC
Webster/Freter/Gonlin	Copán: The Rise and Fall of an Ancient Maya Kingdom	0-15-505808-8	✤ Quilter

▸TC — Available only as custom published options through TextChoice.com

case studies by geographic region

EUROPE

AUTHOR	TITLE & EDITION	ISBN	SERIES
Anderson	The Ghosts of Iceland	0-534-61052-8	
Brogger	Nazare: Women and Men in a Prebureaucratic Portuguese Fishing Village	0-03-043382-7	❋ Spindler/▸TC
Friedl	Vasilika: A Village in Modern Greece	0-534-97165-2	❋ Spindler/▸TC
Galt	Town and Country in Locorotondo	0-03-073327-8	❋ Spindler/▸TC
Krause	A Crisis of Births: Population Politics and Family-Making in Italy	0-534-63693-4	✸ Young
Parman	Scottish Crofters: A Historical Ethnography of a Celtic Village, 2e	0-534-63324-2	❋ Spindler

NORTH AMERICA

AUTHOR	TITLE & EDITION	ISBN	SERIES
Chance	The Inupiat and Arctic Alaska: An Ethnography of Development	0-534-44159-9	❋ Spindler/▸TC
Darian-Smith	New Capitalists: Issues of Law, Politics, and Identity Surrounding Casino Gaming on Native American Land	0-534-61308-X	✸ Young
Dozier	Hano: The Tewa Indian Community in Arizona	0-03-075653-7	❋ Spindler/▸TC
Ennis-McMillan	A Precious Liquid: Drinking Water and Culture in the Valley of Mexico	0-534-61285-7	✸ Young
Finkelstein	With No Direction Home: Homeless Youth on the Road and in the Streets	0-534-62649-1	✸ Young
Gibson	Skin & Bones: Managing People and Natural Resources in Shellcracker Haven, FL	0-15-508476-3	❋ Spindler
Glassow	Purisimeno Chumash Prehistory	0-15-503084-1	ᴀ Quilter
Grobsmith	Lakota of the Rosebud: A Contemporary Adaptation	0-03-057438-2	❋ Spindler/▸TC
Hallowell/Brown	The Ojibwa of Berens River, Manitoba: Ethnography into History	0-03-055122-6	❋ Spindler/▸TC
Hayden	The Pithouses of Keatley Creek	0-534-44186-6	ᴀ Quilter/▸TC
Helweg	Strangers in a Not-So-Strange Land: Indian Americans in the Global Age	0-534-61312-8	❋ Spindler
Hoebel	The Cheyennes: Indians of the Great Plains, 2e	0-03-022686-4	❋ Spindler
Hoffer	Junkie Business: The Evolution and Operation of a Heroin Dealing Network	0-534-64495-3	✸ Young
Hostetler/Huntington	Amish Children: Education in the Family, School, and Community, 2e	0-03-031592-1	❋ Spindler/▸TC
Hostetler/Huntington	The Hutterites in North America, 3e	0-534-44033-9	❋ Spindler/▸TC
Keiser	The Vice Lords: Warriors of the Street	0-534-96931-3	❋ Spindler/▸TC
Kerber	Lambert Farm: Public Archaeology and Canine Burials along Narragansett Bay	0-534-44168-8	ᴀ Quilter/▸TC
Laughlin	Aleuts: Survivors of the Bering Land Bridge	0-534-97119-9	❋ Spindler/▸TC
Lewis	Camden: Historical Archaeology in the South Carolina Backcountry	0-534-51323-9	ᴀ Quilter
Patterson	Toward a Social History of Archaeology in the United States	0-15-500824-2	ᴀ Quilter/▸TC
Prins	The Mi'kmaq: Resistance, Accomodation, and Cultural Survival	0-03-053427-5	❋ Spindler/▸TC
Safa	The Urban Poor of Puerto Rico: A Study in Development and Inequality	0-534-97191-1	❋ Spindler/▸TC
Sano/Sano	Life in Riverfront: A Middle Western Town Seen Through Japanese Eyes	0-15-506421-5	❋ Spindler
Stull/Broadway	Slaughterhouse Blues: The Meat and Poultry Industry in North America	0-534-61303-9	✸ Young
Trigger	The Huron: Farmers of the North, 2e	0-03-031689-8	❋ Spindler/▸TC
Vigil	Personas Mexicanas: Chicano Highschoolers in a Changing LA	0-15-503838-9	❋ Spindler/▸TC
Wong	Chinatown: Economic Adaptation and Ethnic Identity of the Chinese	0-534-97137-7	❋ Spindler/▸TC

▸TC ---- Available only as custom published options through TextChoice.com.

case studies by geographic region

PACIFIC OCEANA

AUTHOR	TITLE & EDITION	ISBN	SERIES
Barker	Bravo for the Marshallese: Regaining Control in a Post-Nuclear, Post-Colonial World	0-534-61326-8	✤ Young
Brewis	Lives on the Line: Women and Ecology on a Pacific Atoll	0-15-501969-4	✻ Spindler
Duffie	Through the Eye of the Needle: The Personal Chronicle of a Māori Woman	0-15-506982-9	✻ Spindler
Glazier	Hawaiian Fishermen	0-495-00785-4	✻ Spindler
Hart/Pilling/Goodale	The Tiwi of North Australia, 3e	0-03-012019-5	✻ Spindler/▸TC
Heider	Grand Valley Dani: Peaceful Warriors, 3e	0-15-505173-3	✻ Spindler
Herdt	The Sambia: Ritual, Gender, and Change in Papua New Guinea, 2e	0-534-64383-3	✻ Spindler
Holmes/Holmes	Samoan Village: Then and Now, 2e	0-534-97120-2	✻ Spindler/▸TC
Keesing	Elota's Story: The Life and Times of a Solomon Islands Big Man	0-534-97146-6	✻ Spindler/▸TC
O'Meara	Samoan Planters: Tradition and Economic Development in Polynesia	0-534-97111-3	✻ Spindler/▸TC
Podolefsky	Simbu Law: Conflict Management in the New Guinea Highlands	0-534-97138-5	✻ Spindler/▸TC
Pospisil	The Kapauku Papuans of West New Guinea, 2e	0-534-97155-5	✻ Spindler/▸TC
Shaw	From Longhouse to Village: Samo Social Change	0-15-502561-9	✻ Spindler/▸TC
Strathern/Stewart	Collaborations and Conflict: A Leader Through Time	0-15-502147-8	✻ Spindler
Tonkinson	The Mardu Aborigines: Living the Dream in Australia's Desert, 2e	0-534-44087-8	✻ Spindler/▸TC
Weiner	The Trobrianders of Papua New Guinea	0-03-011919-7	✻ Spindler
Wormsley	The White Man Will Eat You!: An Antropologist Among the Imbonggu of New Guinea	0-534-44015-0	✻ Spindler/▸TC

▸TC ⋯⋯ Available only as custom published options through TextChoice.com.

author index

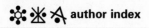

author index